TURKEY
AND THE
WORLD

TURKEY
AND THE
WORLD

Altemur Kilic

INTRODUCTION
WILLIAM O. DOUGLAS

Public Affairs Press, Washington, D.C.

TO THE MEMORY OF ATATURK

INTRODUCTION

We Americans know that the Turks are brave and valiant. But we do not usually think of their nation in terms of democracy. Modern Turkey is, however, a noble democratic society, expressing the faith that government should be of the people, by the people, and for the people.

Ataturk took this nation by the neck at the end of World War II and shook it, demanding that it become modern. After a bitter struggle, equality of women and separation of church and state were realized. Industrialization got under way. A universal franchise was granted and a multi-party system gradually developed. Democratic institutions in the form of honest local government, and independent judiciary, and the parliamentary system were established. A secular state became the way of life, the *mullahs* losing their political authority.

Turkey and other democratic countries lead the way in Asia and the Middle East. Their revolutions have been completed and they are strong in the democratic faith. They prove that peoples of diverse religions and cultural backgrounds can build and work cooperatively even in Asia and the Middle East where the tensions have been the greatest.

Turkey with its press law is going through the phase we experienced in the Alien and Sedition Acts. But her growth is healthy. She is pro-Western partly because of the geographical propinquity of Soviet Russia but mostly because of her democratic faith. This is why in the great days ahead we must come to know her better and to work cooperatively with her.

WILLIAM O. DOUGLAS

Washington, D. C.

PREFACE

This book is primarily concerned with events of the past thirty years. However, neither Turkey's foreign policies nor her relations with the rest of the world can be isolated historically. Accordingly I have attempted to provide historical background and perspective to these events and to reactions toward them.

My main purpose is to explain the developments of the last few decades and the guiding principles of modern Turkey's foreign relations from a Turkish point of view. I want to admit at the beginning that complete objectivity is not, and cannot be, a marked characteristic of this book. As a Turk writing on matters directly related to Turkey, I could not possibly have a detached approach.

Perhaps my subjective approach will to some extent counter-balance certain studies on Turkey's foreign relations which have been biased and lacking in objectivity. In going through many volumes by different authors I have come to the conclusion that Turkey and the Turks have been, to say the least, misunderstood. No doubt many historians and political scientists who have written on Turkey have been motivated by well-meaning zeal, but some have been less than well-informed, and others have been distinctly biased.

Turkey's history, at home and in foreign relations, is not entirely without blemishes; some mistakes have undoubtedly been made. There have been times when Turks reacted forcefully and vehemently under certain provocations, but the majority of Turkish statesmen have had a basic honesty and have been motivated by good intentions— especially in their dealings with the West. Invariably, Turkish excesses have arisen as the result of bitter disappointments suffered in relations with the West.

In particular, two of the greatest Turkish Sultans, Fatih Sultan Mehmet (Muhammed II, 1451-1481) and Kanuni Sultan Suleyman (Suleyman the Magnificent, 1520-1566) actively sought alliances with the West, but they were rejected. The "Capitulations" which the Turkish Sultans accorded Western countries as a gesture of goodwill became in time instruments for the exploitation of Turkey by the West. ("Capitulations", by the way did not, as the term seems to suggest, mean surrender of rights; it is derived from the Latin *Caput, Capitulum* which

means chapter, refering to the articles into which treaties on concessions given by the Ottoman Sultan to foreign powers were divided.)

When Suleyman the Magnificent concluded the first Capitulation
with the French in 1535 he was granting privileges, not surrendering
rights. The Capitulations concluded with Venice in 1540, and with
England in 1579, and renewals or confirmations of these in 1581 and
1593, were similarly not concessions surrendered under pressure, but
concessions given by the free will of the Sultans who ruled the most
powerful empire in Europe. It is paradoxical that the European and
other powers which obtained these concessions used the Capitulation
treaties to shackle and humiliate Turkey economically and politically
when the Ottoman Empire declined. It was then that Capitulations
assumed the connotation of "capitulating".

The basic philosophy of the Ottoman Empire has been overlooked or
ignored by Western writers. Ottoman statesmen, many of them products of the racial melting pot, wished to evolve a federation of races
and religions. True, Islam was the religion of the Empire and the
Turkish race was the core, but both Islam and Turkism were in reality
not the driving forces of the empire. The word "Ottoman" meant all
members of the Empire irrespective of race or religion. To preserve
this, the Millet system of autonomy was evolved, and privileges were
extended to nationalities other than Turks. The best proof of Ottoman idealism was the fact that Armenians, Greeks, and Jews were entrusted with key posts in the state. These and other nationalities enjoyed religious, educational, and economic freedom.

There were many cases of misrule, but this misrule was not directed
against the non-Turkish groups. On the contrary, Turkish Anatolia
suffered more from misrule than any other part of the Empire.

There are Western writers who reluctantly accept the fact that minority groups within the Ottoman Empire were indeed accorded privileges, but they hasten to rationalize by saying that it was "enlightened
self-interest!" Whose self interest? Surely not the self interest of
the Anatolian Turk who was always in the forefront of the Empire's
military operations.

Turkish nationalism came later than the nationalism of the other
groups constituting the Ottoman Empire.

Late in the nineteenth century Turkish intellectuals and others
began to realize that Turkism was being ignored and sacrificed for an
ideal which was being eroded by the 'national awakening' of the Ottoman Millets: the Armenians, Greeks, Kurds, Arabs, and others. The
very Millet system envisaged by the Ottoman idealists as the founda-

tion for a federation had in fact become the basis of nationalistic aspirations which gravely threatened the Empire.

The bitter realization that the Western powers were determined to destroy 'the sick man' made extremists of the Turkish nationalists. It was disappointment with the West and justified suspicion of Western collusion with Russia, which made Turkey an ally of the German-Austro-Hungarian bloc in the first World War. Defeat in the war, and the encroachments by the Western states which followed, spurred this extreme nationalism into an anti-Western attitude and into an alliance with Soviet Russia in 1921.

It was Kemal Ataturk's genius which transformed the extreme nationalism into productive patriotism, put an end to Soviet infiltration, and evolved the pro-Western foreign policy of modern Turkey. This volume is basically the story of this transformation and evolution.

* * *

I would like to express my thanks and gratitude to Mrs. A. S. Sharp and Mrs. Jeanne McLennan for their devoted help in the preparation of the manuscript; to Messrs. T. D. Rivinus, Turkkaya Ataov, and Metin Tamkoc for making available to me copies of their unpublished manuscripts; and to Mrs. Timothy Pfeiffer, Mr. Fred Zusy, Mr. Vincent Joyce, Mr. Marchal Rothe, and Mr. Kerim Key for their invaluable help in reading the manuscript. I think the volume has gained much from their criticisms and the advice of my other friends. My gratitude and thanks also go to Mr. M. B. Schnapper, executive director of Public Affairs Press, for suggestions and criticisms.

Needless to say, the opinions contained herein are entirely personal and should not be construed as reflecting in any way the official views of the Turkish government.

ALTEMUR KILIC

Washington, D. C.

FOREWORD

Events almost daily re-emphasize the importance of the vast and perpetually enigmatic region called the Middle East. Unlike other important regions of bygone eras, this ancient cradle of civilizations and wars continues to be strife-torn and is a focal point in the global struggle of our day.

The Middle East is the natural passageway between three continents; Asia, Europe, and Africa. It has enormous economic potentialities. Having served as the source of great civilizations, cultures, and religions, it is still psychologically and socially receptive to new ideas. Therefore it is a sensitive spot for all humanity.

The Middle East today has rich oil deposits—approximately two-thirds of the known oil reserves of the free world. Although Western Europe might not be entirely dependent on these reserves on a short-term basis, its increasing needs for fuel make the oil of the Middle East essential for the next few decades.

Geographically, Turkey is a Middle Eastern country of major importance to the Western world. But, specifically, her importance in world affairs transcends mere identity and membership in that region, and there are many reasons why she is the most important country in that area.

In the introduction to his *Historical Geography of Asia Minor* Sir William Ramsay says, "Topography is the foundation of history." Indeed, Anatolia's topography has been one of the most important determining factors of its history.

Anatolia (or Asia Minor) is, as Sir William pointed out, "a level and lofty limestone plateau protruding from the main Asian continent towards Europe and the West. The Central Plateau. . . is surrounded by a higher rim of mountains, outside of which is low coast land on north and west and south."

The formidable Taurus and anti-Taurus ranges, which cover the southern approaches, blend with the range of mountains which form a barrier towards the north, along the Black Sea coast and form the complexity of the rugged highlands of eastern Turkey.

It is true that Anatolia forms a land bridge between the East and the West but it is also true that because of its topographic structure it is and can be a "naturally enclosed land unit, a relatively easily defended fortress." It is also because of this topography that peoples who have

11

settled in Anatolia have always asserted and maintained their independence.

Turkey today plays a vital part in the global balance because she
constitutes the link between East and West and she is a member of both NATO and the Bagdad Pact.   Another geopolitical reality
which has been the dominant factor in the foreign affairs of the country
is her proximity to Russia.   Finally, she possesses the southern Black
Sea coast and the Straits which have always been the stumbling block
to Russian aspirations to enter the Mediterranean.   This situation has
brought about a centuries-long conflict of interest between the two
countries.   Turkey, with her strong determination to remain free and
independent, continues to frustrate one of the main aims of Russian
foreign policy and resolutely tries to link the Middle East with the
West.

A passageway for conquerors and often the last stop in mass migra-
tions, the self-contained land unit of Anatolia has served as a melting
pot of many races.   It is therefore more absurd here in Anatolia than
almost anywhere else to seek a pure stock of people.   Scythians, Hit-
tites, Sumerians, Persians, Greeks, Romans, and finally Oghuz Turks
have passed through or settled, and made up the major components of
this melting pot.   But the strong, warrior Turks asserted and maintained their basic Turkish characteristics, their language, their customs, and finally their Islamic religion in this mixture.   Thus Turks
(first the Seldjuk and then the Ottoman) emerged ultimately as the political and cultural masters of the land.   And so today the people of
Anatolia are Turks, regardless of the other ethnic ingredients mixed
with that which is Turkish.

Anatolian Turks from the time of the Seldjuks and the Ottomans
have been very different from their neighbors—the Persians, the Arabs
and even their blood kinsmen who were left on the other side of the
mountain ranges.   They came from the East, but they have always
been oriented towards the West.

These facts about the land and people of Anatolia, which seem to
complement each other, should always be kept in mind while studying
the foreign relations of Turkey.

CONTENTS

ABOUT THE AUTHOR

Altemur Kilic was born in Ankara, Turkey, in 1924. After studying at Robert College in Istanbul he received his M.A. degree in
Social Sciences from the New School of Social Research, New York,
in 1951.

Following his graduation from college in 1944 he began his career
as a reporter on the Istanbul Vatan and soon rose to the post of
foreign editor. Subsequently he worked for the Associated Press in
Ankara, as a consultant for Radio Free Europe in Istanbul, and as a
press officer for the United Nations in New York. In 1952 he served
as a reserve lieutenant with the Turkish Brigade in Korea, acting as
its Public Information Officer. Since 1955, he has been Press Attaché
of the Turkish Embassy in Washington, D.C.

CHAPTER I

HISTORICAL BACKGROUND

During the reign of Suleyman the Magnificent in the sixteenth century the Ottoman Empire reached its zenith, not only territorially but from the point of view of culture and statesmanship. For a time it remained paramount, partly because of gathered momentum and partly because of great men like Sokollu and Koprülüs. After the failure of the second siege of Vienna in 1683 the decline started. By the beginning of the eighteenth century the Ottoman Empire had ceased to be the dominant factor in European affairs. It was receding territorially and crumbling internally. The once glorious empire gradually became the "Sick Man of Europe"—a passive pawn in the struggle for power between the Great Powers. At first the Great Powers were Russia and Austria; later on they were joined by France, England, Germany, and Italy.

However, the "Sick Man"* took a long time to die. There was the glimmer of truth in the rather tragic sarcasm of a Turkish delegate at the Vienna Conference who pointed out that, "Sick Man" or not, the Ottoman Empire was still the strongest empire in the world. He said: "You from the outside, and we from the inside, have still not been able to destroy it."

What caused the decline of the Ottoman Empire? Several volumes could well be devoted to expounding the complex reasons which contributed to its downfall. A major factor was the corruption and abuse of Islam and its institutions which were essentially sound.

The basic characteristics of Islam are little understood in the west, partially because of the Western predeliction to identify religion with politics. In the days of Muhammed the Conqueror and Suleyman the Magnificent enlightened religious leaders supported notable reforms and audaciously decreed *"Caiz degildir"* ("It is not permissible") when the Sultan attempted illegal actions.

"The Ottoman Empire," says Yorga (author of *Geschichte des Osmanischen Reiches*), "formed a happy contrast in . . . regard to the contemporary world. The Slavs were not oppressed as in Greek times. There was no trace of the German anarchy of the same period. Inspectors made their rounds four times a year to see that the non-

---

* It was Tsar Nicholas I who said: "We have on our hands a very, very sick man."

Turkish peoples were well treated. For them there was a change in just one thing that affected their everyday lives: The great land-owners were now of a different race. The Turks paid cash for all they bought. The man who stole a chicken from a peasant made himself liable to the death penalty. In every way, indeed, it was recognized that without such a reign of law, it would be impossible to hold territories where the majority of the inhabitants were Christians."

The courage, drive, and statesmanship which motivated most of the Sultans until Suleyman were non-existent in most of his successors. They lost interest in leading their armies in the field or in ruling their empire. High command posts were turned over to corrupt officials, including eunuchs of the imperial harem. The Janissaries, once the elite corps of the Empire, degenerated into a collection of vagabonds. The administrative system, which had long served as a model to Europe, became a decadent bureaucracy. Judicial and social institutions rotted from within.

The basic cause for the decline was the fact that the Ottoman Empire never really became a homogeneous nation. As the French writer Benoit-Mechin says: "Turkey was an army which conquered an empire without passing through the intermediate stage of being a nation." The Turkish army, which conquered lands and established an effective legal and administrative system, never attempted to Turkify or convert to Islam the conquered peoples. There was a transcendent desire in most of the Ottoman Sultans and statesmen to create an Ottoman Federation. In later years even intellectuals let themselves be deluded by the idea of an Ottoman nation which never existed. In fact the empire was, as Benoit-Mechin, has pointed out, "a true tower of Babel, uncemented by racial, religious, or historic ties," and as such it was destined to disappear as soon as its military power vanished and when the first class legal and administrative system became corrupt. The growth of new powers, especially Russia, in Europe and the awakening of nationalism among the peoples which constituted the empire, hastened the inevitable downfall.

It is noteworthy that even up to the constitution of 1908 all the reforms introduced by successive governments were based on the idea of an Ottoman nation. The master minds of the Tanzimat Reform of 1839-1876, Mustafa Reshid Pasha and his supporters, were thinking in terms of creating a homogeneous Ottoman nation by giving equal rights to all the nationalities within it. The first "Young Turks" (the young revolutionaries against the absolute monarchy of Abdulaziz and Abdul Hamid II were called "Young Turks" abroad but not within the country); Ziya Pasha and Namik Kemal were in reality "Young Ottomans" who never dreamed of Turkish nationalism or Turkish supremacy over other nationalities.

There were, of course, in the nineteenth century some Turkish nationalists who urged recognition of authentic Turkish culture and Turkish elements but their voices were subdued by the Ottoman nationalists. Even the Young Turk movement, which overthrew Abdul Hamid II and brought about, in 1908, the second constitutional regime in Turkey's history, was at first dominated by the Ottomanists who wanted close cooperation with Armenian, Arab, and Albanian nationalists. Intellectuals like Prince Sabahaddin believed they could pacify the nationalists by "decentralization" or by giving complete autonomy to the various nationality groups in the Empire. But by 1912, after a series of events culminating in incidents provoked by minorities during the Balkan War, Turkish intellectuals were jolted into adopting a nationalism of their own. They had fooled themselves long enough with the ideal of creating an Ottoman nation. In vain they had attempted to cooperate with their "brother Ottomans"—Greeks, Armenians, Arabs, and Albanians. (From 1893 onwards the highest posts in the Turkish government were given to Ottomans of Armenian, Greek, Arab, and Albanian origin.)

Dr. Cyrus Hamlin, the American educator who founded Robert College in Istanbul, was a sincere friend of the Armenians. In his book, *Among the Turks*, he points out that the oppressions and incompetence of the Ottoman government "fell upon Moslem and Christian alike," and calls attention to the Christians (mostly Armenians and Greeks) who held high positions in the Ottoman government. We learn from his list of eighty-seven such officials in the 1670's that, for example, the Turkish Minister in Athens was a Greek, the Minister of Public Works an Armenian, the Secretary of the Sultan a Greek. Dr. Hamlin also points out that one of the main impediments to creating a homogeneous empire was the reluctance of the Christians to accept military service although they enjoyed special privileges. But this was not all: Greeks, Armenians, Arabs, and even those who attained high posts did not hesitate to betray the Ottoman state at the first opportunity.

Western writers, often forgetting or denying that there was a genuine desire for Ottoman nationalism, fail to see how deep were the impressions made by betrayals. For instance, the so-called "Armenian Massacres"—which were by no means one-sided—were the result of reactions caused by constant betrayals. Armenian national-

ists and their supporters were ever busy plotting against Ottoman rule
and intriguing with Russian agents.

Of all the nationalities in the Ottoman empire the Armenians enjoyed a special place. Apart from holding high office in the government, Armenians had more national and religious autonomy than perhaps any other minority. The Turks had a deep attachment for the
Armenians with whom they enjoyed a common culture, though dif-
fering in religion and language. The Sultans referred to the Armenians
as "Our faithful Armenian subjects," but Armenian nationalists
betrayed their trust. Armenian terrorists and revolutionaries, coming
from Russia and aided by the Russians, forced Abdul Hamid II to
take drastic action.

When World War I broke out Armenian revolutionaries within
Turkey openly supported the Entente powers and armed themselves in
preparation for "The Day." A documented report of the then Turkish
government states: "As soon as the order of mobilization was issued,
Turkish Armenians crossed the frontiers on their way to Egypt, Bulgaria, Rumania, and Russia, and joined the Russian Army or bands of
Armenian irregulars." After Russia's declaration of war, Armenian
bands raided Turkish villages and massacred many inhabitants. It
was not until fifth column terrorist actions by Armenians threatened
Turkish defenses against Russia, that "deportations" were decided
upon.

In his book *Turkey in the World War*, Ahmet Emin Yalman, the
Turkish journalist, admits that Armenians sometimes became the
victims of regrettable abuses and violence, but he also establishes that
the so-called massacres were initiated by Armenians. What is not
generally realized is the fact that after the Russian revolution the
Armenians massacred some 40,000 Turks in the Turkish territory
occupied by Russia.

Turkish response to Armenian excesses was comparable, I believe,
to what might have been the American response, had the German-
Americans of Minnesota and Wisconsin revolted on behalf of Hitler
during World War II.

Seeking a New Philosophy. While other nationalities composing
the Ottoman empire rapidly developed strong national consciousness
and nationalism most Turkish intellectuals clung to the idea of Ottoman nationalism. They hoped that by reforms of one kind or another
they could still save the empire and Ottomanism.

The "Young Ottomans," (known as Young Turks in Europe) who in
exile were planning the downfall of Abdul Hamid II and the subsequent reformation of the empire, were predominently thinking in terms

of an Ottoman nation. The main cause of division among them was the question of centralization or decentralization of the government.

The ground was not yet prepared for Turkish nationalism. Although some efforts had been made by some intellectuals to bring about a consciousness of Turkish history, language, and race, the majority of Anatolian Turks considered themselves Ottomans and Moslems. In many places the word "Turk" was a derogatory expression. When the Hungarian Orientalist Vambery visited Istanbul and suggested there was an affinity between Ottoman Turks and the Turks of Central Asia his remark was considered in very bad taste.

By 1908, when the second constitution was proclaimed, some Turkish writers became convinced that Ottomanism was a dream. Ziya Gokalp, the intellectual leader of the new "Turkist" movement, lamented in verse:

> "We succeeded in conquering many places
> But spiritually we were conquered in all of them.
> The sword of the Turk and likewise his pen
> Have exalted the Arabs, Chinese, Persians;
> He has created a history and a home for many peoples,
> He has deluded himself for the benefit of others."

The intellectuals under Gokalp's leadership at first started to agitate for the creation of a pure Turkish language, for social reforms and for a national revival in the main spheres of life.

The Balkan War put an end to the tottering dream of "Ottomanism" and Turkish nationalism came to the fore.

To define Turkish nationalism and to make the masses conscious of it was not a simple task. Even Gokalp, who contributed so much to the definition and propagation of the idea, was not clear as to the best course. At the beginning he talked of it as a new kind of Ottomanism, but he had difficulty in reconciling "Turkism" with Islamic precepts and with the reality of the Ottoman empire which still had non-Turkish elements within its boundaries.

There were strong intellectual groups that belittled the new "Turkish" consciousness. Although most of them had given up hope of instilling among Christians the concept of Ottomanism, they believed that the revival of the empire lay in Pan-Islamism. This movement, which sought to "purify the empire of Christian elements and unite the Islamic peoples of the world under the Caliphate," had received some support from Abdul Hamid II.

The Germans saw in this trend a tool for their *Drang nach Osten* policy. When Turkey entered the war Pan-Islamists sensed an oppor-

tunity for the fulfillment of their ideal and Germany urged an appeal
by the Caliph to Islamic peoples of the world in order to hinder the
Anglo-Franco-Russian war effort. But the "Jehad" (Holy War) proclaimed by the Caliph proved to be a mockery. The Moslem soldiers
of the Entente army did not hesitate to shoot at soldiers of the Caliph.
Arabs of the Empire proceeded to plot and rebel against their "spirit-
ual leader"—the Caliph. Obviously, nationalism and particularism
were stronger forces than the call of the Caliph. The British recognized this and capitalized upon it.

Events proved that Pan-Islamism was as hollow a concept as Ottomanism. Turkish nationalism was now the only course left open for
the Turks. There were Turkish nationalists who believed in the
greatness of the Turkish race and in the necessity of returning to pure
Turkism. Theirs was to be an Anatolian Turkish nationalism. While
they accepted common bonds with the Turkish peoples of the world,
they shunned foreign adventures and wanted to devote nationalistic
efforts to the development of Anatolia.

In 1916 Halide Edip, an articulate young authoress, expressed the
trend when she wrote: "The forces of Pan-Turkism seek to induce us
to interest ourselves in the welfare of all Mohammedan Turks, and
Turanians as well. . . We can give the most help to our brothers beyond our borders by concerning ourselves solely with our own home
country. We should not deceive both ourselves and other people.
Every Turk who carries into foreign countries his energy and capacity
puts himself in the position of one robbing his own mother, his own
home." But this realistic approach was relegated to the background
by a kind of nationalism which better fitted the conditions of the day.
Ziya Gokalp defined this appealing and dramatic nationalism in
terms of Pan-Turanism or Pan Turkism:

> *"Fatherland for the Turks is neither Turkey nor Turkistan;*
> *Fatherland is a great and eternal land: Turan."*

At the beginning of the war with Russia, which had within its
boundaries millions of people of Turkish or Turanian origin, it was
obvious that Pan-Turanism, which promised that "The land of the
enemy will be devastated . . . Turkey shall be enlarged and become
Turan!" would have great appeal.

Pan-Turanism originally sought the unification and consolidation
of all races with common Turanian origin including Hungarians, Finns,
and Bulgars. However, it soon became obvious that Pan-Turanism
as such was impractical and the word became synonymous with **Pan-**

Turkism, which called for the unification of peoples of Turkish origin then numbering about 35 millions.

Fuat Koprulu, who served as Foreign Minister from 1951 to 1955, expressed the Pan-Turkish idea in the following words: "I also reject Pan-Turanism; it has no practical value. I have a feeling of solidarity only for those who share both my language and my religion. But this group must be united. We may be a backward people in relation to the west, but we are very advanced as compared with the east. Our brothers are awaiting us impatiently. We cannot let ourselves dwell upon the interests of the Turks in any single region, but must meet the needs of the entire Turkish world between the Mediterranean and China. We should not adhere to the maxim of "sacred selfishness." Our maxim is "One for all, and all for one." If some of us adhere to the dangerously selfish theory of reserving our whole energies for our own field, the primary task of Turkism is to correct such wrong conceptions. The great Turkish world of the future cannot be built in any other manner."

After having influenced the leaders of the government (e.g., the Central Committee of the ruling Union and Progress Party) prior to and during the First World War as militant "Pan Turkism," Turkish nationalism became, under the leadership of Mustafa Kemal, the driving force which restored the independence of the country. Later this nationalism was channeled into the productive patriotism which it is today.

The Eastern Question. European power politics of the nineteenth century revolved around what was called the "Eastern Question." What was to be done with the "Sick Man"—the Ottoman Empire? All the European powers—including Russia, Austria, Great Britain, and France, as well as Germany and Italy—were convinced that the "Sick Man" was to die soon. Indeed sharing the spoils was being considered even while the Ottoman Empire was being used as a pawn in the struggle for supremacy. Sometimes Austria, Britain, and France supported the Ottoman Empire against Russia; they feared that an untimely death at the hands of the Russians would be to their detriment.

The opposite happened when the Tsar came to the "aid" of the Sultan against Britain and France. It was only as a means of delaying the death that the western powers supported Ottoman internal and military reforms. They felt, especially towards the end of the nineteenth century, that by aiding in reforms and thus establishing political and economic influence, their purposes could better be served. But it cannot be said that they were in the least anxious really to save the empire.   One proof of this was the fact that not only the Russians but also the French and the British actively and incessantly supported the separatist nationalist movements of the various elements within it.

Only Germany seemed to have a different attitude.   During Bismarck's time she showed very little direct interest in Middle Eastern affairs, but nevertheless a military assistance group under General von der Goltz established an effective bridgehead of influence in the Ottoman army.

As time went on Germany developed a more active interest in the Ottoman empire and the Middle East, and increasingly gave assistance (material and technical) which Britain and France were reluctant to match.   Kaiser Wilhelm II was pursuing his *Drang nach Osten* policy and to this end developed stronger economic and military relations with Turkey.

While Russia, France, and Britain were determined to bring about the rapid collapse of the Ottoman Empire and to divide the spoils as soon as possible, Germany was aiming at a relatively strong and relatively independent Turkey—dominated by German economic interests.*   The Western powers, on the other hand, were by no means genuinely interested in a solution of the eastern problem beneficial to the Turks—even after the 1908 Constitutional Revolution when the "Young Turks" succeeded by force of arms in imposing the Constitution on Sultan Abdul Hamid II.   The new Constitution promised reformation in all fields and the motto "Fraternity, Equality, and Liberty" stood for a democratic regime and equality for all races and religions. Many of the "Young Turks" believed that the time was ripe to revive Ottomanism, but they and the others who counted on support from France and Britain, (to them cradles of liberty and democracy) were bitterly disappointed when no help was forthcoming.

The non-Turkish elements of the empire continued to press for separatism and sought the support of the major powers.   They were apprehensive that a real reformation might delay the division of the spoils, and turned a cold shoulder to the overtures of the earnestly pro-Western "Young Turks."

The Die Is Cast.   The "Young Turk" leaders had at this time three courses in foreign affairs which they might have followed:

(1) To ally themselves with a group strongly in favor of strengthening ties with France and Great Britain.   (2) To attempt a rapprochement with Russia.   (3) To accept the advice of those—espec-

---

* In his book *The Rising Crescent*, Ernest Jackh contends that there were elements in the German Foreign Office who wanted to make Turkey a German "Egypt."

ially the Turkish military—who would move towards Germany, which they considered Europe's greatest military power.

The second alternative, although not altogether lacking some supporters, was rejected by public opinion. It was a series of external and internal affairs which led to the adoption of the last course.

Separatist pressures and the Tripolitanian and Balkan wars gradually undermined the moderate Young Turks.

Even before 1911 the Western powers (Great Britain, France, Italy, and Austria) had conducted secret negotiations and had reached agreements for the sharing of the spoils of the Ottoman Empire. Raymond Poincaré, an ex-President of the Third French Republic, has called attention to four of these secret agreements:

1. An accord was signed in 1896 between Great Britain, Italy, and Austria for the purpose of "facilitating" the consolidation of British interests in Egypt and those of Italy in Tripolitania.

2. Implied in the formation of the Holy Alliance in 1902 was the understanding that Italy would support the policies of Germany and Austria in the Balkans and that, in turn, Germany and Austria would recognize the right of Italy to invade Tripolitania.

3. In 1900 and 1902 France and Italy signed secret protocols affirming that neither had designs on the other's sphere of influence, that is: Morocco for France and Tripolitania for Italy.

4. In 1909 Italy promised that she would favorably regard Russian interests in the Straits (the Bosporus and the Dardanelles), while Russia in turn said she would favor Italian interests in Tripolitania.

Hikmet Bayur, a Turkish historian, sums up the policies of the Big Powers vis-a-vis the Ottoman Empire as follows:

"They were all intent upon getting a big piece if and when the Empire disintegrated. But, in addition, they each had separate axes to grind:

"Russia wanted to expand towards Istanbul, the Straits, and if possible towards the region of Alexandretta-Yumurtalik, in order to have an opening to free seas. Therefore, her aim was to keep the Ottoman Empire weak by every means possible and even by trying to prevent the construction of railroads in eastern Turkey.

"Great Britain had her reasons to suspect Russian motives. She intended to undermine Turkish influence—through the Caliphate—on other Islamic peoples and for this purpose was intriguing among the Arabs.

"France also feared Russia's motives. Her own ambition was to get Syria, if and when the Ottoman Empire disintegrated. Meanwhile, she considered the empire a vast field for exploitation by her capitalists.

"Italy coveted Tripolitania and the region of Izmir-Antalya.

"Austria, from time to time, had visions of descending upon Salonica. Yet, being afraid that Slavs might become too powerful in case the Ottomans became too weak, she seemed rather in favor of retaining the *status-quo.*

"Germany also considered the Ottoman Empire a field for exploitation and tried to use it as a weapon in her general diplomacy against Great Britain, France, and Russia."

When the Italians attacked Tripolitania in September 1911 some of the well-meaning Turks who thought an alliance with Great Britain might be a solution, experienced their first great disappointment. Cavid Bey, one of the pro-British leaders of the Union and Progress Party, proposed to Winston Churchill an Anglo-Turkish alliance. When Churchill discussed this with Sir Edward Grey, the latter pointed out that such an alliance might estrange the Italians and consequently Churchill's reply was noncommital. After stressing British neutrality in the Italian-Turkish conflict he added that "we cannot enter into new political relations."

During the Tripolitanian War the Balkan Powers had had the time and the opportunity to form an anti-Ottoman Alliance. Kamil Pasha, an old believer in British ties, was then Grand Vizier. He was sure that his English "friends" would never allow an attack on the Ottoman Empire. He even demobilized some 67,000 troops in European Turkey, and when war was imminent made every possible concession, still hoping for the support and intervention of the Allies. But this was not forthcoming and the Balkan War could not be prevented. Kamil Pasha's Cabinet fell as a result of that war. He had trusted too blindly in the Western Powers and he had been betrayed.

It was only as a result of the downfall of the "Great Cabinet" that the Union and Progress Party were able to stage a comeback by *coup-d'etat* on January 13, 1913. The virtual dictatorship of the Central Committee of the Party continued until the Armistice in 1918, but within the Committee the struggle between moderates and militant nationalists continued all through these years. The "Young Turks" had been driven to extremism by the collapse of Ottoman nationalism. The reins of the Ottoman Government fell into the hands of the Central Committee when the support which the moderates expected from the West did not materialize.

Later the pro-German militarists in the Central Committee had their way when the efforts of the moderates to bring about an alliance with the Entente powers were frustrated.

Although, significantly, Cemal Pasha, one of the most powerful members of the Central Committee, was inclined towards an alliance with the West, he was driven, step by step, into the camp of Enver Pasha and Talet Pasha, who represented militant nationalism and were pro-German.

It should not be difficult to understand the feelings of nationalists like Enver, Talat, and Cemal. They had been humiliated by high-handed Western Powers. They had been confronted by demands for concessions of all sorts through their Ambassadors and dragomen and they had experienced the Tripolitanian and Balkan Wars which were results of Entente intrigues. In light of these experiences it is surprising that the moderate elements still clung to the idea of an alliance with the West.

Cemal Pasha himself had worked actively to bring about a Turco-French rapprochement, as he was sceptical of the value of an alliance with Germany. He, as well as the financial wizard of the Central Committee, Cavid Bey, hoped that by such a policy they could obtain financial support from French financiers, and also obtain Anglo-French guarantees against Russia. To this end the already existing French Commission for Reformation of the Gendarmerie and the British Naval Mission were cultivated. A French Inspector-General for the Ministry of Finance was invited to Turkey. A Franco-Turkish friendship committee was founded under the auspices of Cemal Pasha. When he went to France in 1914 to attend naval maneuvers, he bluntly told the French Foreign Office: "If you want to close your iron ring (around the Central Powers) you must . . . take us into your Entente and at the same time protect us against the terrible perils threatening us from Russia. . . If you support us in our upward strivings, you will soon have a faithful ally in the East."

But this proposal was rejected to the bitter disappointment of Cemal Pasha. A French newspaperman wrote at the time: "If Cemal Pasha now goes home without having done anything for his country, we shall have no right to be angry if he finds himself compelled to take steps which may not be to the taste of France."

Even in trying to negotiate a loan, Cavid Bey was confronted with unbelievably difficult conditions in Paris and a point-blank refusal even to consider the abolition of financial Capitulations.

This, though, was not the first rejection. Previous overtures in London for an Anglo-Turkish alliance were, as an English author writes, "politely turned aside."

It was evident that the British and French were not eager for an alliance with Turkey and therefore were not prepared to give her guarantees against Russia, or to satisfy her demands concerning the abolition of the Capitulations and the return of the Dodecanese. They just wanted to keep Turkey neutral in the imminent war.

Churchill admits in his *World Crisis, 1911-1914* that neither he nor Sir Edward Grey considered Turkey an important military factor and that he personally thought that Greece would be a more valuable ally. In fact, it was Churchill who went so far as to promise Cyprus to Greece in order to win her to the Allied side.

An Alliance Is Signed. As might have been expected, when the effects of pro-Entente Ottoman statesmen failed, pro-German leaders were able to maneuver Turkey into an alliance with Germany.

The basis for such an alliance was well prepared by the Germans, while the Entente powers made surprisingly little effort even to keep the Ottoman Empire neutral. A German diplomatic mission made a very favorable impression on public opinion. Germany never missed an opportunity to sympathize with and to support Turkey on military questions. When France refused a loan, Germany gave both money and arms.

Negotiations for a Turkish-German alliance were started secretly between the German Ambassador, Baron von Waggenheim, and Enver and Talat some time before the outbreak of the first World War. Signing of this document was kept a secret from most of the Cabinet including the Grand Vizier and Cemal Pasha.

According to Jackh (then in the German Foreign Office), the German Foreign Office and the German Ambassador in Istanbul were reluctant at first to have the Turks as an ally. They thought Turkey would be a burden and a drain on German resources, especially if the Russians started an offensive. But these misgivings were overruled by Kaiser Wilhelm himself and the alliance was signed.

The moderates in the Cabinet, the Grand Vizier, Said Halim Pasha, the Sheik-ul-Islam Hayri Bey, and Cavid Bey were opposed to it. Cavid Bey had some misgivings about the religious minorities, but later his unhappy experience with the Allies made him feel that this was the only course to take against an imminent Russian attack.

The principal points in the alliance were as follows:

1.   The two contracting powers agree to observe strict neutrality in the present war between Austria-Hungary and Serbia.

2.   If Russia intervenes and takes active military measures, and the necessity arises for Germany to carry out her pledges of alliance

to Austria, Turkey is under obligation in such a case to carry out her pledges made to Germany.

3.   In case of war the German Military Mission will remain at the disposal of Turkey.   As agreed between the head of the Military Mission and His Excellency the Minister of War, Turkey will grant to the German Military Mission an active influence and authority in the general management of the army.

4.   In case Turkish territories are threatened by Russia, Germany agrees to defend them if necessary by force of arms.

5.   The present agreement has for its purpose the safeguarding of both empires from international complications which may rise out of the present war.   It will take effect immediately after it has been signed by the delegates mentioned above; and its mutual and identical pledges will remain in force until December 31, 1918.

However, what literally threw Turkey into the arms of Germany and into the ranks of the alliance was not the pact but rather a blunder on the part of the British Admiralty.   For years the Turkish people, who, to a man were very conscious of the weakness of their fleet, had been contributing towards the building of two Turkish dreadnaughts in England.   These ships were in Portsmouth dockyards on the eve of war and near completion.   They had even been named the *Sultan Osman* and the *Reshadiye*.   Probably thinking that these two battleships might upset the balance of power in the Aegean in Turkey's favor and against Greece, the British commandeered them.   Perhaps the logic of the Admiralty was correct, but Vere-Hodge in his *Turkish Foreign Policy (1918-1948)* contends: "The harm done to English prestige in Turkey was far greater than any material destruction these ships might have caused if used in action against the Entente."

It may well be that had Britain not taken this step the alienation of the Turkish people might have been prevented and Turkey's joining the war might at least have been delayed.

Let us look at the German side of this story: "The confiscation let loose throughout Turkey an immense wave of indignation and even hatred against England.   All those Turks who had given subscriptions felt personally cheated.   England could not have done better propaganda for us, for her behavior sensibly increased Turkish gratitude for the warships Germany sent them as compensation."

Ironically, it was the two battleships sent by Germany, the *Goeben* and *Breslau*, renamed *Yavuz* and *Midilli*, that were responsible for the incident which brought Turkey into the war.

There is, however, one other incident which underlines the apathy shown by the Entente toward Turkey's alliance with Germany.   After concluding the Turco-German alliance, the leading Germanophile, Enver Pasha, in an inexplicable move, offered the Russian Ambassador in Istanbul a Turco-Russian defensive alliance, to be based on the following points: The Turks would withdraw their troops from the Caucasus; they would dismiss the German instructors. In return they would receive compensation in the form of a return of the Aegean Islands and of territory in Thrace up to the 20th Meridian.

The Russian Ambassador Giers urged Sergei Sazanov, Russian Foreign Minister at that time, to accept this alliance, pointing out that "this would be the easiest way for Russia to establish dominance over Constantinople."

However, Sazanov could not act independently of the Allies. Delcassé, the French Foreign Minister, and Grey of Great Britain, were immediately consulted, but their reply was in the negative—out of opposition to making any territorial concession to Turkey.

It is conceivable that Enver made his proposition—knowing very well that it would be refused—in order to convince the moderates in Turkey once again that the members of the Triple Entente were against any link with Turkey and that only Germany and Austria had displayed any feeling of friendship toward her.

The signing of the alliance with Germany and subsequent mobilization and closing of the Straits did not put an end to the efforts of moderates in the Ottoman cabinet to keep Turkey out of the war and even to steer her back to neutrality. They believed that by remaining neutral they could still obtain concessions from both sides and profit politically and economically. They hoped that the capitulations could be abolished and the Aegean Islands taken back. But, as explained above, the Entente powers did nothing to encourage the moderates in these hopes. The Germans on the other hand were strengthening the hands of the extremists by promising concessions which would lead to the aggrandizement of the Ottoman Empire. Thus, the Pan-Turkish ideal would be realized!

In spite of these pressures the moderates were successful in having the Liberal Cabinet make several important decisions: 1. To reexamine the alliance with Germany. 2. Seek tripartit alliances with Bulgaria and Germany. 3. Limit the influence of the German Ambassador and the German Military Mission. 4. Finally, to wait and see, and thus to convince the Entente of Turkey's determination to remain neutral.

But the *Goeben-Breslau* incident, and the rapid developments resulting from it, made all these decisions meaningless. When these two German battleships, fleeing from British pursuers, took refuge in Turkish waters, the moderates wanted to refuse them sanctuary. But Enver Pasha made a strong case for keeping the ships there and purchasing them—of course at a nominal price—to make up for the loss of the two battleships kept by the British.

Public sentiment concerning the British action on the *Sultan Osman* and the *Reshadiye* made this suggestion generally welcome. On the other hand, even at this stage, when Cemal Pasha was approached by the British Ambassador and was asked the conditions for Turkish neutrality he enumerated them as follows: complete abolition of the Capitulations; restoration of the Aegean Islands; solution of the Egyptian question; assurance that Russia would refrain from interfering in Turkish domestic problems; effective British and French protection in case of a Russian attack.

However, the British Ambassador could not give definite and convincing responses to such conditions. But the Entente asked Turkey to give assurance that she would not close the Straits and that she would send the German Missions home.

There is much truth in Cemal Pasha's appraisal of the situation: "The Entente did not want to have the Ottoman Empire as an ally because this would, to say the least, complicate Russian plans and hopes for the eventual conquest of Istanbul and with it the Straits. However, if the Ottoman Empire did not enter the war it was believed that at the end of hostilities Istanbul could be handed over to the Russians, and other territorial and economic demands could be made on neutral Turkey"

Therefore, the only course left for the extremists was to join the Central Powers and to assist in the destruction of Russia, the real foe. Cemal Pasha's explanation of this move was: "There was of course a possibility that the Central Powers might be beaten—in which case a catastrophe was a certainty. But it is also an undeniable fact that if we had remained neutral and left the Straits open, the inevitable victory of our enemy would have sealed our fate with equal certainty."

Such reasoning was perhaps justified. The Entente had simply pushed even some of the moderate Turkish statesmen into this desperate extremist view. Nevertheless there was still a moderate like Rifat Pasha, the Ambassador in Paris, who burned up the diplomatic wires with appeals to reason. "Hostility to the Entente may endanger our very existence," he warned on September 4, 1915 "The only sane policy for Turkey consists in obtaining advantages from the Entente and pursuing strict and sincere neutrality." And a few days later, on September 28, he stated: "German interferences must be brought to

an end. The Entente is ready to condemn us to death if we act as her
enemy. Germany has no interest in saving us. She considers us as
a mere tool. In case of defeat she will use us as a means of satisfying
the appetite of the victors; in case of victory she will turn us into a
protectorate. The Entente is in a position to injure us even in the
event of an Entente defeat. We are on the direct road to dismemberment. We should recall the fact than an extremist foreign policy has
always been the cause of our misfortunes."

But it was too late. On October 28 the *Goeben* and the *Breslau*
under the German Admiral Souchon and flying the Ottoman colors
at their mastheads, struck across the Black Sea and bombarded Russian ports.

Although Enver Pasha and Cemal Pasha both claimed that Admiral
Souchon made the decision to attack the Russian ports without their
knowledge or consent and as a reprisal for Russian attacks on the
Ottoman fleet, there is reason to believe that at least Enver Pasha
knew and approved Souchon's plans in advance.

Moderates in the Cabinet still sought to prevent Turkey's entry into
the war. They thought Souchon's action provided an excuse for
abolishing the German Alliance and dismissing the German Missions.
But Enver and Talat Pasha reminded them of the threatening guns of
the *Goeben* and the *Breslau* which were lying in the Bosporus. As a
compromise measure it was proposed to the Entente that a full enquiry
into the "Black Sea incident" should be made. Russia refused to
discuss the matter and a few days later declared war on Turkey.
This was followed by declarations of war by France and Britain.

Whatever the explanation of the Black Sea incident may be, the
verdict of the Independence Tribunal, set up in Ankara in 1926 to
judge the question of war guilt on Turkey's entry into World War I,
seemed to be an objective appraisal:

"The whole Turkish nation was dragged into the war as a result of
a *fait accompli*, the work of a German admiral, who received his orders
from the Kaiser . . . In other words, a great and historic empire had
become the toy of this German admiral whose very name was unknown
to the Turkish people.

"Turkish Ministers who submitted to such steps look more like
obedient submissive servants of the Kaiser than Ministers responsible
for the welfare of Turkey. Could not these so-called Turkish patriots
punish the folly of a German officer who had played with the self-
respect of the Turkish State?"

The entry of Turkey into the war was received by the British ambassador with some joy and by the French ambassador with indif-

ference. But both the joy and the indifference were unwarranted. There were definitely disadvantages for the Entente: They were obliged to commit two to three million troops for action against Turkey, thus lessening the pressure they could bring to bear on Germany and Austria. Furthermore, as a result of the Straits' closure, war materiels from the Allies could not reach Russia, a factor in prolonging the war for at least two years.

The second disadvantage gave rise to further disadvantages for the Western powers:

1. Prolongation of the war and the inability of the Russian armies to wage a successful war against Germany hastened the Revolution and the rise of Soviet Russia.

2. The prolongation of hostilities resulted in the inability of British, German and Belgian industries to supply finished goods to many parts of the world. These potential markets then turned to the industries of the United States and Japan, and this in turn helped immensely the development of American and Japanese industries.

3. The prolongation of the war forced Britain and France to draw off additional men from their colonies and territories. While these Powers were obliged to promise more and more priviliges in return for manpower, the troops, by coming into closer contact with Europeans began to lose their respect for white men. This was perhaps the starting point of the nationalistic movements in India, southeast Asia and Africa.

The role played by the Turks in World War I was obliquely acknowledged later by leading Entente statesmen. M. Millerand, the French Prime Minister at the time of the Sèvres Conference (1920) for a Peace Treaty with the Ottoman Government, said: "The responsibilities of the Ottoman State are so great that they cannot be measured by the sacrifices made for the Allied successes achieved against the Ottoman armies. By closing the Straits and thus cutting the supply lines between Russia and Rumania on one side, and by their allies in the west on the other side, Turkey had caused the prolongation of the war for at least two years and thus had caused losses of manpower reaching millions and of material damages amounting to billions."

War and its Aftermath. During World War I Turkish armies fought on several fronts. As Vere-Hodge points out, they "proved more than a match for Western armies equipped with modern arms".

The Turkish victory at Gallipoli was one of the most important factors in the prolongation of the war. On the southern front, the Turks threatened Egypt and annihilated at least one British army at Kutal-Amara. On the eastern front, in spite of Enver Pasha's Sarikamish

disaster, they advanced up to Batum. In addition, the Turks fought
successfully in Rumania and Galicia. The war, as a matter of fact,
gave the Turks an opportunity to prove that they were still a fighting
nation.

E. G. Mears in his *Modern Turkey* states: "The Ottoman Empire
had nearly four million men under arms in the course of the World
War—of which almost 1½ million were at the fronts. This means
that the most gigantic army in Ottoman history was welded together.
When considering this unprecedented phenomenon of Ottoman history it is not difficult to praise and assess the wonderful success and
virility shown by the Ottoman Empire."

The World War had taught a number of lessons, moral and political
as well as military. In the first place, although they took a certain
pride in being comrades in arms with the Germans, the Turks resented
the fact that so many of them had to die, sometimes needlessly, while
serving under the orders of German commanders. Mustafa Kemal
(Ataturk) in particular—who, incidentally, was certain from the beginning that Germany could not be victorious—resented the attitude
and meddling of German generals.

Secondly, the fact that many Moslem peoples fought in the ranks
of the Allies against the armies of their Caliph—although the Caliph
had issued several *fetvas* (edicts) calling them to the *Jehad*—made
them bitter against the other Islamic countries and skeptical of any
proposed Pan-Islamic unity. Wrote one Turkish author: "No one
bothered to listen to the *fetvas* and other religious proclamations . . .
Indian, Algerian, and Tunisian Moslems, feeling no religious conscience, came as soldiers to fight against the Caliph and his armies."
This skepticism was to be one of the foundations of the future secular Turkish state.

Thirdly, the betrayal of the Arabs made it clear that the "Ottoman
Nation" was only an illusion. Henceforth, Turkish nationalism would
be based upon Anatolian patriotism and the ethnic entity of the Turkish people.

In the course of World War I, and later during the armistice when
Britain and France actively worked for the partition of the Ottoman
Empire, Turkish nationalism crystallized as anti-Westernism. It
was Mustafa Kemal who picked up the pieces and rebuilt the Turkish
state after its crushing defeat.

In his famous seven-day speech in 1927 to the Grand National Assembly after the Turkish War of Independence, Mustafa Kemal gave
the following picture of the general situation at the end of World War
I:

"The group to which the Ottoman State had belonged was defeated in the World War. The Ottoman army had been mutilated on every front and an armistice of harsh terms had been signed. Due to the long years of the war, the nation was tired and poor. Those who were responsible for bringing the nation and country into war, had fled in fear of their lives. The person who occupied the throne as Sultan and Caliph was a degenerate who was in quest of ways and means to preserve his throne. The Cabinet was weak, dishonest, without any pride and was completely subservient to the will of the Sultan—willing to comply with any condition under which it might preserve its position. The weapons and ammunition of the Army had been or were being confiscated . . .

"The Entente powers did not even feel the necessity of complying with the provisions of the Armistice Agreement. Under some pretext or another, the Entente fleets and soldiers were in Istanbul. The Adana Province had been occupied by the French, and Urfa, Marash, Aintab by the British. In Antalya and Konya there were Italian troops; in Merzifon and Samsun, British soldiers. Everywhere foreign officers, officials and private persons were active. Last, but not least, on May 15, 1919, a Greek army was landed in Izmir, by agreement with the Entente powers.

"On top of all this, in every corner of the country, Christian elements were doing their utmost, both openly and clandestinely, to hasten the collapse of the Ottoman State."

The terms of the Mudros Armistice, signed on October 30, 1918, were severe. They provided for: immediate opening of the Straits by an Allied occupation force along the Bosphorus and the Dardanelles; immediate demobilization of Turkish troops; general withdrawal of Turkish troops and surrender of certain specific garrisons to the Allies; and the right for the Allies to occupy strategic points.

At the first few meetings of the Supreme Council of the Peace Conference at Versailles, it became evident that peace terms would be made harsher yet than those set down in the armistice. It was also clear that the Allies were determined to amputate large slices of Turkey in order to set up the independent states of Kurdistan and Armenia and to create mandate areas in various regions of Anatolia.

Damad Ferid Pasha, who was allowed to speak to the Supreme Council at the Versailles Conference, did not try to minimize the culpability of the leaders of the *ancien regime*, but he argued that Turkey had a right to be judged according to the same principles which were to govern the settlement of other nations' problems—i.e., according to the Wilson Doctrine.

He told the Conference: "All peoples at the heart of the Ottoman Empire are firmly decided not to be downtrodden by the circumstances of the hour. They are firmly decided neither to accept the dismemberment nor the repartition of the Empire into various mandates. No government can act in this way against the resolve of a nation."

These were encouraging words for the Turks. Outside Istanbul, especially in Anatolia and Thrace, resistance groups began to spring up to counteract the activities of Armenians and other Christian elements, and Kurds, all of whom had Allied backing. These groups called themselves the "Defense of Rights Committees."

The occupation of Izmir by the Greeks on May 15, 1919 gave the necessary impetus to the Turkish resistance movement and committees increased a dozenfold in all parts of Thrace and Anatolia. The man who unified the resistance groups into one great independence movement, later incorporated into the Ankara Grand National Assembly, was General Mustafa Kemal, hero of the Gallipoli campaign.

CHAPTER II

WAR OF INDEPENDENCE

It is true that in times of crisis nations somehow produce men to pull them through. Ability to do so is the evidence of the vitality of a nation. The leader should, of course, be able to assess the potentials and limitations of his people. History, and even our own times, has not been lacking in leaders who failed to appraise their own nations accurately and mistook their own aspirations for those of their people.

Mustafa Kemal, who emerged as the leader of the Turks after their defeat in World War I, was a perfect example of a leader finding a nation and a nation finding a leader. His success stemmed from his extremely realistic appraisal of the situation, his profound knowledge of the innate desires of his own people, and, finally, the ability to know his people's potentialities and limitations. This was true when he rallied them for the War of Independence, when he embarked on his reformation program, and when he laid the groundwork for Turkey's present foreign policy.

Turkey's new leader was born as Mustafa[1] in 1881 in Salonica, which was then a part of the Ottoman Empire. Like most of the Turks of his time, he entered a military school in his early teens and graduated a captain from the Staff College in Istanbul in 1904. And like many of his contemporaries, he joined the secret society of Young Turks who were plotting against the "Red Sultan" Abdul Hamid II. He played an important part in the revolt which deposed the despot only to find himself pitted against some old collaborators who had assumed dictatorial powers. When these new leaders pushed Turkey into World War I on the side of Germany, young Colonel Kemal opposed subservience to the Kaiser and his military advisers, but this did not prevent him from becoming one of the war's most successful field commanders. His brilliant actions in the Gallipoli campaign won him world fame.

After the war, Kemal, now a renowned General, wrangled an appointment from the Istanbul government as an Inspector-General in Anatolia, ostensibly to administer the terms of the armistice. His real objective, however, was to rally various patriotic forces under one banner; within a short period he was able to crystallize the movement of national liberation forces at two momentous meetings

at Erzurum and Sivas. These meetings, attended by representatives
of practically all national groups, culminated in the centralization in
Ankara of resistance to foreign occupation of Turkey and the Sultan's
policies.

The principal points of the declaration issued by the Erzurum
Congress on July 23, 1919, were: (1) The nation is an indivisible unit.
(2) In the event that the Sultan's Government falls as a result of
invasion or due to foreign political pressure, the Turkish nation will
offer full resistance. (3) Political rights that may endanger the
social equilibrium of the nation cannot be granted to Christian minorities. (4) No foreign mandate will be accepted. (5) The immediate formation of a National Assembly is essential.

The details of these principles were worked out later at the Sivas
Congress held in September. One interesting aspect of the Sivas
meeting was that some delegates discussed the possibility of an American mandate over Turkey as "an acceptable alternative."[2] However, the majority of delegates, including Kemal, were firmly opposed
to such an idea. They wanted American support—in fact, general
Western support—for their independence movement, but not an American, nor any other, mandate. For them, it was independence or
nothing.

The principles of the independence movement were embodied in a
new national pact (*Misaki Milli*) at Istanbul. This pact is a highly
important document since it is the foundation of modern Turkey's foreign policy. The first article stipulated that "areas inhabited by an
Ottoman Moslem (Turkish) majority, united in religion, race and
aim did not admit of division for any reason." The fourth article stipulated: "The security of the city of Istanbul and of the Sea of Marmora
must be protected from every danger. Provided this principle is maintained, whatever decision may be arrived at jointly by all other governments concerned regarding the opening of the Straits to the commerce and traffic of the world is valid." In the fifth article, Turkey
guaranteed the rights of minorities "dependent on similar concessions
being made to Moslem minorities in neighboring countries." The last
article stated: "It is a fundamental of our life that we, like every
other country, should enjoy complete independence in assuring the
means for our development. For this reason we are opposed to re-
strictions inimical to our development in political, juridical, financial
and other matters."

Two factors which stiffened the resistance of the Turks, however,
were the Allied coup in Istanbul against the last Ottoman National

Assembly on March 16, 1920 and the signing by Damad Ferid Pasha, the Grand Vizier, of the Sèvres Peace Treaty.

The Istanbul National Assembly, which had convened in spite of the warnings of Mustafa Kemal, was dispersed by the Allied occupation forces, who arrested the leading members and deported them to Malta. This provided Kemal with a reason to convene the Ankara Grand National Assembly on April 23, 1920. The Sultan thus became a monarch without subjects and Istanbul a capital without a country. Henceforth, the Ankara "Grand National Assembly Government" would determine the fate of the Turkish nation.

The terms of the Sévres Peace Treaty gave Turkish nationalists further proof that Wilson's principles were empty words, that the Allies intended to dismember the Turkish nation, and that the Sultan and his government were incapable of defending their interests. The main provisions of the Sévres Treaty were:

1. An international commission was to control the Straits. Turks were not to be represented on this body.

2. The Sultan remained in charge of Constantinople and Turkey's remaining littoral on the Asiatic side of Marmora while Greece gained control of the European side.

3. Iraq, Syria, and Arabia were separated.

4. Most of Thrace was ceded to Greece and Smyrna was to be administered by Greece for a period of five years after which time a free plebiscite was to be held.

5. Turkey gave up all claims to the Aegean Islands in favor of Italy.

6. Most of the Turkish Army was to be disbanded and disarmed and the remaining security forces would come under the control of Allied officers.

7. The Capitulations would continue and special steps were to be taken to ensure full civil rights for minorities.

8. Armenia was to be independent and was to include Erzerum, Trabzon, Van, and Bitlis.

9. An independent state of Kurdistan was to be formed in eastern Anatolia.

10. An international finance commission was to supervise the financial, economic and administrative policy of the country.

11. A tripartite agreement, signed on April 20, defined three separate regions of influence for England, France, and Italy.

Although the Sèvres Treaty was never enforced, Greek, French, and Armenian military intervention began even before the treaty was actually signed.

An Aggressor Defeated and Friends Made. Under the command of

Mustafa Kemal nationalist forces, which at first comprised irregular bands, fought on several fronts. The most important front was in the west where strong Greek armies were trying to seize the territories which were promised them by the Allies and later specifically mentioned in the provisions of the Sèvres Treaty. In the southwest, in Cilicia, French troops were trying to consolidate their share. In the east, the Tashnak Armenian Republic was preparing to make the dream of a Greater Armenia a reality. In addition, the so-called "Security Army of the Sultan" was both engaging the nationalist forces directly and abetting anti-nationalist elements in the region just east of Istanbul.

The new Soviet Government, which at that time was busy denouncing imperialism and the imperialist secret agreements of the Czarist regime, was likewise threatened by the Western powers. Thus it was a natural ally of the nationalist Turkish government. Hence Kemal's first step in diplomacy was directed towards reaching an understanding with Soviet Russia. This was designed to relieve to some extent the eastern frontier and also to obtain some material aid from Russia. Soviet leaders at first were reluctant to commit themselves to an alliance with the new Turkish government. One reason for this was that the Russians, posing as champions of wronged peoples, would not join Turkey against the Armenians at a time when the future of the nationalist movement was uncertain.

Soviet Russia had proclaimed its decision "to allow Armenia, Kurdistan, Lazistan, the Batum Province . . . to decide their own destiny." Also she wanted the Straits question "submitted to a conference of states bordering the Black Sea." Furthermore, Soviet leaders were still hopeful of being able to turn the Turkish independence movement into a class war—a war of the workers and peasants against the landlords.

Kemal was successful in persuading the Soviets to accept the conditions that the relations be based on the idea of cooperation against "foreign imperialism." A Turkish "nationalist" mission to Moscow under Bekir Sami, Foreign Minister of the Ankara government, finally reached an agreement with Chicherin, the Commissar for Foreign Affairs, on a draft treaty. There was a delay of several months, however, before the treaty was signed. The Armenian Republic of Erivan, established after the Russian Revolution, was actively seeking to realize her territorial aspirations in Transcaucasia and eastern Turkey. Even while the Bekir Sami Mission was in Moscow, Russia supported Armenian aspirations and demanded that Turkey cede some of her territory to Armenia. Lenin and Chicherin obviously were playing for time, hoping perhaps that Mustafa Kemal's movement would collapse—and had their agents busy in Anatolia trying to spread communism in preparation for such a collapse.

Also there was the Enver Pasha interlude, which for a time hindered the clarification of Soviet-Turkish relations. Enver Pasha, the military dictator of the Ottoman Empire during the First World War, had escaped to Russia. There he hoped to rally the Turkish and perhaps the Islamic peoples of Asia to his banner and attempt the "liberation" of Anatolia. In the beginning the Soviet leaders supported this movement. At that time self-determination for Asian peoples "under Soviet sponsorship" concurred with Soviet policies, and a conference of the delegates of Asian peoples was organized with the help of Enver in Baku.

Mustafa Kemal and Enver had never been friends. From the days of the clandestine Young Turkish movement, Mustafa Kemal had resented the vanity and "prima donna" methods of Enver. He held him responsible for dragging Turkey into the war and for allowing the German officers a free hand in running the Turkish armed forces. When Enver tendered cooperation to the liberation movement in 1920 his offer was refused. Kemal would have nothing to do with the remnants of the Union and Progress Party. He wanted his movement to be unblemished by war guilt. Therefore Enver's "Asiatic" activities in Moscow and Baku were in contradiction to Mustafa Kemal's aims.

Mustafa Kemal drew the attention of Soviet leaders to this. At first the Russians hesitated, but when they realized that Enver's plans would eventually run counter to their imperialistic aims, they turned against him. Although guilty of forcing Turkey into war and of mismanagement of the Turkish armed forces, Enver was also a true Turkish nationalist who earnestly desired to restore the grandeur of Turkey. He died heroically in pursuit of this ideal while leading a cavalry charge of Basmachi Turks in Central Asia against the Red Army. But his dream of Pan-Turanism or Pan-Islamism was patently unrealistic. Had Mustafa Kemal cooperated with him or left the stage to him the collapse of the Anatolian liberation movement would surely have been the result.

A fully fledged Turco-Russian Treaty was signed on March 16, 1921, after Turkish forces had defeated the Armenians, and after their victories over the Greeks on the Western Front had convinced the Soviet leaders that the Turkish star was in the ascendant. The Armenian threat on the eastern front was eliminated by force of arms. At first, forces of the Armenian Republic, strongly supported morally and materially by Americans and the English, advanced as far as Oltu, occupying Kars and Sarikamish, massacring the Turkish population which lay in their path. This advance, however, was halted by the offensive of the Turkish Army under General Kazim Karabekir which re-occupied Sarikamish, Kars and Gumru (Alexandropol). It was at Gumru that, on December 3, 1920, Turkey dictated peace terms to the Armenians, putting an end to their dreams of a Greater Armenia. This, incidentally, was the first treaty the new Turkish State signed with a foreign power.

The Turks, simultaneously with their victory over the Armenians, put an end to the attacks of the irregular forces of the Georgian Menshevik Republic. Thus, Turkey, early in 1921, was relieved on her eastern frontiers and had gained a friend—the Union of Soviet Socialistic Republics—with whom she could have trade relations and from whom she could obtain war materials.

On The Western Front. The war with Greece in many respects was full of anachronisms. Although the Greeks at first were urged by all three members of the Entente to land in Izmir, both France and Italy later showed themselves reluctant to give her continued support. Great Britain, under Lloyd George, was the only power that gave nominal help to Greece during the Greek-Turkish war. But this support was never completely overt nor was aid offered on a very large scale. This half-heartedness was due to opposition at home and to advice of military experts. There were many attempts, both by England and the other Entente powers, to bring an end to hostilities between Greece and Turkey. So far as Lloyd George was concerned, however, all these efforts were made primarily to appease public opinion at home and never in the belief that the Turks would win.

Turkey refused the terms proposed during the first negotiations held in London. Then the Greeks refused the second set of proposals which were agreed upon by the Entente powers at the Paris Conference (June, 1921) as a basis for compromise between Turkey and Greece. King Constantine, reinstated on the Greek throne, was confident that even without the aid of the Allies the Greek Army "could break the backbone of the Kemalists." The Allies were then obliged to proclaim their neutrality (August 10, 1921) and 13 days later the decisive battle of Sakarya, near Ankara, took place. It was this engagement that diminished the offensive capability of the Greek Army.

When the third bid for an armistice was made in the Spring of 1922, again by Allied ministers, it was Mustafa Kemal's turn to refuse. He saw this as a last effort to save the virtually defeated Greek Army. Turkey's final offensive, therefore, began on August 26, 1922, with his famous order: "Turkish Armies, your first objective is to reach the

Mediterranean." The order was carried out. On September 9 the Greek Army in Western Anatolia was destroyed and Izmir recaptured.

Turkey Makes New Friends. During the war with Greece a number of important diplomatic developments had taken place in other sectors. France, always reluctant to support the Greeks, perceived earlier than Great Britain that the Kemalists might be victorious. She was intent on securing some concessions, economic and financial, from the new leaders of Turkey. In June, 1921, a French representative, M. Franklin Bouillon, arrived in Ankara and started negotiations. There was some hesitation on the French side, due to the Turkish determination that the capitulations should come to an end. However, after Kemal's triumph at Sakarya, a pact amounting to a separate peace treaty was signed between Turkey and France. Under its provisions, France evacuated the Cilicia region, thereby relieving large forces of Turks on the southern frontier. A settlement fixing the future boundary between Syria and Turkey was reached, and France received concessionary rights to the Baghdad railway between Pozanti and Nusaybin in the province of Adana. An article of the pact regulated the temporary status of the Alexandretta region, which the Turks considered to be within the boundaries stipulated in the national pact; a special administrative regime was to be established and Turkish inhabitants were to enjoy every facility for the development of their cultural needs.

The third member of the Entente, Italy, had from the beginning of Turkey's war of independence supported the nationalists, more or less openly, by supplying them with war material. The port of Antalya, which was under Italian occupation, had become the main supply port of the Ankara Government. However, a treaty signed between Count Sforza and Bekir Sami, Turkish Foreign Minister, on March 12, 1921, whereby Turkey recognized preferential Italian rights in the vilayets of Antalya, Burdur, Mugla, and Isparta, in return for Italy's promise of support in an eventual peace conference, was declared null and void by Mustafa Kemal, with the explanation that Bekir Sami had acted without the consent of the Ankara Government.

After the defeat of the Greeks and the recapture of Izmir, Turkish armies continued their advance toward Istanbul. For a time there was danger of war with Great Britain as Lloyd George was determined to prevent Turkey's seizure of the Straits. Great Britain called for troops from the British Dominions and from the Allies, with this official explanation: "If the advance of Kemalist forces on Istanbul and the Dardanelles and the demands of the Ankara Government are to be accepted, the benefits of the victory won over the

Turks in the last war will have been lost. The deep, salt water passage which separates Europe and Asia and which joins the Black Sea and the Mediterranean is strongly linked to most important world and British interests." Although Australia and New Zealand agreed to send troops, and France and Italy were willing to cover the retreat of the Greek forces in Thrace, Great Britain did not muster enough support to defend Istanbul and the Straits.

On October 11, the Mudanya Armistice was signed whereby the Turks were allowed to re-occupy the Straits, Istanbul, and Thrace as far as the Maritza River. This was an inglorious defeat for England, and for Lloyd George in particular. Frank Simonds in his *History of Post-War Europe* says that never before had British prestige "sunk this low." The Cabinet under Lloyd George was consequently forced to resign.

A Conference is Convened, a Treaty is Signed. Invitations to a peace conference at Lausanne were issued by the Allies on October 27, 1922. The Western powers, still reluctant to recognize the Ankara Government as the sole representative of the Turkish people, had made it a point to invite representatives of both the Ankara and Istanbul governments. Mustafa Kemal's regime, however, proved that the Istanbul regime was "de facto" defunct, by a resolution of its legislative body. The Grand National Assembly in Ankara abolished the Sultanate of the Ottoman Dynasty and proclaimed instead the "Sultanate of the People" on November 2, 1922. (The Republic was established October 29, 1923).

This meant that at Lausanne the delegates of the Western powers would be confronted by the delegates of a regime which was determined to break loose from all the stagnant traditions of the Ottoman Empire. The Lausanne Conference, and the subsequently signed Lausanne Treaty, would therefore be one of the foundation stones of modern Turkey's foreign relations, as well as the keystone for a new and progressive Turkish diplomacy.

Ottoman statesmen of nineteenth century vintage had always accepted the fact that they were representing a "Sick Man." To them their geographical link between East and West, their control of the Straits and their long borders with Russia were all extreme disadvantages. They therefore adopted a vacillating policy of playing the big powers against each other in order to avoid the brunt of these physical disadvantages. Their aim was to gain time, or, in their own words, "manage the affairs" and pass the day. They accepted without questions the right of the Western powers to obtain all sorts of concessions, to meddle in the internal affairs of the empire, and to infringe on the sovereignty of the Turkish state. It is a sad thing to read, for instance, that the prime minister or a minister of the once glorious empire would listen patiently to, and more often than not, comply with, the outrageous demands of the ambassadors, or even dragomen, of the Western powers.

The Young Turks had wanted to break away from this tradition. They resented foreign meddling in the internal affairs of the Turkish state. They wanted to abolish the capitulations and all the other concessions which were infringements of the sovereignty of the state. But nevertheless one reads in the memoirs of Cemal Pasha that even he listened patiently to the French Military Attaché, who was demanding that a certain person who had plotted against the Turkish government be "pardoned"; or to the Italian Ambassador who "demanded" that Italian surveyors be allowed to survey Turkish lands.

It was at Lausanne and after Lausanne that a new forward-looking Turkish statesmanship emerged which was jealously conscious of Turkey's national sovereignty, with all its ramifications. This sensitivity on national sovereignty would prove to be a dominant factor in modern Turkey's foreign relations.

It is true that Turkish diplomacy at Lausanne made some use of the rivalry between the Western powers themselves, and also between the western powers and Soviet Russia. But this was not done to "manage the affairs" or pass the day; it was done to ensure adamantive foundations for the new Turkish state and its foreign policy.

Roderic H. Davison, who has written a stimulating monograph on Turkish diplomacy, *From Mudros to Lausanne*, says: "The nationalists from the start limited their aim to the preservation of control and complete sovereignty only over those areas which were predominantly Turkish in character. Nationalist diplomacy used all means possible to attain these limited but almost rigid objectives. Its workings can be understood only by following the sequence of events from the establishment of nationalist policy in 1919 to the triumph of its diplomacy at Lausanne in 1923."

Lausanne Conference. The Lausanne Conference started on November 20, 1922. The gathering broke up from February 4 to April 24 because the Turkish delegate refused to accept certain terms which the Allies were trying to impose. The Peace Treaty was finally signed on July 24, 1923.

The man who led the Turkish delegation to Lausanne was Ismet Pasha (later Ismet Inönü, President of Turkey), then the foreign minister. Primarily a soldier, with only staff duty as his main experience, he was confronted by some of the most experienced states-

men of the Western countries, among them Lord Curzon of Britain.
Ismet Pasha was quite conscious of the fact that he represented a
victorious nation, but he had some difficulty in making the Allied delegates accept this fact.   They still insisted on treating Turkey as a defeated nation entitled to only limited sovereignty.   The conference
dragged on for eight months, during which time all efforts of Lord
Curzon to bully Ismet Pasha failed.

At Mustafa Kemal's directions Ismet Pasha showed justified
obstinacy in asserting the independence and sovereignty of the new
Turkey.   He demanded the abolition of all controls over her finance,
economy, judicial system, minorities and her territory.   "Turkey is
rightly sensitive on the question of sovereignty," he declared, "her
misgivings are well founded for, up to the present day, Turkish sovereignty has always been infringed upon the plea of humanitarian
considerations.   The integrity of Turkey was frequently guaranteed
by the highest authorities and by solemn treaties, yet her sovereignty
was repeatedly violated."

Ismet's emphatic insistence on complete sovereignty irked Lord
Curzon time and time again.   "Cannot the Turks realize that theirs
is not the only sovereignty in the world"? he asked.   The contrast
between Curzon's flamboyant brilliance and eloquence and Ismet's
timorous but obstinate stand was well marked.   Ismet also used his
deafness as a stratagem to gain time, but he always heard what he
wanted to hear.   And, of course, as he himself admitted, via continuous telegraphic communication, he had the brilliance of Kemal to
save him from being cornered on numerous occasions.

Ismet made good use of the rivalry among the Western powers, and
between the Western powers and Soviet Russia.   During the Conference Chicherin was ready to give advice to Ismet and seemed to be
the benevolent protector of the new Turkish state, and Ismet appeared
ready to take advice.   "Turkey could look to the East and the North
as well as to the West," he said.   But he managed to avoid being
made a satellite of Russia at the conference.   The test of this was the
Straits question.   Russia wanted Turkey to assert full control over
the Straits and close the Black Sea to vessels of non-Black Sea powers.
This seemingly pro-Turkish view was in reality for the benefit of
Soviet Russia.

As will later be expounded, the Turks accepted the Western suggestion of opening the Straits to all, even though it meant the demilitarization of the waterway.   Although there was agreement on
many disputed questions, there were many others, such as the Turkish-
Iraq boundary in the Mosul region, the sharing of the Ottoman debt,

reparations, and the liquidation of the capitulations, which caused a break in the negotiations on February 4.

There were many extremists in the Turkish Government and Grand National Assembly who were opposed to the resumption of the negotiations. Soviet Russia supported this view, hoping that Turkey would thus continue on a course of anti-Westernism. However, Mustafa Kemal favored the resumption of the negotiations and eventual rapproachement with the Western powers, and the conference re-convened on April 24. Three months and many wearisome sessions later, as a result of concessions and counter-concessions, the Lausanne Treaty was finally signed on July 24, 1923.

The Lausanne Treaty was the first post-war treaty that the Allies had to sign with a former enemy on equal terms and, in every respect, it contrasted sharply with the Versailles, Neuilly, and Sèvres treaties. Turkey had come to this conference as a victor and rightly considered it the continuation of her war of independence in a new phase. She was determined to make the utmost use of her military victory and of the fact that the Allies were unable to undertake the prolongation of the struggle.

On the other hand, the British and the French were determined to prevent Turkey from gaining complete sovereignty or entering the Russian sphere of influence, and they had difficulty in accepting the fact that the delegates speaking for Turkey were, both in spirit and professional standing, quite different from the Ottoman delegates they had been accustomed to deal with throughout the 19th century until Sèvres.

In general it was a positive diplomatic victory for the new Turkish government. It abrogated the humiliating Sèvres Treaty in toto. Turkey was to pay no reparations. Her boundaries, except for the Mosul and Syrian frontiers which were either left unsettled for further negotiations or regulated by a special regime, were those fixed by the national pact of the Turkish nationalist movement. The idea of an Armenia on Turkish territory was eliminated; Izmir and southern Turkey would remain Turkish; the Greek population in Anatolia would be exchanged for the Turkish population in western Thrace; capitulations and all the humiliating concessions granted to European powers would be abolished; the complete economic freedom and sovereignty of Turkey were recognized; and there were to be no limitations on Turkish armed forces. As an American author wrote: "If the treaty arising from the Lausanne Conference had sounded the death knell to the old Ottoman Empire by cutting away vast territories, it had signaled the coming of the new Turkish Republic which was freed from ancient institutions, in the process of becoming a modern nation."

The price paid for this victory at Lausanne, in addition to the blood of the Turkish warriors in the War of Independence, were some serious concessions on the Straits question. The Straits settlement at Lausanne—which will be discussed in more detail—provided for the demilitarization of the Turkish Straits and for the establishment of an international commission to regulate matters pertaining to the passage of ships. This was obviously not compatible with Turkey's national sovereignty nor did it adequately safeguard Turkey's defenses. Ismet Pasha explained at the time: "We have abandoned the principle of the closing of the Straits, a principle which, as has been proved by past experience, is historically that which most adequately secures the safety of our capital and we have agreed that the waters of the Straits shall be open to the ships of all nations. Further, in spite of the fact that in many cases where both shores of an open waterway belong to a single power, that power retains by usage the right of fortification, but we have agreed in the present instance to demilitarization. We have also abandoned our request regarding the maintenance of a garrison in the Gallipoli peninsula."

These sacrifices were undertaken, in spite of Soviet opposition, in order to conciliate the Allies. Turkey desired peace and rapprochement with the Western powers. Lausanne, despite its shortcomings, would pave the way. Indeed, Turkish leaders were able to use the treaty as a symbol of achievement by which they enhanced their prestige, both at home and abroad, and also as a starting point for the social revolution.

CHAPTER III

BETWEEN TWO WORLD WARS

"If the Turkish Empire," Lord Palmerston wrote in 1839, "could be given a decade of peace and if the time is profitably used for its internal reorganization, there is no reason whatever why it should not become again a respectable Power . . . Half the wrong conclusions at which mankind arrive are reached by the abuse of metaphors, and by mistaking general resemblance of imaginary similarity for real identity. Thus people compare an ancient monarch with an old building, an old tree or an old man, and because the building, tree or man crumble, or decay or die, they imagine that the same holds good for a community . . . All that we hear about the decay of the Turkish Empire, and its being a dead body or a sapless trunk, and so forth, is pure and unadulterated nonsense."

Yet this very sympathetic attitude was not shared by the majority of European statesmen, even after Lausanne. In 1918 and 1919 even the friendliest Europeans were sure that the Turks would cease to exist as a nation. The successful War of Independence and the Lausanne Treaty were rude awakenings for those European statesmen who had some trouble in adjusting themselves to the reality of a new and different Turkish state, one which could and did act independently and resisted all forms of foreign interference.

After Lausanne the determination and character of this new state were put to a number of tests. There was the joint demand made by England, France, and Italy that the capital of Turkey not be moved to Ankara—apparently for the reason that a capital on the sea could be brought under the threat of enemy naval guns.[1] There was an attempt to prevent the Turkish government from controlling the curricula of foreign schools. Then a move was made to name a Greek Patriarch who would be subservient to the interests of the Allies. Finally, there was the "Mosul" incident between Britain and Turkey. The Turkish government took a firm stand in the face of all these circumstances and, ironically, the first British Ambassador to Ankara found himself admitting that "there certainly is a very different climate in Ankara."

As was to be expected, during the years immediately following Lausanne a feeling of intense nationalism dominated both the domestic and foreign affairs of the new state. Suspicion of Europeans and

47

animosity towards all Western-held concessions and Western firms constituted the *leit-motif* of the first decade.   This antagonistic attitude was so marked that Europe was sure Turkey was being drawn into the Soviet sphere of influence.   The Russian leaders on their part certainly did their best to make this a reality.   Soviet Russia had helped the Turkish nationalist movement by providing financial and military aid.   There was a feeling of a common front against the west.   Russian representatives and experts were welcomed virtually as brothers and heroes wherever they went in Turkey.

In its hatred of the West, Turkey could easily have become the first Soviet satellite, or, in the era of Hitler and Mussolini, extreme Turkish nationalists could have followed a course of irredentism, claiming the lost provinces of the Ottoman Empire.   Least dangerous of probabilities would have been for Turkey to smoulder in unproductive nationalism, to remain a backward, stagnant Oriental country—a dangerous power vacuum.

It was Mustafa Kemal's vision and forceful personality which prevented Turkey from taking these dangerous courses.   He freed the country from Russia's bear-hug and allied himself with the West.   He guided the extreme nationalism into constructive patriotism.   Utilizing this patriotism he transformed a backward, medieval country into a modern republic.   The enormity and full meaning of his internal reforms can be better appreciated if conditions in the Turkey of thirty-five years ago are kept in mind.   In a country where the Ottoman Sultans ruled for centuries as Allah's Shadow on Earth, Mustafa Kemal had the courage and vision to wipe out centuries of tradition—and corruption—by announcing that "The Turkish State is a republic."   The abolition of the Sultanate was rapidly followed by the abolition of the Caliphate, another expensive luxury.

The next logical step, that would have been considered unthinkable in the pre-Kemal days, was the separation of religious and state affairs.   The law of the Koran had been entrenched and dominated all segments of the society and state.   Kemal proclaimed that the new state was to be secular.   He then replaced the *Sheria*, the law of the Koran, with a modern civil code, adapted from the Swiss civil code, and a penal code adopted from the Italian penal code.   The entire legal system was based on Roman law.

These reforms had their greatest impact on the status of women.   Most of the women in Turkish society thirty-five years ago were confined behind latticed windows, were not permitted to have jobs, could be divorced at the whim of their husbands, or could be made one of four wives in a harem.   The new civil code gave Turkish women complete equality; emancipated women were encouraged to get into the professions, and in 1934 they acquired the right to vote and to be elected to parliament.

Mustafa Kemal accomplished these reforms rapidly and dramatically. For instance, when he decided to abolish the fez, headgear considered by the people as the symbol of Islam, he simply put on a Western hat and drove into one of the most conservative towns in Anatolia. He got out of his car in the town square and coolly addressed the gaping crowd, "This, gentlemen," he said, "is called a hat, and it is the headgear of civilized people." That marked the end of the fez in Turkey.

Another of his dramatic reforms was the abolition of the Arabic script and adoption of Latin characters. Turkish intellectuals had known for a long time that the Arabic script was not suitable for the Turkish language and that it was very difficult for Turks to master this script. This in turn accounted for the high illiteracy rate. But in the face of strong conservatism no one had dared to suggest a change. Kemal, however, had made up his mind. He asked his advisers how long it would take to adopt the Latin script. The minimum period suggested was seven years. Kemal cut the discussions short. "We'll do it in seven weeks," he said, and within a short time the new Turkish script was being used in schools and in all the newspapers. Still another important development was the institution of a limited, planned state economy. This arose partly as a result of the nationalist urge for economic independence and partly from the lack of private capital within Turkey.

But the greatest achievement of Mustafa Kemal was his ability to organize the intense nationalism of the twenties so that it became productive patriotism. This patriotism was the driving force of his internal reforms and had prepared the ground for a rapprochement with Turkey's former enemies in the West. For, even during bitter negotiations of the Lausanne Conference, Mustafa Kemal had decided that Turkey's fortune lay with the West. In 1923 he expressed himself thus: "The West has always been prejudiced against the Turks and has always tried to destroy us, but we Turks have always and consistently moved towards the West. . . In order to be a civilized nation, there is no other alternative!" How he implemented his desire for a rapprochement with the West and how he managed to evade the "friendship" of both the Soviets and the Axis powers will be explained later.

Before setting out a detailed examination of the foreign relations of the new Turkey, two important tenets of Mustafa Kemal's world outlook must be mentioned. These were his sincere desire for world peace, and his no less sincere determination to avoid foreign adventures. It would seem paradoxical that a successful general like Kemal would hate war so intensely, but it is a fact that the basic philosophy of this general was based on peace. He once said: "There are two means of conquering; one is the sword, and the other the plough. . . The nation whose only means for victory is the sword will be ultimately defeated. The real conquest is the one achieved by the plough. The plough and the sword—of these the second has always been defeated by the first." On another occasion he expressed the aim of his foreign policy in a nutshell: "Peace in the country, peace in the world."

Perhaps his dramatic discarding of his general's uniform at the end of the war was also symbolic of his passionate desire for peace and peaceful methods. While Hitler and Mussolini, who were not professional soldiers, were always in uniform, Mustafa Kemal, who had earned his medals and uniform in the field, was in mufti. This desire for peace kept him from irredentism and all other kinds of foreign adventures. Like his contemporaries he could very well have claimed, and perhaps obtained, some of the old territories of the Ottoman Empire, or he could easily have succumbed to various offers and temptations and led adventures into Pan-Turanism and Pan-Islamism. But he did not follow these courses. He had drawn the frontiers of the real Turkey, the land inhabited by Turks, and beyond these frontiers he would not go. He realized that progress, the well-being and happiness of his people were more important than territorial aggrandizement or personal glory. He also knew that all his and his people's energy was needed for the gigantic task of developing Turkey into a Western country. It was on these principles that Mustafa Kemal embarked on the implementation of his new foreign policy.

Toward A Balkan Federation. Mustafa Kemal often said that a Balkan federation should be the ultimate aim of Turkish foreign policy. He visualized a strong federation as a third power in Europe, which would keep the solidifying Axis bloc and the Western powers in a peaceful balance and also prevent piece-meal attacks against each of the Balkan states by Germany or Russia, in case of war.

Kemal's efforts for Balkan unity, however, were made in an extremely hostile atmosphere and received little encouragement at the first. Greece was primarily a frustrated former enemy, and the Lausanne Treaty had not solved all the problems between the two countries, the most outstanding of which was the minority question. The wholesale exchange of Turkish and Greek minorities had caused a great social upheaval in both countries and Turkish-Greek relations had become strained. Violations and counter-violations of exchange agreements, and reprisals and counter-reprisals made any rapprochement between the two countries impossible for a long period. Italy at the time was aiming at a tripartite pact with Turkey and Greece but was compelled to give up the idea and signed bilateral treaties with Turkey and Greece instead, in 1928.

In 1929 expulsion of the subservient Greek Patriarch, Constantine, from Istanbul and the reconditioning of the Turkish battleship *Yavuz* further aggravated the situation.[2] Suddenly, however, as if by magic, the situation changed. Prime Minister Elefteros Venizelos of Greece, who in 1920 said that for Greece's security "Turks should be thrown back to the Anatolian plateau and their country should be partitioned," pointed out in a speech delivered in the Greek Parliament in 1929 that friendship with a "strong Turkey" would provide the best foundation for Greek security. Conversely, the Turkish press, which for years had attacked Venizelos bitterly, began to refer to him as "Turkey's friend." The magic word, to all appearances, was the joint good sense and farsightedness shown by Ataturk and by Venizelos coupled with conciliatory efforts on the part of Italy.

On June 10, 1930 the minorities problem was solved by the signing of a new agreement. When, in October, Venizelos paid Turkey a visit on board a Greek battleship, he was enthusiastically welcomed. On October 30 a treaty of "neutrality, conciliation and arbitration" was signed in Ankara. This treaty, followed in 1933 by a "Cordial Friendship Pact," was to lay the basis of the Balkan Entente and, even today, constitutes a foundation for close relations between the two countries.

The Balkan situation outside the sphere of Turkish-Greek relations, however, appeared less bright. Bulgaria was the object of revisionist claims by Yugoslavia, Rumania and Greece. In addition, the Turco-Greek accord could not fail to displease her, especially since one of its clauses specifically guaranteed the Greek frontiers. Rumania and Yugoslavia, in turn, felt the pressure of Hungarian and Italian threats; and Greece, suspicious of the motives of both Bulgaria and Yugoslavia, war prompted to come to an understanding with Turkey.

Turkey had signed treaties with all the Balkan States separately (with Yugoslavia in October, 1925 and November, 1933; and with Bulgaria in 1929; with Rumania in October, 1933; and with Hungary in 1927). Nonetheless, after reaching her accord with Greece, she started working for Balkan unity, which she envisaged as a bulwark against any potential aggressor, notably Mussolini's Italy and Soviet

Russia. Both Italy and Russia, and later Germany, took a negative attitude toward the Entente and schemed in many ways to break it up.

As has been mentioned earlier, the second agreement between Greece and Turkey, the Cordial Friendship Pact of 1933, became one of the foundation-stones of the Balkan Entente. Article 3 of the Pact read as follows: "In all international meetings the membership of which is restricted, Greece and Turkey are prepared to consider that it will be the duty of the representative of one of the two parties to defend the common interests of both parties; and they undertake to endeavour to secure such joint representation, either alternately or, in particular cases of special importance, by the country most closely concerned."

Several efforts were made towards a Balkan unity. The first Balkan Conference in 1930 avoided controversial issues and was concerned with plans for economic, cultural and technical cooperation. The second Balkan Conference (1931) was concerned with the task of formulating a non-aggression pact and reaching an agreement on pacific settlement of disputes. The third conference (1932), however, was a political failure because of the negative attitude by Bulgaria who was harassed by minority and frontier disputes. On the economic side, at least, it succeeded in setting up a Balkan Chamber of Commerce in Istanbul. Not withstanding Bulgaria's negative attitude and her eventual refusal to join, the Balkan Entente was signed in February, 1934. The preamble to the pact stated that "in the spirit of the Briand-Kellogg Pact," the four signatories (Turkey, Greece, Rumania, and Yugoslavia) wished to contribute to the consolidation of peace in the Balkans (1) by binding themselves to a mutual guarantee of security of all their joint Balkan frontiers; (2) by agreeing to hold joint consultations in emergencies to agree on measures to be taken; (3) "not to embark on any political action (in respect of any Balkan state) without previous mutual discussion and not to assume any political obligation towards any other Balkan state without the consent of other signatories."

The new Entente received the approval of England and France, and the Turkish press in particular was very enthusiastic about the result. In October, 1934, several new statutes were adopted in Ankara: The permanent council was to hold regular sessions; an economic council was to be set up, and a legal commission formed for the purpose of unifying the legal codes in the Balkans; discussions for postal and customs unions were started. Nonetheless, enthusiasm gradually waned and it became evident before long that the Entente had failed to unite the Balkans.

Theodore Geshkoff, in his *Balkan Union,* had this explanation: "The Balkan Entente is a fragile combination of small states having a definite and limited objective; namely, to guarantee some of the frontiers against the possible aggression of certain small and weak states. The members of both ententes seem to have completely ignored the fact that they have other frontiers to guard against the aggression of great and predatory states."

The weakness of the Pact had indeed become evident from the very outset. A protocol, signed along with the Pact but kept secret for some time, stipulated that if a signatory were attacked by a non-Balkan power and later assisted by a Balkan power, the other Entente signatories would be obliged to go to war against the Balkan aggressors. However, both Turkey and Greece reassured Russia and Italy, respectively, that the clause would not operate against them in case they became involved with a Balkan State.

Vere-Hodge points out that "the effect of the reservations made by Ankara and Athens greatly decreased the value of the general guarantee of security to Yugoslavia and Rumania." It is quite apparent, however, that it was not only these reservations which made the Balkan Entente as ineffective as it was. The non-participation of Bulgaria and Albania (the former because she interpreted it as being an anti-Bulgarian instrument, and the latter because of Italy's influence) was also instrumental in the failure of the Pact, as were the German economic offensive and intrigues in the Balkans which resulted in a series of bilateral agreements, and in the feeling of isolationism which was rife among all the signatories except Turkey, who continued to hope to the end that the Balkan Entente would work. On July 14, 1937, the Turkish Prime Minister, Ismet Inonu, stated: "The special policies of the four Balkan states which from time to time are made manifest because of their different tendencies give rise to propaganda to the effect that their obligations emanating from the Balkan Entente are diminishing or growing feeble. We have taken notice of this propaganda; it should not nevertheless receive credulity. We have ascertained through personal and intimate contacts that the four Balkan States are sincere and persistent in the ideal of peace which unites."

As it became tragically evident during Hitler's onslaught in the Balkans, Inonu's statement constituted wishful thinking. However, "right up to the outbreak of the world conflict, Turkish policy remained unswervingly loyal to the principles of the Balkan Entente; and her statesmen sought all possible means to avert a break-up of

Balkan unity." Nevertheless, as the Turks saw the weaknesses, they attempted to seek other security arrangements outside the Entente.

Deterioration of Relations. When the Turks were struggling for their independence, their northern neighbor, Soviet Russia, was also fighting against foreign intervention. The two countries, in point of fact, had common enemies. They were both "outcasts" from the Western community, and for both of them the chief villain and major cause of their troubles was England. Thus it was only natural that two new governments, the Turkish Grand National Assembly government and the Soviet Russian government, should be drawn together.

As previously pointed out, the Soviet leaders were at first doubtful of the chances for success of the Turkish independence movement and did not hasten to sign a formal accord with the Turks. The first military victory of the Kemalist forces against the Greek Army, the first battle of Inonu in January, 1921, was the main reason for the change in heart at the Kremlin in regard to the new Turkey.

The Soviet leaders thereafter were aware of the existence of "ulterior" justification for a rapprochement with Mustafa Kemal. By supporting the independence movements of peoples who were once subjects of the Tsar and of peoples neighboring on Russia such as Iran, and Afganistan, they were already forming a "friendly" sphere of influence around them. A friendly "nationalist" Turkey would be far preferable to an Ottoman government which would be subservient to the Allies, as were the Armenian and Georgian governments of the time. Furthermore an anti-Western Turkey was susceptible to communism, and with adequate propaganda and agitation there was the possibility of transforming the Turkish nationalist movement into a communist movement.

On their side, the Turks were desperately in need of friends both for moral and material support. If they could achieve an accord with the Soviets, they would feel relieved at least on one important frontier and be free to transfer their forces from there to the western front. Also, they could obtain military and civilian supplies, and perhaps monetary aid, from Russia. The Turks had always been suspicious of Tsarist Russia, knowing that she had had ambitions regarding both the Straits and Istanbul and some of the eastern territories. Perhaps as a mere temporary tactical move, the Soviet government had renounced all claims of the Tsars and all secret agreements concluded between Russia and the Allies, including those which pertained to the partition of the Ottoman Empire. This gesture had made a favorable impression on the Turks, and gave them the feeling that they could make a fresh start with a new Russia.

Concurrent with this optimism was the apprehension felt by Turkish leaders that communist agitation and infiltration, following upon close friendship with the Soviets, was easily possible. Mustafa Kemal, besides inserting provisions against such a possibility into the treaty, (signed March 16, 1921, in Moscow) was shrewd enough to anticipate future difficulties. When the Soviets suggested that Turkish communists should be allowed to form a Turkish Communist Party, he did not refuse. Instead, he instructed some of his close friends, who were no more communist than he, to form the Turkish Communist Party which was abolished when its usefulness was ended.

This first Turco-Soviet treaty, pact of "friendship and brotherhood," in its 16 Articles, defined the Turkish border on the northeast in accordance with the "National Pact"; recognized the identity of interest of the two countries; gave suzerainty over Batum to Russia (with a proviso that the Turkish community there should enjoy full freedom and that the Turks should be allowed to use Batum as a free port); declared null and void all previous treaties concluded between Tsarist Russia and the Ottoman government; denounced the capitulations and envisaged cooperation and collaboration in all fields and treaties regulating economic, financial and other questions.

Further, Article VIII states: "Both parties undertake not to allow on their respective territories the formation and sojourn of groups that would lay claim to the role of government in the country of the other party."

In regard to the Straits question, the Pact contained the following stipulations: "With a view to guaranteeing the freedom of the Straits and their free passage for commercial purposes to all countries, both parties agree to entrust to a special conference, composed of delegates of all the riparian states, the drafting of the definitive and international status of the Black Sea and of the Straits, on condition that its decisions shall not prejudice the absolute sovereignty and safety of her capital, Istanbul."

But in spite of the treaty and in spite of the aid given by Soviet Russia, there was a mutual and tacit understanding that the "friendship" was to be a limited and pragmatic one. Zinoniev, the President of the Congress of Eastern Peoples held in 1921, had said: "We give patient aid to groups of persons who do not believe in our ideas, who are even opposed to us on some points. In the same way the Soviet Government supports Kemal in Turkey. Never for one moment do we forget that the movement headed by Kemal is not a communist movement. We know it!" Mustafa Kemal, on the other hand said: "We are on the same side with Russia. Her enemies are our enemies, but we have no intention of fighting exploiters in order to be enslaved by others."

The subtle point underlying this friendship was emphasized by a Turkish writer: "Nationalist Turkey could not allow the spreading of Bolshevist revolutionary doctrines into her own terrain. Bolshevist Russia too, did not find it convenient to allow the spreading of the Turkish nationalist (Pan-Turkish) movement into Russia . . . On both sides this feeling prevented a real entente."

During the years of the war of independence the Soviets did their best to increase their exports to Turkey. In view of the fact that Turkey especially needed finished goods, Soviet-Turkish trade reached unprecedented heights in the decade 1921-31. By 1923, however, Turkish leaders had misgivings regarding Soviet economic aims and difficulties subsequently arose in commercial relations (as, for example, when the Russians insisted that Russian trade bureau personnel enjoy diplomatic rights to which Turkey objected; or when Turkey did not exempt Russian exports from protective tariffs).

In addition to encountering difficulties in trade relations, Turkey entertained a growing suspicion in regard to Communist propaganda. Despite Kemal's ruse in having his friends organize the Turkish Communist Party, by 1924 some real Bolshevik sympathizers were gaining power. During 1924 and 1925, the Ankara Government took action against the so-called "Green Army" and a newspaper with leftist tendencies. Many Communists were tried by the famous "Independence Tribunals" which had been formed to combat opposition to Kemal and Kemalist reforms. In spite of the commercial difficulties, the Communist agitation in Turkey, and the anti-Communist measures taken by the Turkish government, a non-aggression pact was signed between Turkey and Russia on December 17, 1925 in Paris. The main factor prompting the Turks to take this action was their renewed suspicion toward "British" imperialism, which, on the Mosul issue, had indeed alarmed them.

Article I of this Pact reads: "Both parties agree to observe neutrality toward the other in case a military action should be carried out by one or more powers against one signatory party." The most important article insofar as it would have much influence on future foreign relations of Turkey was Article II, which states: "The High Contracting Parties engage to avoid all forms of aggression against the other party. Both parties bind themselves not to participate in any alliance or entente of a political nature directed by one or more powers against the other Contracting Party. Likewise, the Contracting Parties agree not to participate in an alliance or entente directed by one or several powers against the military and naval security of the other party."

In 1927 a commercial treaty was also signed and hailed by the Soviet press as "another mark and evidence of Turkish-Soviet solidarity." Yet, although the volume of trade between the two countries increased between 1927 and 1930, relations were not always amicable. Even while treaty negotiations were being carried out, some friction had arisen as a result of Soviet insistence on establishing "branches of the commercial delegation" in many Turkish cities. The Turks were successful in rejecting the establishment of such offices in Kars and Artvin. They had reason to suspect the motivation for these branch offices, and were especially sensitive to the idea of having them established in such important cities as Kars and Artvin.

Then, after the new commercial treaty had been concluded in 1931, further similar difficulties arose, such as the blocking of the funds of Turkish merchants in Russia and Soviet dumping practices. These obstructionist actions on the part of the Soviets created much ill feeling in Turkey, especially in the Turkish press. One newspaper wrote: "The invasion of the market by Russian coal, the ruin of our cement industry, the fact that the exportation of Turkish tobacco to Germany and of Turkish wheat to Greece is now impossible owing to Soviet competition, and the threat to our cotton textile industry make an inquiry into Soviet dumping necessary."

As far back as Lausanne, the Turks had indicated that they were inclined toward making a rapprochement with the West. By 1928 the pro-Western attitude in Turkey had begun to alarm the Soviet leaders who imagined Turkey as forming a part, in the role of junior partner, of the Western sphere of influence. Although the Mosul incident had brought Turkey and Russia closer together for a time, the Anglo-Turkish accord reached in 1926, the Turkish-Greek agreement of 1930, and Turkey's joining the League of Nations in 1932 were milestones in Turkey's rapprochement with the West. One reason for this new turn in Turkey's foreign policy may be found in her increasing suspicion of Soviet underground activities within her borders —a situation which limited relations between the two countries to an official plane.

When Litvinov, the Foreign Commissar of Soviet Russia at that time, visited Istanbul in 1931 and spoke of the western capitalistic menace, few Turks showed the enthusiastic reaction they might have shown earlier, say during 1921. The Turks, as a matter of fact, were now alert to the menace from another direction, and were cautiously scrutinizing Russian trade offices for subversive activities. By 1932

Turkish-Soviet trade volume had noticeably declined. Nevertheless, when in May of that year Ismet Pasha visited Moscow, he was enthusiastically welcomed. The Soviets, in a new move to prevent Turkey's rapprochement with the West, offered her a credit of $8,000,000 for the purpose of buying machinery in the USSR. Turkey had been unable to obtain these from the West, including America, because of the current world economic crisis. In addition, the Soviets made free gifts of military planes, tanks, trucks, and armaments and loaned the services of experts to set up industrial plants.

Notwithstanding these various expressions of "good will." Soviet Russia was unable to prevent the shift of Turkey's sentiments toward the West. One other reason for Turkey's suspicion of Soviet motives, besides that of the activity of Communist agitators, was the realization once again that they might be cherishing imperialist claims to the Straits and Istanbul. Trotsky had explicitly stated: "We must cry aloud that we need Constantinople and the Straits"; and the Soviet attitude at Lausanne, which appeared more pro-Turkish than the attitude expressed by the Turks themselves but which was actually aimed at making the Black Sea a closed Russian sea, had revived the traditional fears of the Turks. These fears were primarily responsible for the fact that Turkey began to express dissatisfaction with the Lausanne Convention on the Straits.

Although the terms of the Montreux Revision of 1936 were more favorable than those of the Lausanne Convention insofar as the Soviet was concerned, the USSR was vexed at the intimate collaboration of the Turks with the British delegation. The Soviet press from that moment on began to complain about Turkey and charged her with playing the game of the "imperialist powers." Soon after that, when Turkey's Foreign Minister, Dr. Tevfik Rusdu Aras, and Minister of the Interior, Sukru Kaya, visited Moscow to assure the Soviet Government that the Saadbad Pact just signed between Turkey, Afghanistan, Iran and Iraq was not intended as a weapon against Soviet Russia, Litvinov made the following sarcastic statement:

"It sometimes happens that one state menaces the territorial integrity or the political independence of another by invoking sacred revisionist principles, or by some historical claim, or simply a racial tie. Sometimes even, if this state finds it impossible to realize these threats owing to insufficient military preparation or an international situation that does not favor her plans, she proposes to this other state that they should pass as friends. What is even more astonishing is that this other state tolerates this trumpery whilst fully comprehending that the false maneuver is giving the aggressive state the possibility of strengthening herself so as to better prepare for a premeditated aggression against her 'friend.' Cases can even exist where friendship is concluded between two parties of very unequal strength. Then, the more feeble of the two, in exchange for the friendship of her protector is forced to sacrifice a part of her real independence. Such relations between states can never be defined as friendship in a relative sense. Need I point out that the relations existing for 18 years between the USSR and the Turkish Republic have nothing in common with the types of friendship that I have been enumerating. The basis of our relations and our purposes are entirely different."

In short, the close friendship and collaboration during the first years of relations between Soviet Russia and Turkey had begun to deteriorate as the Turkish leaders' realization of the real motives of Soviet Russia grew. They were by no means willing to be a junior partner in a Soviet sphere of influence. Although they were at all times cautious not to antagonize and break with the Soviets completely, they steered a course toward closer relations with the Western world. Mustafa Kemal (now Ataturk by virtue of the decision of the Grand National Assembly) was fully convinced that the real and eventual danger to the West lay in Soviet Russia, and in 1935 he tried to warn the Western nations of this peril: "I am afraid a catastrophe will not be prevented unless European statesmen will deal with the major disputes, completely free from the pressures of national egotism and in a spirit of good will. European questions have ceased to be disputes between France, England and Germany. Today in Eastern Europe there is a power which is menacing the whole civilization and even the whole of humanity. This power which can mobilize all its moral and material forces totally for the purpose of a world revolution, pursues methods yet unknown to Europeans and Americans. The victor of a possible war in Europe is neither France and Britain nor Germany. The victor will be simply Bolshevism. As Russia's closest neighbor and as a nation which has fought much with this country we follow these events closely and see the dangers clearly. Bolsheviks know how to exploit the mentality of awakening Eastern nations and are today menacing not only Europe but also Asia."

But the real reversal in Turkish-Soviet relations was to come after Ataturk's death in 1938. After Molotov replaced Litvinov as Soviet Foreign Minister, Moscow's negotiations between Turkey and Russia in 1939 for a new mutual assistance pact reached an impasse. Deterioration of relations reached its climax immediately after the war in 1945 when the Treaty of Friendship and Brotherhood of 1925 was denounced by Moscow, and when official and semi-official claims on the Straits and Turkey's eastern provinces were advanced.

From Hate to Understanding: British-Turkish Rapprochement. The attitude of Turkish public opinion toward Britain was complex. Turkish intellectuals always had a great respect for the democratic institutions and traditions of Britain. To them British democracy, with a constitutional monarch as a traditional symbol, was an ideal. They earnestly hoped that the Ottoman Empire would evolve into something like the British Empire. To the Turkish people in general the traditional pomp of the empire and the strength of the British navy appealed very much. To many Turkish statesmen, Britain was the only hope against Russia. But then, there were also bitter disappointments. Britain's actions outside her own territory did not seem to gibe with the long-respected traditions of honesty, fair-play and democracy. It seemed evident more than once that Britain, while seeming a friend, intrigued against the Ottoman Empire, even in concert with Russia. It also seemed evident that she coveted the Ottoman territories and that she was not really interested in saving the "Sick Man," but rather was trying to hasten his death. Kamil Pasha's disappointment in Britain before the Balkan War left deep and bitter impressions on the memories of the Turks.

Later, during the First World War and the Armistice which followed, the antagonism to Britain increased. The excesses of the British Occupation Forces caused further ill-feeling even among the Turks, who still respected the traditions of British democracy and fair-play. The British attitude toward Turkey after the Lausanne Conference did not change immediately. Lord Curzon, like many of his contemporaries, could not comprehend the change in Turkey, nor the sensitivity of the new Turks on matters pertaining to their sovereignty. The British Foreign Office, for a while, could not free itself from the momentum of its established attitude towards "The Turkish Question."

"The Turkish Question" for Britain, immediately after Lausanne, centered around the Mosul question: Britain insisted that oil-important Mosul, which was predominently Turkish, be awarded to Iraq which was her protectorate. Turkey on the other hand insisted that Mosul was within the National Pact boundaries. The matter was left unsettled at the Lausanne Conference and it continued to be a source of friction and animosity between Britain and Turkey. There were aerial bombings by the R.A.F. in the area, there were threats of war by both sides, and the British Intelligence Service carried on intensive clandestine activities in Eastern Turkey, especially among the tribes of Kurdish origin. There was apparently a strong clique in the British Foreign Office and Intelligence Service which believed that Arab and Kurdish States under British influence might check the strengthening of a new Turkey.

In and out of the League of Nations there were endless negotiations on the Mosul question. At one point a League Commission, under the Estonian General Laidoner, studied the matter on the spot and prepared a report. It was on the basis of this report that the Council of the League of Nations awarded Mosul to Iraq, with the proviso that the British Mandate in Iraq continue for 25 years. Turkey contested the legality of this decision—which was instrumental in Turkey's hastening to sign a new Treaty of Friendship and Non-Aggression with Soviet Russia, on December 17, 1925, in Paris.

It was, however, second thoughts by both the Turks and the British on Turkey's establishing closer ties with Russia that made them reconsider their differences. Britain did not want Turkey to fall under the influence and domination of Soviet Russia. Turkey herself did not feel very tranquil about establishing closer ties with her northern neighbor. Consequently both Turkey and Britain showed a definite spirit of reconciliation in reconsidering the Mosul question, and managed to solve it finally and definitively, to the disappointment of Russia, in June 1926. Turkey relinquished her claims on Mosul in return for ten percent of Mosul oil production. Britain promised to relinquish her sponsorship of Kurdish independence and autonomy and did not insist on the return to Turkey of some expellees.

Once the problem of Mosul was removed, attempts at a rapprochement were allowed to proceed more smoothly. In 1929 ships of the British fleet visited Istanbul and a British admiral visited Mustafa Kemal in Ankara; and, in March, 1930, a British-Turkish treaty of commerce and navigation was signed. Meanwhile, the appearance of Italian expansionist ambitions on the horizon set in motion a definite pro-British trend both in the press and in government circles in Turkey.

The British Government took a sensible attitude toward Turkish claims for the revision of the Straits convention. This was demonstrated during the Montreux Conference itself and helped to increase the pro-British feelings in Turkey and by 1937 a seemingly well-established Anglophobia and the bogey of "intrigues of the British intelligence service" almost disappeared from Turkish minds. Dr. Tevfik Rusdu Aras, Turkish Foreign Minister, was now saying that there existed a complete "identity of interests" between the two countries.

Evidences of the new friendship could be found in the fact that many important consignments of armaments were bought from British firms; a contract for the rearmament of the Straits was awarded a British firm; likewise a contract for the construction of steel and iron works at Karabuk was awarded to a British company. The visit of King Edward VIII of England to Turkey in the summer of 1936 symbolized the climax of the rapprochement. The most cordial personal relations (between the King and Ataturk) were established in the course of that short visit.

Ismet Inonu, the Prime Minister, when he visited London in 1937 for the coronation ceremonies of King George VI and Queen Elizabeth of England, said: "We find England's conduct in pursuit of the cause of peace fully in conformity with our spirit. The sentiment of confidence between our two countries will be very useful for the development of our reciprocal relations and will be a precious factor tending towards the cause of international peace and towards the atmosphere of security."

For a time a silent struggle was waged between Great Britain, Germany, and Russia to win Turkey's confidence and friendship. Following the eight million dollar loan by the USSR, England granted sixteen million pounds sterling; later, Germany gave a loan of one hundred and fifty million Reichsmarks. By 1938, Turkey found herself somewhat estranged from Russia and maintaining steadier and more favorable trade as well as diplomatic relations with Germany and Great Britain. However, in 1939, the pendulum was definitely on England's side. In the spring of that year, an identity of views had been reached by the Turkish, British, and French government. This constituted the first big step leading toward the tripartite mutual assistance pact which was to come after the failure of Saracoglu's Moscow mission and after the Soviet-German non-aggression pact.

The French Touch: Turkish-French Relations. France has always been a source of inspiration in the arts and general culture for Turkish intellectuals. When the Young Turks initiated their attempts to bring about political reform and a renaissance in Turkish art, modes of thought and culture, it seemed natural that they should turn to the French. But, as it was with the British, the Turkish intellegentsia was bitterly disappointed by French actions towards Turkey. France, together with Britain, had rebuffed the efforts of some Turkish statesmen to bring about an alliance. French occupation troops had acted outrageously during the armistice. The French General, France deEsperey, who had entered Istanbul on a white charger in 1918, had become the symbol of foreign oppression and the excesses committed by the French troops in the southern provinces of Antep and Marash were fresh in Turkish minds. But nevertheless it was France which realized the strength of the nationalist movement and acted first to recognize it.

The visit of Franklin Bouillon to Ankara during the war of independence and the subsequent recognition of the national pact by France seemed to usher in a new era of Turkish-French relations. France's unequivocal acceptance of the abolition of the capitulations was especially well received in Turkey. Yet France was one of those most interested in the capitulations inasmuch as her capital holdings in Turkey were greater than those of any other outside power. Both the eventual abolition of the capitulations and Turkey's nationalist movement, which became evident immediately after Lausanne, harmed French commercial interests and led to a liquidation or *turkification* of many French firms as well as some French-supported institutions, hospitals and schools. Those French citizens who had become permanent residents of Turkey—the so-called Levantine community—were adversely affected by both high taxation and intense nationalistic feelings. Yet the French Foreign Office in Paris gave only feeble support to her citizens in Turkey for she was busy elsewhere in the Middle East, namely, in Syria. Ironically, it was precisely in that area that a motive for friction between France and Turkey arose. The Franklin Bouillon agreement had stipulated that a special regime be instituted in the *Sanjak* of Alexandretta which would be granted autonomy. In a way Turkey was, for the time being, leaving perforce a territory which she considered within the national pact frontiers under the trusteeship of France. This was Turkey's understanding when the special status of the Sanjak was confirmed at Lausanne; it never occurred to the Turkish government that the Sanjak would be considered a part of Syria. But from 1925 on Syrian agitation in the Sanjak and along the Turkish-Syrian frontier became a source of irritation. When the France-Syria accord was signed in 1936 its provisions concerning unified Syria were interpreted by the Syrians as incorporation of the Sanjak into Syria. France did little to correct this interpretation, but rather provoked Syrian nationalists.

The Turkish government always considered the Sanjak (the Turks called it Hatay) predominantly Turkish since the Turkish population was the largest single ethnic group. Hatay and the port of Alexandretta (Iskenderun) were vitally important to Turkey's strategy and security. Held by weak or hostile hands, this region could be an ideal beachhead for enemy forces attacking Turkey. The first target of such forces would be the rich and fertile fields of the Adana region.

A hostile navy or navies, operating from the excellent port of Iskenderun could control all the southern approaches of Turkey.[3] Conversely, if Turkey controlled the Hatay region, she would have a
natural first line of defense. Iskenderun would be an excellent defensive naval base and, most important of all, this port would be the
only defensible port open to logistical support of the Turkish army by
friendly allies.

Turkey therefore vehemently objected to the Franco-Syrian interpretation, which meant the transfer of France's responsibilities in the
Sanjak to Syria, that is, the Sanjak's incorporation in Syria. She
demanded that France conclude a separate treaty with the Sanjak
similar to those concluded with Syria and Lebanon. Eventually, it
was pointed out, the future of the Sanjak should be decided by bilateral treaties between Turkey and France.

Ataturk's speech in the Turkish Assembly on November 1, 1935
marked the beginning of the Turkish campaign for Hatay: "The
important topic of the day which is absorbing the whole attention of
the Turkish people is the fate of the district of Alexandretta, Antioch
and its dependencies, which in point of fact belong to the purest
Turkish element. We are obliged to take up this matter seriously
and firmly." Ataturk elaborated this in another speech: "I am not
interested in territorial aggrandizement. I am not a habitual peace-
breaker. I only demand our rights, based on treaties. If I do not
obtain these, I cannot rest in peace. I promise my nation: I will
get Hatay."

The French, on the other hand, held the opinion that separation of
the Sanjak from Syria would in effect mean dismemberment of Syria
and consequently an abuse of the trust confided in them.

From 1936 on there was a long period of violence in the Sanjak
with bloodshed and rioting between the Arabs and Turks. Then
there even arose the possibility of a Turkish military operation
toward the Sanjak. An agreement was reached, however, in January,
1937 according to which Alexandretta and Antioch were to form a
separate political entity (although linked with Syria in customs,
monetary exchange and maintenance of foreign relations) and Turkish
and Arabic would be recognized as the official languages. But there
was a dispute over the new electoral system of the *corpus seperatum*
of the Sanjak and tension flared up again. By that time, France had
become fully preoccupied with the European situation and was urged
by Great Britain to reach an agreement with Turkey. The Turks
took advantage of this situation and intended to conclude a French-
Turkish agreement on their own terms. On July 4, 1937, a Turkish-

French treaty of friendship was signed. The contracting parties undertook not to enter into an entente of a political or economic order
directed against either one of them and, in the event of attack from
a third power, they were not to enter the conflict on behalf of the
aggressor.

The following year the two countries agreed to proclaim the Sanjak
a Franco-Turkish condominium, and Turkish troops were stationed in
the Sanjak pending the result of a general election. In September,
1938, elections were held and the Turks gained a majority in the
assembly which promptly proclaimed autonomy under the name of
Hatay. The president of the new republic and all the members of the
cabinet were Turks. The flag of the new state was modeled after the
Turkish flag, and the new government immediately decided to ask a
union with the mother country. France was forced to keep silent in
the face of all these developments, particularly since German and
Italian moves were increasing the importance of Turkish cooperation.
In June, 1939 at a meeting between France's Ambassador Massigli
and Turkey's Minister for Foreign Affairs, Saracoglu, France agreed
to the cession of Hatay. In this manner, the last obstructions to
good French-Turkish relations were removed and the way was open
to a tripartite agreement among Turkey, France, and Great Britain.

Thus Ataturk had attained posthumously the only territorial aim
he had ever entertained, an aim which was dictated both by the
national pact and by the value placed on Alexandretta as a strategic
port on the Mediterranean.

Drang Nach Osten: Turkish-German Relations. In reviewing
Turkish-German relations, both before World War II and during the
war itself, the somewhat paradoxical attitude of Turkish statesmen
and people towards Germany and her people should be kept in mind.
Although the Turks were bitter against the Germans for having em-
broiled them in the first World War and because of the high-handed
attitude of the German generals during the war, their rancour was
tempered on several counts: Turkish professional soldiers were full
of admiration for German army and technical efficiency. To have
been comrades-in-arms once with such a well-disciplined army was
a matter of pride for them. On the whole, however, both the government and its people were determined that they should not be coerced
into a second world conflict as a pawn of Germany. Mustafa Kemal
himself had bitter memories of German high-handedness during the
First World War. He never forgot that most German generals considered the Turkish army *Kannonenfutter.*

Another factor to be kept in mind in connection with Turkish-

German relations is that trade between the two countries had been gradually increasing since 1925. One reason for this was the continued sympathy evinced by the Turks for their former German business "associates" (comrade-in-arms in civilian attire), and the confidence they felt in German products. With the passing of time dependency on German industry increased because neither Great Britain nor France could satisfy all the needs of the Turkish planned economy. Russian products, on the other hand, were not very popular.

After Hitler came to power in 1934 trade relations with Germany, hitherto of purely commercial significance, assumed political and diplomatic importance. It was quite evident from the intrigues initiated in the Balkans that it was Hitler's intention to revive the old *Drang Nach Osten*. In 1934, following the visit of a German commercial mission, a long-term credit of 20,000,000 Turkish liras, applicable toward the purchase of German machinery, was accorded the Turkish Government. Turkish statesmen, Ataturk in particular, were not blind to German intentions. Ataturk had resented German interference during the first World War and he did not fail to see that Hitler's motives were suspect. In 1936 he explicitly told his close friends: "Beware of these megalomaniacs [i.e., Hitler and Mussolini]; they will stop at nothing to satisfy their personal ambitions. It will mean nothing to them if both their own countries and the rest of the world are destroyed, in the course of satisfying their ambitions."

It would have been conceivable for the "strong man of Turkey" to join the "revolutionist" camp of Germany. But Ataturk did not have territorial aims and saw clearly the dangers of arousing national passions for external adventures. He said, "This man (Hitler) will lead a dynamic nation into disaster by spurring its passions." But, in spite of these misgivings, Turkish-German trade relations were proving rather profitable to Turkey—both for general economic reasons and the relative ease in obtaining armaments which could not be obtained elsewhere. It was not any less true, however, that beneath the surface of these advantages, the conditions imposed upon the Turks were considerable—resulting from Dr. Schacht's machinations during his trip to the Balkans in 1936. Repayments of loans were to be made according to Schacht's wishes and prices were to be set at levels above world markets.

Meanwhile Turkey did not desire an exclusive German monopoly over the Turkish economy. She contracted for the construction of Karabuk steel and iron mills by a British company instead of the Krupp firm. Germany's negative attitude toward the Montreux Convention, and her close collaboration with Italy, who was in the course of conducting continuous intrigues against the Balkan Entente, gave the Turks further cause for annoyance. In 1937 Dr. Tevfik Aras, Foreign Minister of Turkey, felt the necessity of countering German-Italian pressure. He visited the European capitals and made particular efforts to increase Balkan solidarity to counter these German-Italian intrigues.

At this time there was also a strong desire in certain Turkish circles to form an alliance with Great Britain, which, from being a "despicable imperialist power" of the mid-twenties, had now moved into the position of a "dependable friend" in Turkish sentiments. The Chamberlain government in the year 1937, however, politely refused a Turkish bid for alliance—although England attempted to counter German economic influence. It was with this intention in mind that in 1938 she extended the equivalent of an $8,000,000 loan to Turkey—which was only to be offset in turn by a 150,000,000 Reichsmark German credit.

In 1939 the Germans increased their efforts, both through press propaganda and economic pressure, to bring Turkey into their sphere of influence, and thus prevent her from becoming a factor in what they called Anglo-French "encirclement." It was this situation which motivated von Papen's appointment as ambassador to Turkey—although Turkey in 1939 was more concerned about her relations with Russia and with tightening her ties with France and Great Britain.

Mare Nostrum: Turkish-Italian Relations. Mustafa Kemal Ataturk had never admired Mussolini. The Italian leader's bombastic speeches about *mare nostrum*, about Italy's historic "role" in various regions of Asia and Africa, accompanied by the actual fortification of the tiny Meis Island—an Italian possession just off Antalya in southern Turkey—had irritated him in the extreme. It was during this period that the Italian Ambassador at Ankara was called one day to Ataturk's residence at Cankaya, to be received by the President in mufti except for his military boots. At the end of their conversation, Ataturk pointedly remarked: "Tell your Duce that I can wear the boot very quickly!"

Surprisingly enough, Turkish-Italian relations until the year before (1938) had been extraordinarily good. In 1921, Count Sforza had reached an agreement with Turkey, and Turkish-Italian trade relations from that time on had continued to flourish. With Mussolini's advent to power, however, Turkey became uneasy and during the Mosul dispute it was feared the Italians might take advantage of the situation and make a landing at Antalya. But relations improved in the following years, and in 1928 Italy was striving for a tripartite pact in the eastern Mediterranean among Turkey, Italy, and Greece. Italian diplomats were trying to bring about Greek-Turkish understanding for this purpose.

In May, 1928 a bilateral Turkish-Italian agreement was signed stipulating among other things that in the event one of the contracting parties was attacked by one or more other power, the other party would remain neutral. The following month Mussolini praised the pact in the following glowing words: "During the last two years, since the intrigue of elements alien to Turkey but hostile to Italy had ceased, Italo-Turkish relations have greatly improved . . . Italy meets Turkey in a sincere and friendly spirit. Now, one must get into the habit of looking at Turkey in a new light, as a nation boldly creating a new spirit within herself after having established a new Constitution, as a strong and populous nation guided by a leader whose prestige is linked with historical events of extreme importance."

Ismet Pasha's reply to this statement a few days later in the Turkish National Assembly was in no less glowing terms: "The treaty has been a blessing for the two countries as well as for real friends of peace . . . I can assure you that since the signature of the treaty, this confidence has steadily increased on both sides." Italian "conciliation" played such an important part in the Greco-Turkish accord of 1930 that both parties thanked Italy for her help.

Italo-Turkish collaboration, however, had reached its climax. In the course of the following years the increasing aggressiveness of fascism and Italian intrigues among the Balkan countries resulted in a considerable cooling of Turkish-Italian friendship. Mussolini's speeches in the Italian Senate on March 19, 1934 brought Turkish suspicions to the surface. Il Duce had said: "The historical objectives of Italy have two names, Asia and Africa . . . The South and East are principal areas which most absorb the interests and aims of the Italians." It was also about this time that huge maps began to be displayed on the walls of Rome with the Mediterranean Sea marked as *Mare Nostrum.*

These events aroused considerable criticism in the Turkish press—so much so that Mussolini had to clarify his position to the effect that he had never included Turkey in his plans for the future.

Italy's attack on Ethiopia further increased Turkey's suspicions, and both the Turkish Government and press openly favored the Ethiopians. Turkey, who had favored collective action mechanisms within the League, voted in favor of sanctions against Italy. An observer at that time wrote: "Tevfik Rushdu was clearly more concerned with keeping Turkey's relations with the international community on a good footing than with preventing a partial Turkish-Italian rupture."

This attitude was rewarded when Turkey's demand for a revision of the Lausanne Straits convention was favorably received. The Italians, on the other hand, objected both to the revision conference and to the Montreux convention itself. This objection served to increase Turkish suspicions regarding Italy.

Relations between the two countries from 1937 until 1939 remained cool although Count Ciano and Dr. Aras held several conversations in the course of which Italy hinted that Turkey's adherence to the Axis might prove to be "useful." But the Italian invasion of Albania —the culmination of Mussolini's intrigues against the Balkan Entente —was one of the factors which induced Turkey to join the Anglo-French camp in 1939.

Turkey and Her Eastern Neighbors. A heritage of religious rivalry, jealousy, misunderstanding, and fear formed a wall more formidable than her eastern mountain ranges between Turkey and her eastern neighbors. The wall was somewhat more rugged on the other side.

The Ottoman Turks were mainly interested in westward conquests. They had even started their western probes before completely consolidating their power within Anatolia. After having eliminated a few feudalities within the natural borders of Anatolia, they would have been perfectly content with stopping at these borders. But at the beginning of the 16th century the Ottomans had to turn to the east, temporarily, to counter the threats of Shah Ismail of Persia and the Mameluke Kingdom of Syria and Egypt. From then on Ottoman policy in the East was to prevent the recurrence of such threats from the East and South East.

Constant wars with Persia, although basically arising from this policy, assumed the aspect of a religious struggle between the Sunnite Turks and the Shiite Persians. The fact that a great number of Anatolian Turks were Shiites should be enough reason to show that the religious rivalry was by no means the main factor involved. But even after the wars and border frictions had come to an end, at the beginning of the 19th century, Turkish-Persian relations continued to be marred by the specter of Sunnite-Shiite hatred. Years of friction had left a residue of mutual distrust.

With the Arabs it was a different story. There was generally no rivalry of sects between them and the Turks.[4] Nevertheless, the inevitable friction between the conquered and the conqueror was very much in evidence.

The Ottoman Turks had conquered Arab lands to protect themselves. But, having done so, they earnestly tried to consolidate them as equal partners in the Ottoman nation. As the empire declined, there was Ottoman misrule in Syria, Egypt, Arabia, as was the case in Anatolia and the Balkans. But there was never a conscious effort to oppress, "to divide and rule," or to assimilate the Arabs.[5] They could and did attain high positions in the Ottoman hierarchy and they did enjoy special privileges as the "race which had given birth to Mohammed." Many leading Ottoman statesmen, including the famous Grand Vizier of the Young Turk Revolution of 1908, Mahmud Shevket Pasha, were Arabs.

In spite of all this, Arabs developed a growing contempt for the Turks. They said that "grass did not grow where the Turkish horse-hoof trod." They could never tolerate being dominated by a people they considered culturally and socially inferior. Perhaps the bitter remarks of an Arab nationalist to Cemal Pasha exemplifies this contempt: "What have you Turks done for us Arabs, that you should now expect friendly treatment on our part?" he asked. "Are you forgetting that in Constantinople, when you want to call a dog you shout 'Arab, Arab.' When you say that anything is obscure it is like the hair of an Arab."

If it is true that there are in Turkish usage many such sayings and phrases which might seem derogatory to Arabs, it should not be forgotten that there are also Turkish sayings which are extremely derogatory to the Anatolia Turk. The slightest of these is the saying, "To the Turk realization comes late." This was particularly true in the case of Turkish-Arab relations.

Abdul Hamid II's attempts at Pan-Islamism, which heaped favors and special privileges on the Arabs and which overcrowded the ruling circles with Arabs, did not stop the tide of Arab nationalism, neither did the concept of equality-fraternity of the 1908 revolution. Thus the resulting Turkish nationalism was especially bitter against Arab betrayals. The Arab Revolt conspired by Lawrence during the first World War, the revolt which the Turks considered "the stab in the back," increased this bitterness immeasurably. Consequently, the modern Turkey of 1923 was determined not only to be aloof diplomatically from the East, but was determined to purge the Turkish language, culture and society of all Arabic and Persian influences. This determination widened the already existing gulf between the Turks and their eastern neighbors. Turks wanted a Turkey for the Turks and were determined also not to get into unprofitable entanglements. It was in this spirit that the caliphate was abolished, as Ataturk realistically decided that the caliphate was but an empty title. It could not be the rallying point for Islamic countries and no sovereign Islamic state could recognize the overriding authority of the caliph. The Turkish Republic was made a secular state forthwith.

The abolishing of the caliphate and the secularization of the state, together with Turkish nationalism and the westernization of modern Turkey, increased the bitterness in Persia and Arab countries. On their part the Turks assumed a policy of disinterestedness in the East. But it is important to remember that there were no unsolved border questions, no economic or political aspirations, and the social-cultural antagonisms were, although bitter, not deep and insurmountable. In fact, Ataturk soon realized that it was a mistake to assume complete indifference towards the East. Although he persisted in westernization and in breaking social and cultural ties with the East, he saw the growing importance of, and at the same time the great weakness in, a very important strategic flank.

Paradoxically the first step toward the normalization of Turkey's relations with her eastern neighbors was instigated by Soviet Russia. The Treaty of friendship concluded in 1926 among Turkey, Iran and Afganistan was Soviet-sponsored. Prior to the signing of this treaty, border disputes and Kurdish uprisings had caused considerable friction between Iran and Turkey. In 1927, again, frontier disputes caused a new rupture in the relations and a few years elapsed before the frontier problem was definitively settled. Riza Shah's visit to Turkey in 1934 confirmed the Turkish-Iranian friendship treaty not only on paper but in reality.

Afghan-Turkish friendship followed an easier course. There were no complex issues involved in the relations between the two countries. On the contrary, racial affinity between the two nations made co-operation easy. Turkey furnished military and technical advisors to Afganistan for many years, and continues to do so.

The solutions of the Mosul question on the other hand made friendly relations possible between Iraq and Turkey. The growing threat of Soviet imperialism after the Sixth Comintern Congress at Moscow (it was at this Congress that Russia adopted Stalin's "Socialism in One Country" policy which marked the beginning of the nationalist expansionism) and Mussolini's aspirations in the Middle East brought about the realization that some sort of collective security arrangement was necessary. The pact which resulted from this realization, however, was not an armed assistance pact. Although Ataturk and his Middle Eastern contemporaries realized the necessity of a collective security arrangement they also realized their own limitations. There was, furthermore, some caution so as not to irritate the Soviet Union.

The Saadabad Pact, signed in 1937, was quite limited and cautious in its provisions; it merely guaranteed mutual acceptance by the signatory states (Iran, Afghanistan and Turkey) of each other's borders and a mutual agreement by all not to interfere in internal problems. They also agreed to consult each other in all international conflicts "affecting their common interests."

Article 6 of the pact was quite interesting: "If one power commits aggression against a third power, the other powers can without warning denounce the present treaty as far as the aggressor in concerned." This was perhaps the sharpest tooth in the whole treaty. One can very well understand why a real collective security arrangement could not have been undertaken at that stage. It would not have been logical for Turkey to get involved, without any obvious advantage, in a Middle Eastern arrangement which might prove a liability.

It was Ataturk's intention to continue to build on modest foundations. As was reflected in the Turkish press comment of the time, he saw the pact enhancing Turkey's position as a link between Balkan and Middle Eastern groups. The Saadabad Pact group in due time could become a bloc against the pressure of Soviet Russia on the one side and the Axis on the other.

But these long-range hopes were never realized. The pact never went beyond the 1937 stage. Although it was instrumental in the maintenance of friendly relations among the signatories, when it was put to the test during the second World War it proved to be of no use whatsoever. The fault was not only due to the diluted provisions, but also to the spirit of the signatories, most of whom resorted to individualism rather than to developing collective security arrangements. Turkey, for one, desired more cooperation and collaboration, but she was left alone, and therefore she had to resort to her own brand of individualism, both in the Near East and the Balkans, in order to escape the flames of war.

The years between the two world wars saw the spectacular transformation of an anti-western, anti-British, anti-Greek, and anti-Middle Eastern nationalist Turkey into a state with a western outlook, which succeeded in staying outside the Soviet sphere of influence, in reconciling her differences with Great Britain, Greece, and the Middle Eastern countries, and in being the chief pioneer for two regional pacts designed against German, Italian, and Soviet activities in the Middle East and the Balkans. By 1939 Turkey, despite economic dependency on Germany, and in the face of increasing Soviet criticism, was drawing closer to Great Britain and France.

It was at this stage that the second world conflagration broke out.

CHAPTER IV

THE WAR YEARS: 1939-1945

Mustafa Kemal Ataturk died on November 10, 1938. In his comparatively short lifetime he had achieved what many before him had failed to accomplish in a long stretch of years. "Even if he had achieved only one of his many reforms, he would deserve to be called a great man," as a French journalist observed.

In comparison with the sense of accomplishment he must have felt on his internal achievements, his disappointment in foreign affairs was great. Neither the Balkan Pact nor the Saadabad Pact had become the effective collective security arrangements he had envisaged. International cooperation, which he considered the only effective means for curing the ills of humanity and for preventing wars, had proved to be a fiasco in the debating halls of the League of Nations. The Axis, in default of preventive measures and due to the apathy and weakness of the Western powers, was threatening the little nations and, perhaps more important in Ataturk's eyes, the real threat to humanity, the growing Soviet power, was lurking behind the apathy of the West and the hopeless but destructive passions of Mussolini and Hitler. All these prophesies, aspirations, and fears can be traced in Ataturk's speeches.

In urging world organization and international cooperation, he declared in 1935: "If war were to explode suddenly, like a bomb, nations would not delay combining their armed forces and national potentials to prevent it. The fastest way and the most effective measure is to establish an international organization which would prove to the aggressor that its aggression would not pay." These were prophetic words.

Years before Roosevelt became a world leader Ataturk said: "The whole of humanity should be considered as a body, and a nation, one of its organs. We should not say, 'What do I care if there is trouble in a remote corner of the world?' If there is such trouble, we should be concerned with it as if it were our own . . . If everlasting peace is desired, international measures should be taken to improve the conditions of the human masses. The prosperity should replace hunger and misery in the entire world. Future world citizens should be brought up free from envy, greed, and hate."

He was irked by the apathy and weakness of the West. "I do not believe in the merits of lines such as the Maginot Line," he said when Western hopes were entrenched there. "Wars are fought by men. Therefore men have to be on the surface. A force which is confined like hedgehogs in concrete pipes and armored towers is already *hors de combat*. I cannot see what can be gained—except defeat—by destroying ones own maneuverability."

To him the real and lasting danger was the Soviet danger, and it is chiefly due to his realization of this threat that Turkey moved towards an alliance with France and Great Britain. Ataturk had also urged the contemporary leaders of the Western world to put aside or resolve the disputes among themselves and to devote more attention to the real menace from Soviet Russia and Communism. He pointed this out in no uncertain terms in his various speeches and in his messages to his Western contemporaries. As much as he deplored Hitler and Mussolini and could not condone their regimes and methods, he favored a settlement between France, Great Britain, Germany and Italy; he was apprehensive that Soviet leaders and communism would profit from the disputes among Western countries and would emerge as real victors of a possible war.

Turkey was dependent economically on Germany and there was an undeniably fertile atmosphere for closer cooperation with Germany in Turkish mass psychology. But Ataturk steered clear of involvement with Hitler's regime. He could see clearly that the German dictator considered Turkey a part of his *Lebensraum* and closer relations with him would be to the detriment of national interests. Thus, on the eve of the Second World War, Turkey's relations with the USSR were without incidents, yet remained somewhat complicated in view of Turkey's orientation towards Great Britain and France.

On the other hand, Turkey's relations with Germany and Italy were correct but by no means cordial.

Turkey has been accused of cannily biding her time throughout the Second World War with intention of jumping in at a moment which would be most appropriate for her own interests. This "accusation" seemed more serious during the war years and immediately after when the war neurosis was still prevalent, but in retrospect it shows common sense rather than opportunism. Indeed, it would appear that if this was the intention of the Turkish statesmen and generals of the time, they were both wise and successful. There are, however, other variations to accusations on Turkey's wartime record. It has been said that it was difficult to keep Turkey from entering the war on

Germany's side! Also, that if Turkey had entered the war earlier on the side of the Allies, it might have shortened the war considerably. But the train of events of the Second World War will, I think, show the opposite of these accusations.

In order to comprehend fully the significance of the events of World War II, one has to look at the situation immediately preceding the world conflagration.

Prelude to War. The Turkish Republic, after a brief period of isolation verging on xenophobia, had become an active enthusiast of internationalism and of collective security arrangements against aggression. Her policies in the League of Nations, her support of the sanctions taken against Italy, her part in the Nyon patrol, her interests in the Balkan and Middle Eastern Ententes were indications of this enthusiasm. It was precisely because she realized that the League of Nations was useless as an agency of collective security, and that both the Balkan and Saadabad Pacts despite the best intentions were ineffective, that Turkey first sought the revision of the Straits Convention and then a definite arrangement with the French and British.

Her first attempts at *rapprochement* with Britain were not enthusiastically reciprocated by the Chamberlain government. The explanation of what amounted to the spurning of Turkish moves in this direction was that the British Prime Minister was preoccupied elsewhere and Turkey's position did not rank high on his priority list.

From the outset, all the moves of Turkish governments toward the West precluded any designs against Soviet Russia. In fact, Turkey took pains to stipulate orally or in writing in all her negotiations and agreements that in no case would she become belligerent against the Soviet Union. These reservations were voiced in Turkey's alliance with her Balkan and eastern neighbors. But as Lewis V. Thomas states in his *Turkey & The United States,* this by no means meant that Turkey was a Russian satellite, or that she felt within the sphere of Russian influence, or in gratitude for Russia's past aid. On the contrary, as pointed out earlier, both the Turkish people and her leaders were extremely wary of Russian intentions and no amount of aid could dispel the traditional dislike and suspicion against Russia.

Turkish leaders, with their reservations and insistence on not being committed against Russia, were trying not to give any excuses to the Communists. Also, Ataturk's unwritten legacy to the effect that Turkey should align herself with Great Britain, was taking on special significance in the rapid development of events—events that showed that she was being seriously threatened by Axis moves.

The occupation of Albania by Italy confirmed Turkey's apprehensions, and she felt it necessary to strengthen and consolidate her ties with England and France mainly against a possible German-Italian encroachment in the Balkans. Furthermore, the Turkish government sincerely thought that she might serve as a link between the Soviet Union and Great Britain and France, thus forging a strong chain against the Axis in the Balkans and the Black Sea area. For this purpose the Turkish government attempted once again to consolidate the Balkan Entente. Before the Soviet-German *rapprochment* both these intentions were favorably received by Moscow. Litvinof, Molotov's predecessor, was even enthusiastic.

Two declarations, (the Turkish-British and the Turkish-French Declarations,) were made in the spring of 1939 announcing that "identity of views" had been reached and that a mutual assistance pact was to be worked out. Turkey kept Moscow faithfully informed of the negotiations between herself and France and Great Britain. She made it clear that simultaneously with a Tripartite Pact, Turkey was desirous of a mutual assistance pact with Russia which would reaffirm both the *status quo* in the Balkans and Black Sea region as well as her independence and territorial integrity.

However, this genuine desire was in a sense dwarfed by the events which followed. The Saracoglu Mission to Moscow, which he had undertaken for the purpose mentioned, was doomed to failure from the outset. First let us briefly review the events which led to this tragic failure:

On April 29, 1939, two foreign diplomats arrived in Ankara. One was Germany's new Ambassador, Baron Franz von Papen, one-time Chancellor of Germany who had ushered in Hitler's regime and who had been one of the instigators of Germany's *Anschluss* with Austria. Hitler believed that von Papen, having once served with the Ottoman Army on the Palestine Front, might keep Turkey in line with German policy or at least might get her to take a neutral position in case of war.

One German preoccupation at the time was to have a free hand in the Balkans, or, to use their own word, to prevent an "encirclement" of that area. Von Ribbentrop, Germany's Foreign Minister, had instructed von Papen before the latter's departure that, "if the encirclement ring were closed, this time with the participation of Turkey, in contrast to 1914, there would be no alternative to war." In compliance with these directives, von Papen played on the theme of traditional German-Turkish friendship and tried to disperse Turkish fears of German intentions. Although the Turkish-British declaration was made public a few days later, von Papen was not discouraged. He sought now to prevent a more definitive agreement between Turkey, Great Britain, and France. While threatening Ankara that Germany would cease to export supplies, he suggested to the Italians that they return the Dodecanese Islands to Turkey so as to convince her of the good intentions of Germany and Italy in the Balkans. Both the German government and von Papen feared that a formal British-Turkish-French treaty might allow the free passage of British ships to Soviet Russia, in case that country were attacked by Germany.

Concurrently with these efforts of von Papen, M. Vladimir Potemkin, Soviet Vice-Commissar for Foreign Affairs, was in Ankara urging Turkey to consolidate her relations with the Balkan states and the Western Allies against a possibility of German aggression. Turkey, on her part, with the intention of linking Russia with France and Great Britain, proposed to the USSR a new Mutual Security Pact similar to the one she was then negotiating with the two Western Allies. As David J. Dallin pointed out, "No government was better qualified for that office." In view of the military talks being held at that period in Moscow between Voroshilov (USSR), Admiral Drax (England), and General Doumene (France), there appeared for a time a good possibility of forming a strong bulwark against Germany. However, before Sükrü Saracoglu, Turkey's Foreign Minister at the time, arrived in Moscow at the invitation of the Soviet government "to negotiate a pact of mutual assistance," Soviet policy had already changed in favor of a pact with Nazi Germany.

The Soviet-German Non-Agression Pact had in fact been signed on August 23. Soviet leaders had, in the words of Churchill, "shown remarkable skill in concealing their true intentions till the last possible moment." As late as August 4 the German Ambassador to the USSR, Count Schulenburg, was still uncertain about the outcome of the talks. In a message to his Foreign Office, he wrote: "My overall impression is that the Soviet Government is at present determined to sign with England and France if they fulfill all Soviet wishes. Negotiations, to be sure, might still last a long time, especially since the mistrust of England is (also) great . . . . It will take a considerable effort on our part to cause the Soviet Government to swing about." It took 19 days!

Thus, when Saracoglu began official conversations with Molotov on September 26 the days of Potemkin were well a thing of the past. The Turkish view of the contemplated pact with Russia, based on the talks with Potemkin, was that it should be limited in scope: "aggression being understood in the broadest sense of the term; that it should cover land war as well as war at sea; and that it could be concluded either as a corollary of the Franco-British-Turkish Pact, or independently."

The Soviet Union, however, replied that this view which had seemed acceptable as a basis for negotiations during the Ankara conversations was no longer acceptable since the Anglo-French-Soviet conversations had come to a halt and the situation was "no longer the same." Doubtless the new Soviet-German agreement was implied in this last phrase. Therefore it was decided that negotiations should concern themselves with questions of assistance in the Dardanelles and the Black Sea, consultation regarding the Balkans, and the situation of the two countries vis-a-vis Great Britain and France. The implications of the Soviet-German treaty came into the picture when the Turkish delegation insisted that a reservation, which would establish that any obligation assumed in the pact by Turkey could not involve her in an armed conflict with either of the two Western powers, should be inserted in the pact. When Molotov faithfully reported this suggestion to the German Ambassador, Germany counselled strongly against it, and hinted that emphatic Russian opposition could prevent the proposed Turkish-Anglo-French tripartite pact. Molotov, in reply to repeated representations to this effect by von Schulenburg, promised that Soviet Russia would work for transforming the "vacillating policy" of the Turks into a permanent neutrality. The impasse resulted when Soviet Russia demanded the inclusion of a reservation regarding Germany similar to the one regarding France and Great Britain, i.e., a provision to the effect that, because of the arrangements which the Soviet had assumed by virtue of the German-Soviet pact, she could not be involved in any aggressive act against Germany.

Furthermore, and most important of all, the Soviets demanded that Turkey sign a bilateral protocol which would in effect modify the international Montreux Convention in accordance with Russia's favorite view that Turkey should not allow warships of non-Black Sea powers to pass through the Bosphorous into the Black Sea and, by implication, that Russia should control all Turkish decisions relating to these seaways. Behind all this were German and Russian designs concerning the Balkans, the Black Sea, and the Straits, and their effort to use Turkey as a pawn.

Russia no longer cared about Turkey's desires to strengthen the Balkan Pact against the Axis or to be linked with France and Britain. Her pact with Germany had cleared the way for her plan to capture Bessarabia from Romania[1]; independence of the latter was guaranteed by France and Britain who could send their navies to her aid. Turkey, the guardian of the Straits, was obliged by the provisions of the Montreux Convention to let these navies through as they were to assist Romania, a Black Sea Power. Russia now wanted to get Turkey on her side, or pressure her into closing the Straits, which she had tried before without success at the Lausanne and Montreux Conferences. Also, she in concert with Germany, or rather on Germany's instigation, wished to neutralize the Balkan Pact and dominate it. Russia, furthermore, wanted Ankara's approval of the dismemberment of Romania by herself and the Bulgarians. Last, but not least, she wished Turkey to recognize the partition of Poland.

Turkey could not accept any of these points as they would, in the long run, undermine her own security and independence. Saracoglu pointed out that Turkey could not ignore the Montreux Convention[1] nor could she have the Balkan Pact dominated by Russia. Negotiations therefore collapsed on October 16, 1939, with Turkey suggesting as an alternative a general treaty, again with the reservation that it could never be construed as a move against France or Britain. Russia refused.

Saracoglu remained in Moscow for nearly a month and was rebuffed and ignored with studied discourtesy on many occasions. It was evident that the USSR was not very intent on signing an agreement based on goodwill.

As early as October 1, Molotov was expressing the opinion that the mutual assistance pact "would not be completed." Nevertheless, when negotiations failed, both Molotov, in his speech to the Supreme Soviet and the Soviet press, upbraided the Turks "for preferring the Western Alliances to entering into a mutual pact limited to the Black Sea and Straits." In the same speech, Molotov also emphatically denied that the Soviet Union had demanded the cession of Kars and Ardahan provinces and a "privileged" position regarding the Straits; all Russia wanted by a mutual pact was "sufficient guarantees."

The Anglo-Franco-Turkish Tripartite Pact. The failure of Turkish-Soviet talks was a disappointment for Germany. As we have attempted to point out in the above passages, she had hoped that Soviet Russia would be able to prevent Turkey's alliance with the Western powers. She was quite certain that as a result of the conclusion of the Soviet-German treaty, Turkey would have to revise its previous position and that "a new attitude on the part of Turkey would upset all the stategic plans of the French and English in the eastern Mediterranean."

Negotiations nevertheless collapsed and three days later, October

19, 1939, the Anglo-French-Turkish Mutual Assistance Treaty was signed in Ankara. The pact pledged mutual assistance on the part of the three signatories: (1) in the event Turkey were involved in hostilities with a European power in consequence of aggression by that power against Turkey, France and Great Britain would cooperate with her and would lend her all necessary aid and assistance; (2) in the event that an act of aggression on the part of a European power occurred leading to war in the Mediterranean area in which France and Great Britain were involved, Turkey would collaborate with France and Great Britain and would lend them aid and assistance; (3) in the event that an act of aggression on the part of a European power occurred leading to war in the Mediterranean area in which Turkey is involved, France and Great Britain would collaborate with Turkey and would lend her aid and assistance.

Although well aware of Soviet intentions regarding the Straits and although quite annoyed by the Soviet attitude in recent negotiations, Turkey insisted upon a protocol which stated: "The obligations undertaken by Turkey in virtue of the above-mentioned Treaty cannot compel that country to take action having as its effect, or involving as its consequence, entry into armed conflict with the Soviet Union." Along with the treaty a special agreement providing for a joint Anglo-French loan of 25,000,000 pounds sterling "for supplies of war material" to Turkey was also signed.

In commenting on the Pact Molotov declared: "I wonder whether Turkey will not come to regret this?" German reaction was surprisingly milder. Knowing that they could not afford to attack Turkey merely because the pact had been concluded, yet willing to make the best of the situation, the Germans simply stated that they "had no wish to quarrel with the pro-British line which Turkey was following." Yet von Papen, when he returned from Berlin after explaining the Tripartite Pact to Hitler, said that he thought "there were some things which Turkey could do to oblige Germany without infringement of the Anglo-Franco-Turkish alliance"—Turkey had to keep neutrality as much as possible, in order to be accepted into the New Order which Hitler intended to set up in the Balkans.

The War Period—Prior to the Soviet-German War. In April, 1939, Great Britain's Prime Minister, Neville Chamberlain, following the offer of a guarantee to Poland, had announced that Great Britain "attached the greatest importance to the avoidance of disturbance by force or threat of force to the status quo in the Mediterranean and the Balkan Peninsula." Later, the Turkish-British and Turkish-French declarations preceding the Tripartite Pact of October, 1939, provided for "consultations to ensure the speedy establishment of Balkan security." This, however, was a conspicuous failure, and despite all efforts on the part of both Turkey and Great Britain, the Balkan Entente could not be consolidated. Two inherent flaws in the Balkan Entente were: Bulgaria's attitude based on her perpetual grievance because of her loss of Dobrudja to Romania and failure to acquire an outlet to the Aegean Sea, and the isolationism of individual member states.

The visits of M. Gafencu, Foreign Minister of Romania, and M. Kosseivanof, Prime Minister of Bulgaria, to Ankara for the purpose of bringing about a conciliation between the two countries brought no results. By the end of 1940 all hope had vanished, and it was evident that Germany was winning over Romania, Yugoslavia, and Bulgaria.

After the visits of the Bulgarian king and Prime Minister to Germany, Turkey delivered, at the suggestion of the British government, a communication to Sofia expressing her confidence that "Bulgaria would undertake no hostile action of her own violation" and warned that events might put the two countries in opposite camps. The Turkish-Bulgarian declaration of February 17, 1941, a mere confirmation of the treaty signed on October 18, 1925, therefore added nothing to the general security of the Balkans. Turkey on her part, continued to warn Bulgaria against her current connections with Germany. The fact is that even before the Declaration, Bulgaria had already become involved to the extent of allowing the infiltration of German troops within her boundaries.

Similar Turkish moves, supported by Great Britain, concerning Yugoslavia were of no avail either. In the face of increasing German pressure in the Balkans, the British Foreign Secretary, Anthony Eden, came to Ankara, February 26 to March 1, 1941, to confer with the Turkish government on the Balkan situation. He and Mr. Saracoglu met again on March 18 in Cyprus to decide on the instructions to be sent to the Turkish Ambassador in Belgrade. It was too late, however, as a swift change of events had taken place: Prince Paul had accepted Hitler's demands (he was deposed by a *coup d'etat* of pro-allied army officers who placed young King Peter on the throne) and the German invasion followed on April 6. Before long, the eventuality which had been most dreaded occurred—the Balkans were completely dominated by the Axis. In consequence of this and various Allied setbacks elsewhere, Turkey was left completely to her own devices. Sir Hugh Knatchbull-Hugessen said of the situation: "If Romania had shown more courage and more public spirit, Bul-

garia less passionate nationalism, and Yugoslavia less exclusive individualism, things might have been different." Turkey and Greece
alone had remained faithful to the Balkan Entente to the end.

An Unapplied Pact.—Popular Turkish enthusiasm for the Tripartite Pact was short-lived. The Germans had always been very popular in Turkey and even if at first pro-Western elements had managed
to create a feeling of enthusiasm for the new Allies playing on the
theme of German menace in the Balkans and of Anglo-French invinci-
bility, the setbacks suffered by the Allies eventually upset the balance.
Even before Allied defeat in the West, a number of Turkish newspapers
had been emphasizing the necessity of Turkey's neutrality in the war.
In addition, negotiations between the Allies and the Turkish Government were not proceeding so well. The British were experiencing difficulty in rearranging and redirecting their foreign trade so that they
could compete with the Germans on the Turkish market, and supplies
of war material promised to Turkey were not "flowing smoothly."
The Turkish Government pointed out that due to equipment short-
ages she would not be able to fulfill her Tripartite Pact commitments.

From January, 1940, onwards continuous military talks between
Allied and Turkish officials created some tension in Turkey, but the
Turkish Premier's assurance in February that Turkey would only
enter the war if her "zone of security" were menaced had a calming
effect on the public. Then came German successes in Norway, the
Netherlands, and later Mussolini's "stab in the back" to France. Under the terms of the Tripartite Pact, Turkey was now obliged to declare war against Germany and Italy. When the British and French
Ambassadors requested her to do so, the Turkish Government replied
that its policy towards her Allies remained unchanged, and that it
nevertheless preferred for the moment to remain non-belligerent. But
the Germans were quick to note that Turkey did not hasten to "subject her policy to a thorough revision" due to the collapse of the Allied
front in the west and to the Russian moves in the Balkans.

Von Papen in a telegram to his Foreign Office in June 29, 1940
pointed this out and added that Turkey was then mainly concerned
with possible Russian moves in the Straits and was refusing implied
conditions of the Soviets for a Turkish-Soviet rapprochement, and
that she turn her back on England.

Von Papen suggested to the Foreign Office that it would be better,
especially for Italy in the Mediterranean, to have Turkish Straits
rather than Russian Straits and to that end that he be allowed to
attempt to "exert appropriate influence to improve Turkish-Russian

relations before it is too late." Ribbentropp's reply to this suggestion were instructions to Von Papen that he "do nothing but observe."

The British Ambassador, Sir Hugh Knatchbull-Hugessen, comments that although Turkey's obligation to become a belligerent was evident, "....in a world upheaval such as that through which we were passing, when nothing could be foretold with certainty and when, as Numan Menemencioglu (who later became Foreign Minister) remarked to me in a different connection, *'il faut se metier de la logique, nous sommes dans l'illogique jusqu'au cou,'* it would have been worse than quixotic to look for so much direct sequence."

Sir Hugh himself admits that Turkish statesmen were then better informed on the situation than were the British: They were aware that France could not be saved, that the Balkan Entente had virtually collapsed, that Germany having finished the business in the west might turn her attention, (as she subsequently did) to southeastern Europe and they knew they were not equipped to fight the German army. "To plunge thus handicapped into the melee at a moment when one of their allies was down and out and the other in deadly danger might have earned for Turkey imperishable memories of heroic self-sacrifice," Sir Hugh contends, "but it would have done very little good. Indeed by becoming a liability to their already strained ally they might have done incalculable harm."

Lord Halifax also recognized the reality of Turkey's position when he said on July 11, 1940, in the House of Lords: "His Majesty's Government fully appreciated the circumstances which lead to this decision of the Turkish Government, who throughout have kept in close contact with His Majesty's Government. Meanwhile our Treaty with Turkey stands as does the friendship and sympathy between our peoples on which the Treaty is based and which has rendered it in the past, as it will in future, a fruitful basis for constructive co-operation between us both as long as the war continues and in the years of peace to come."

On the other side, von Papen defended Turkey's attitude from perhaps a more realistic point of view: "It is interesting to read in Sir Hugh Knatchbull-Hugessen's memoirs that he considers the chief reason for the Turkish non-fulfillment of their treaty obligations lay in the inadequate equipment of the Turkish Army. Where they were expected to fight is not clear. It seemed a lot to ask Turkey to expect her to enter the war at the time of France's debacle and the disaster to the British Expeditionary Forces at Dunkirk."

The tone of the official communications of Von Papen during the same time were different. He blamed Sükrü Saracoglu (then Foreign

Minister) for maneuvering against the Axis. According to a message dated July 10, 1940, Saracoglu warned Russia, both through the Russian Ambassador in Ankara and through the Turkish Ambassador in Moscow, about the dangers of a German-Italian hegemony in Europe and tried to bring about a Turkish-Russian-British understanding.

The German Ambassador in Moscow, Von Schulenburg, concurrently reported that the British Ambassador in Moscow, Sir Stafford Cripps, was working along the same lines and advising Molotov that Russia resist the German-Italian efforts and restore the balance of power in Europe. Although the Turkish Ambassador in Moscow, Haydar Aktay, on instructions from Ankara kept in close touch with Sir Stafford concerning these efforts, apparently the British went a little further without informing the Turks. In his memoirs, Von Papen contends that Molotov had told the German Ambassador that the British had expressed their readiness to accept the Balkans as the Russian sphere of influence and had even acknowledged Russian aspirations on the Dardanelles.

The main German efforts in Ankara at the time seem to have concentrated on getting rid of Sükrü Saracoglu, the Foreign Minister (later Premier), whom they considered too pro-Allied. Ribbentrop even prepared a plot to discredit Saracoglu and also bring Russian pressure to bear upon Turkey. When the Germans occupied Paris they reportedly found a report from Rene Massigli, the French Ambassador in Ankara, in the Archives of the French Foreign Office in which he described an interview with Saracoglu who reportedly suggested the idea of a Turkey-based air attack on the Russian oil fields of Baku. The Germans published this in the form of a White Book. Although both Massigli and the Turkish government denied the authenticity of the document, there was considerable embarassment in Ankara.

In his memoirs Von Papen denies knowledge of or complicity in Ribbentrop's plot, but it is evident from reading the official messages to German Foreign Office, that he did his utmost to use the White Book in order to get rid of Saracoglu.

Evidently the Germans overplayed their hand. Van Papen admitted this when he wrote to the Foreign Office "that anybody familiar with the Turkish psyche would know that the liberation of Turkey from the Capitulations, only 20 years ago, had left behind a particularly sensitive feeling against ever doing anything, anywhere, which might appear to be the result of pressure exerted by a European Great Power."

There was immediate and sharp reaction in official circles and in the

Turkish press to the German hints which followed the publication of the German White Papers. At a social gathering in Istanbul during those days a German newspaperman said: "Very soon important discussions between Germany and Russia are to take place. These will concern Turkey and the Straits. Russia has a number of demands to make to Turkey, especially a base in the Straits. But Turkey should not be alarmed, as Germany will support her against Russia. But in order to assure this Turkey must demonstrate her friendship and sympathy with Germany. This must begin with the weeding out of Turkish ministers who are anti-German, starting with the Foreign Minister, Saracoglu."

The efforts of von Papen led to a state of emergency in Turkey and partial mobilization was declared. A few days later, on July 12, Turkey's Prime Minister, Dr. Refik Saydam, said pointedly in the National Assembly: "Turkey will remain faithful to her commitments made to England. Turkey will not bow herself before threat and insult. Turkey, the Kemalist Turkey, is not the Ottoman society of Viziers and Grand Viziers; no longer can ministers be dismissed or promoted at the express desire of foreign governments. Let this be clearly understood everywhere."[1] This attitude irked the Germans greatly. Von Papen reported to Berlin that although Turkey had perhaps not fulfilled "all the expectations" of the Allies, she "retained her decisive importance for saving the [British] Empire in this last phase of the struggle." According to Papen, Turkey assured the status quo in the Near East.

Turkey was finding it increasingly difficult to preserve her neutrality. German pressure, both on the Balkans in general and on her in particular, was increasing. Allied defeats were discouraging to pro-Western newspapers; pro-German commentators, on the other hand, had cause to rejoice. When Italy attacked Greece in October, 1940, tension reached a climax. Again Turkey, according to the provisions of the Balkan Entente, should have entered the war. Yet she did not. Although blackouts were imposed in the principal cities and a state of siege was declared in important nerve centers, the Foreign Minister made another announcement of Turkey's non-belligerence. This attitude was even more criticized than Turkey's stand in connection with Italy's declaration of war at the time of the French collapse.

Sir Hugh Knatchbull-Hugessen defended Turkey's position: It would have been impossible for Turkey to denude herself of defense to the extent of sending an expedition to Greece, nor would it have been possible for us to provide the necessary naval support or to participate in action in the Dodecanese. Nor was there yet sufficient

progress in the building up of equipment for Turkey. When these
points were considered it was found best to leave matters as they
were, not to call on Turkey for action until we could give her more
support, but to look to her for as favorable an attitude as possible
without risk of being attacked. The Turkish government were indeed
able to do something for Greece by assuring the Greek government
that they could safely withdraw their troops from their eastern borders in Thrace." Greece was also informed that she could count on
Turkish support if Bulgaria attacked.

Profiting from the war in Greece and infiltration of Romania, Germany made a new move to draw Turkey into the Axis. Von Papen
had suggested on August 1, 1940, that since the attempt to bring about
a change of course in Turkey through the publication of the Massigli
Documents had not been successful, Germany should seek other means
to do this—namely, to try to neutralize Turkey by giving her joint
assurances and promising her the Dodecanese Islands. Von Papen
pointed out that "Turkey remained as an extremely unpleasant threat
to the flank of any operation against the British Empire in the Middle
East."

Later in the course of conversations held between Molotov, Hitler,
and Ribbentrop in November, 1940 in Berlin, the Germans recommended that Turkey should be induced to free herself from British
ties and suggested that adoption of a common platform by Germany,
the Soviet Union, Italy, and Japan would help in this direction. They
"understood" Soviet dissatisfaction with the Montreux Convention and
believed that the Soviet Union should have certain privileges in the
Black Sea and that Soviet warships and merchant vessels should have
free access to the Mediterranean. On November 13 Ribbentrop for-
mulated all these points in the form of a draft declaration. According to the files of the German High Naval Command, Molotov during
these conversations had requested not only bases in the Turkish
Straits but also demanded the Kars-Ardahan region.

Soviet Russia, further, was annoyed by Germany's diplomatic and
military moves in the Balkans, notably in Hungary and Romania (especially the pressure on and German guaranty given to Romania and
the military occupation of the country). She now wanted as an additional measure of security for the Soviet Union in the Straits a
mutual assistance pact to be concluded between the USSR and Bulgaria. Molotov also would have amended the Ribbentrop draft so
as to "guarantee a base for light naval and land forces of the USSR
on the Bosphorus and the Dardanelles by means of a long term lease,
including—in case Turkey declares herself willing to join the (pro-

posed) Four Power Pact (between USSR, Germany, Italy and Japan) —a guarantee of the independence and of the territory of Turkey by the three countries named. This protocol should provide that in case Turkey refuses to join the Four Powers, Germany, Italy, and the Soviet Union agree to work out and to carry out the required military and diplomatic measures, and a separate agreement to this effect should be concluded."

In July, a few months prior to these secret negotiations between Soviet Russia and Germany, Stalin had accepted the good offices of Sir Stafford Cripps, the British Ambassador in Moscow, for the improvement of Turkish-Soviet relations. Von Papen was immediately instructed by Hitler to prevent a Turkish-British-Russian rapprochement.

The demands set forth by Molotov concerning Bulgaria and the Straits displeased Hitler inasmuch as they conflicted sharply with German intentions of creating an exclusive sphere of influence in the Balkans, and he ordered the Army to prepare for Operation Barbarossa against the Soviet Union. The factor which made him take the final decision was the set of proposals offered by Russia to Bulgaria on November 25. This provided for a mutual assistance pact which would assist Bulgaria in realizing its national aspirations both in Greek and Turkish Thrace, and under which Bulgaria would assist the Soviet Union in case of a threat to Soviet interests in the Black Sea or in the Straits. Germany was informed by Bulgaria of these proposals.

On February 17, 1941, Germany occupied Bulgaria. One month earlier Molotov had given voice to a serious complaint: that German troop movements in Romania were aimed at occupying Bulgaria, Greece, and the Straits, and that, owing to British opposition, Bulgaria might be turned into a theatre of war. The Soviet Government, he said, would consider the appearance of any armed forces on the territory of Bulgaria and on the Straits as a violation of the security interests of the USSR. Following the occupation of Bulgaria, Molotov expressed regret that Germany had done "injury to the security interests of the USSR" by this move.

The new development compelled Soviet Russia to approach Ankara as a possible counterweight to German encroachment in the Balkans. Turkey was at that time also being courted by Hitler, who sought to sever her relations with Great Britain and replace the British Alliance with a German one—but now without the "common platform" with the Soviet Union. Hitler had therefore, in November, tried to make best use of Molotov's demands concerning the Straits in order to show Turkey Germany's good intentions by informing the Turkish ambassador in Berlin about them.   Yet Turkey did not hesitate to issue a joint declaration with the USSR on March 25, stating that "the reports appearing in the foreign press to the effect that, if Turkey were led to enter war, the Soviets would take advantage of her difficulties to attack her . . . in no way correspond to the position of the Soviet Union." In such a case, she could, "in accordance with the terms of the non-aggression pact between herself and the USSR, count on the full understanding and neutrality of the USSR" and the USSR on her part "could count on the full understanding and neutrality of Turkey if she found herself in such a situation."

For a complete perspective of the post-war attitude of the USSR towards Turkey this declaration should be kept in mind, together with some other events, such as Soviet Russia's reluctance to sign a mutual assistance pact with Turkey in 1939; her opposition to Turkey's Alliance with France and Great Britain; and her "secret" demands concerning the Straits in November 1940.

Turkish-British efforts to consolidate the Balkans were of no avail and German encroachment, as a result, could not be checked.

When Greece and Yugoslavia were attacked by Germany in April of 1941, Turkey had to declare again that she was "non-belligerent." Thus isolated, inadequately armed and equipped, she was now under the direct pressure of Germany.   But Hitler assured Inonu several times that his country had no intentions whatsoever concerning Turkish territories.   German propoganda, meanwhile, played on the "former ally, former comrades-in-arms" theme and was attaining some success.   The stage was set for a new and subtle German move on Turkey.

Hitler and Ribbentrop considered it extremely necessary that Ankara should at once come into the Axis orbit, especially with a view to the coming attack on Soviet Russia, yet they conceded that "it is outside the realm of doubt that any action whatever directed against Turkey would provoke the military reaction of the Ankara government."   One means of attracting the Turks, Hitler then thought, would be to offer them Syria.

By June, 1941, Turkey's position had become very precarious.   She was cut off from friends and the Rashid Ali rebellion in Iraq, which was instigated against the British by German agents, was threatening her with complete encirclement.   Thus Turkey was now obliged to reassure herself as regards Germany.   On his side, Hitler needed Turkey badly.   Von Papen was instructed to try to force Turkey's acquiescence regarding the secret passage of arms for Iraq through Tur-

key. Preliminary talks on a Turkish-German pact took place on May
14, 1941, between von Papen and the Turkish President, Ismet Inonu,
who is reported to have said: "with such all-round good-will, a formula
can certainly be arrived at."

According to the original Ribbentrop proposal, there was to be a
treaty of friendship which was to be represented to the Turks as a
German guarantee for any Russian designs on Turkey. With this official treaty another secret agreement was simultaneously to be signed
by which Germany was to have the right to transit without limits of
arms, materials of war, and some armed forces which were to be sent
to Iraq in a disguised form. Turkey, in return, would be offered some
territory from Bulgaria and one Aegean island.

It soon became apparent that the Turkish government was not receptive to such terms. It was not willing to let either German arms
or German soldiers in disguise through their territory. It desired to
maintain alliance with Great Britain; and it did not intend to de-
mobilize its armed forces.

A non-aggression treaty was signed on June 18, 1941 which contained provisions for mutual respect of territorial inviolability and
integrity, abstention from action, direct or indirect, by one party
against the other, and friendly settlement of all questions affecting
common interests. It did not contain any secret commitments or any
wider implications. It clearly reaffirmed Turkey's prior obligations
under the Anglo-Franco-Turkish Pact of October 19, 1939. In commenting on this treaty Inonu stated: "It was now understood that the
Germans had put off their attack on Turkey to a later and more suitable time. Turkey also considered it necessary to gain time, both
for its own security and for the benefit of the Allies." Von Papen
declares in his memoirs that Ribbentrop did, at first, object violently
against such a clause concerning prior obligations. But Von Papen
convinced him that no alternative was possible since "Turks were
gentlemen, and gentlemen had the habit of keeping their word."

Although the British were kept fully informed of the talks preceding
the signing of the Treaty and although the Anglo-Turkish alliance
retained its position of preference, there was much criticism among
the Allies regarding the Tukish attitude. According to Sir Hugh
Knatchbull-Hugessen, however, "It was evident that the Turks were
driven by hard practical considerations into making their Treaty with
Germany. It was in no sense due to inclination or sentiment that
they did so . . By the end of the year it had become obvious that the
German Treaty was meant to stave over a dangerous period and represented no fundamental change of policy."

Four days after the Treaty was signed, Germany attacked Soviet Russia. Thus a new phase in the second World War began, a phase implying more threats, temptations, and provocations for Turkey.

A Period of Threats and Temptations. Up to the time of the German attack on Soviet Russia, both the Turkish Government and its people had the best intentions regarding the maintenance of close relations with Great Britain. This was considered a part of Kemal Ataturk's legacy. Despite the setbacks suffered by the Allies, despite the promise of British military aid which never assumed adequate proportions, despite the increase of German political and economic pressure and traditional sympathy for Germany, the official Turkish attitude was to do everything possible for an eventual Allied victory while refraining from antagonizing Germany or providing any excuses for her aggression.

Even the Turkish-German Non-Aggression Pact as such was not a deviation on Turkey's part from this fundamental attitude of friendship for the Allies. Sir Hugh Knatchbull-Hugessen admits that the Pact had "introduced a certain delicacy" into his relations with the Turkish government, but he hastens to add: "I had to realize more than once that things were being said to me, not from a desire to favour Germany or to obstruct the allies, but merely in order to be able to tell the Germans that a firm line had been taken with me, or that my suggestions had been refused. It was as likely as not that, on such occasions, the refusal was a matter of words and in due time whatever I asked was quietly done."

When the question of the Turkish-German Pact came up for debate in the British House of Commons on July 24, 1941, several members asked that the Anglo-Turkish position be clarified. Churchill countered criticisms with this statement: "It is unsuitable to continue in this way a discussion about the general interests of another country. We do not seek to predict the line of policy to countries undergoing grave difficulties, who do not, and do not wish to, clarify their own positions." Eden assured the House that "Our relations have continued to be on a very special footing [since conclusion of the Mutual Aid Pact in October 1939]... Turkey is our friend and ally. As we were fully informed of the negotiations between the Turkish and German governments, the agreement comes to us as no surprise at all." Thus was consent given to Turkey's "perforce" understandings with Germany.

Despite Ribbentrop's ambitious first draft and von Papen's hopes that the Turks might allow the passage of aid to the Rashid Ali uprising[3] in Iraq (May 2, 1941), neither the text nor the protocols contained any commitments or implications, nor were there any secret protocols. It was merely stipulated in Articles 1, 2 and 3 that the two countries agreed to respect reciprocally the "integrity and sanctity of the territory of their respective States," and that they would not take any measure which could be "directly or indirectly" turned against the other party; that they would establish contact on all problems that "touch their mutual interests; and that an economic agreement would be entered into." Nor was the Pact an anti-Russian action, as such, on the part of the Turkish government. It is granted that the signing of the Turkish-German treaty on June 18 and the German attack on Soviet Russia on June 22 were not isolated events and that the main reason which prompted Hitler into taking immediate action against Russia was Germany's aspirations concerning Turkey and her interest in the Straits and the Balkans. It was equally evident that "drawing Turkey away from the British camp" was an important prerequisite of a German operation against Russia. But all German intentions and ambitions in this connection were not fulfilled by either the text or implications of the treaty.

An indication of what the British, and especially the Soviet Government, felt regarding Turkey is the joint British-Soviet note of August 10, 1941 to Turkey, which implies a tacit acceptance of Turkey's "faithful guardianship of the Straits." The two governments reaffirmed their fidelity to the Montreux Convention and assured Turkey that they had no aggressive intentions or claims concerning the Dardanelles. They would "scrupulously" respect the territorial integrity of the Turkish Republic and "fully understood" the desire of the Turkish Government not to be drawn into the war.

In any case, Turkey had declared her neutrality in the German-Russian conflict from the very outset. Both the signing of the Turkish-German Pact and the German-Soviet war, ushered in a new era when the position of Turkey "took on a new significance." Using the Pact as a spring-board, Germany would increase her pressure through commercial transactions, through the press, and through diplomacy. Nor would this pressure be merely of a crude nature; it would rather, involve temptations towards which the Turks could not remain altogether indifferent. It should also be kept in mind that the fact that Turkey's former ally and former comrade-in-arms was actually fighting and defeating her traditional enemy made her susceptible to all sorts of propaganda possibilities. Even Turkish Premier Saracoglu enthusiastically shouted *"Ce n'est pas une guerre, c'est une crusade"* when he heard about the German attack on Russia. German successes on the Eastern front, one must admit, added fire to the

dormant ambitions of Turanism in Turkey and even tempted some of
the Turkish leaders. Germany therefore once again could hope to
use the same tool she used in the First World War in order to draw
Turkey closer to herself. Despite the explicit heritage of Ataturk and
stipulations in the National Pact against "foreign adventures," there
was in Turkey a strong Pan-Turanist movement which included some
generals and statesmen. Russian defeats had revived the inherent
desire for unity of "all the Turks in the world" and the restoration of
the Turkish Empire in a realistic way—which Suleyman the Magnificent had ignored—by conquering lands with more or less homogenous
populations.

Gone therefore were the first years of the war when Turkey was
disinterested in any material or territorial gains and she could stand
adamant against German pressures. Strong temptations were leading
her in a specific direction.

Another aspect of the pressure on Turkey which followed in the
wake of the German-Turkish Pact was the increase in German-Turkish
economic relations. By May, 1941, Germany returned to her position
as the foremost importer from and exporter to Turkey. A trade mission headed by Dr. Claudius arrived in Turkey immediately after
the signing of the Pact and by October an agreement was signed under
which Germany was to provide (transportation costs included) steel
and war materials (to the value of about 1,000,000 Turkish liras) in
exchange for Turkish raw materials, especially chrome. Chrome deliveries of 90,000 tons a year, however, would start only with the expira-
tion of the Anglo-Turkish Treaty of 1939 by virtue of the provision
that Britain would get the entire output. As Sir Hugh expressed it:
"the renewal clause" of the agreement made it possible for the
British "with the aid of the Turks" to defeat German aims in this field.

In another field, the field of temptations, the situation was different.
By October 1941, many Turks, including government officials, were
sure that the defeat of Soviet Russia was in the offing. With that eventuality there would be two main problems. Considering that by the
establishment of the German army in the Caucasus, Turkey would be
flanked on all sides, there would be necessity for a different, and as
they put it, "more stable" *modus vivendi* with Germany. By friend-
lier relations with Germany, some immediate Turanist goals, such as
creation of independent Turkish states under Turkish auspices, could
be attained.

There is no doubt that at the time even Turkey's Prime Minister
hinted at these aims during conversations with von Papen, who sent
several memoranda to Berlin concerning these hints and detailed sug-

gestions as to the administration of Turkish regions of Russia. On the other hand, the Turkish Ambassador at Berlin, Husrev Gerede, allegedly made similar hints during his conversations with the German Foreign Office.

The Turanist movement in Turkey at that time existed in several strata of the Turkish intelligensia. There were even the beginnings of such aspirations, due to the success of the German Army, among government officials who had been up to that time opposed to foreign adventures in general. But in view of the new developments, they believed that to work in the direction of Turanism would be the realistic approach. Some top army officers were in favor of such national aspirations. There was also a young Turkish group which was extremely active in conditioning the minds of the people in general by various publications. Finally, there were the several groups of émigrés from the Crimea, Azerbaijan, and other Turkish regions of Soviet Russia working on all these levels.

"Participation in the war against Russia . . . would be very popular in the army and in many sections of the population," wrote a German observer in December, 1941. Yet a few months later the slowing down of the German offensive in Russia would have a sobering influence on the Turks.

In order to understand this and other factors which were foremost in the minds of the Turkish leaders, let us consider the *Tour d'Horizon* written by von Papen on January 5, 1942: "The enlargement of the theatre of operations, both due to the explosion of the American-Japanese conflict and due to the declaration of war against the Axis powers by the United States, has provoked here an immediate sentiment of profound deception. As I have told you on many occasions the Turkish government had hopes of compromise between the British Empire and the Axis countries, a compromise which according to them was still possible as America had not decisively passed to the adverse side. Now all those possibilities are closed up. As a result of these developments Turkey reiterates and repeats her unchanged desire to keep out of hostilities and to refuse to let herself be drawn into the struggle for any conditions which do not directly concern Turkey."

Von Papen added that the Anglo-American entente with Russia had given a new turn to German-Turkish relations and that Turkey's real interests are linked with the outcome of the Russo-German war.

"The fact that England, as is clear, has decided to establish a New Order with the aid of Bolshevist Russia appears a considerable blow. It is impossible to imagine that a civilized State like England which, more than any other Continental State, ought to employ all its forces to fight for the maintenance of principles established through thousands of years, can take these plans seriously. This declaration of England is considered a measure of propaganda in the aim of sustaining by every means Soviet Russia's resistance.

"According to Turkish opinion only America amongst the participants of the Anglo-American bloc would appear to be invincible. The Axis countries as a consequence would have been able to turn the issues of war to their sole advantage in inflicting a defeat upon the British Empire. Such a total defeat does not coincide with Turkey's interests for the interest of Turkey is the maintenance of an equilibrium in the Mediterranean and not in the total predominance of Italy, which would be the possible consequence of a complete victory of the Axis.

"Another possibility would be a complete victory of the Anglo-American bloc with the aid of Soviet Russia. According to Turkish opinion this would signify the total collapse of Europe; neither England nor the United States of America would be in a position to stop the territorial expansion of the Russians or to preserve from Bolshevism a Europe that was starving, impoverished and exhausted by war."

In his book *Diplomat in War and Peace* Sir Hugh Knatchbull-Hugessen confirms this picture of the period. Although the Pan-Turanism of the previous year had been transformed into a cautious attitude by the beginning of 1942, and although the entry of the United States into the war, despite initial setbacks in the Pacific, had bolstered this attitude, the Turkish pendulum had not entirely swayed back from the Axis. One reason for this was the suspicion felt for any alliance which included the Russians.

The conversations at Moscow between Soviet Russia and Great Britain, which incidentally were attended by the British Ambassador at Ankara, increased these suspicions. As Sir Hugh himself stated: "on any occasion where there was any cause to think, however mistakenly, that Turkish affairs were being discussed between the great belligerent Allies behind Turkey's back, Turkish susceptibilities were not unnaturally aroused." Also, as von Papen states, the Turks feared the day when the Soviets would be the "unconditional victors" in Europe and the Balkans. Ismet Inonu frankly told von Papen that Turkey was very much interested in the total destruction of the Russian colossus. But it must be pointed out that this was a mere expression of a wish shared by all the nation and could not be considered as an indication of Turkey's actual participation in activities against Soviet Russia. There were, it is true, even on the governmental level, contemplations of various schemes for administering the Turkish

provinces of Soviet Russia, but the Government was always careful
not to commit itself too much and not to antagonize Soviet Russia by
indiscreet moves.

However, several events in the course of 1942—including Axis victories both in the Middle East and in the Pacific, and suspicions concerning the conversations at Moscow—increased Turkish leanings
towards Germany. Sir Hugh's statement to the press to the effect
that Turkey would have nothing to fear from an Allied victory did
not offset these suspicions. The bomb plot in Ankara in February,
1942, against Von Papen, a plot designed by Soviet directives in order
to create an incident between Turkey and Germany, did not help
Allied prestige. Neither did the sinking of some unarmed Turkish
merchant ships in the Black Sea, by Russian submarines and mines,
increase Turkey's affection for the Soviet Union.

From December 3, 1941, Turkey had been a recipient of Lend-Lease
aid. This was a part of the Allied strategy, designed both to increase
economic activities and to give military supplies to encourage her, and
also to counteract German Economic and diplomatic influence on
Turkey. Turkey's Foreign Minister, Numan Menemencioglu, however, was strongly anti-Russian and hence very much in favor of
strengthening, especially the economic ties with Germany. In fact,
he actually had approached von Papen with the idea of improving
and enlarging the scope of Turco-German relations, yet he emphasized "without in this way complicating the relations of Turkey with
the Soviet Union and without rendering her relations with the Allies
more precarious." Pointing out that Lend-Lease was not functioning
well, he proposed rejuvenation of the *Funk Agreement* (for credits
to be used in purchase of war material from Germany) which had not
been put into effect. To this von Papen replied by saying that "the
transport of war goods would have to be compensated by some political
equivalent."

This move, sponsored by Menemencioglu, did not get anywhere.
The Germans, who had been so busy promising large pieces of territory to Turkey, now even cancelled the delivery of some war materials
ordered by the Turkish army from the Krupp firm.

Pan-Turanism was not yet dead. Allegedly, talks between von
Papen and Saracoglu and Menemencioglu again took place on the
details of plans for governing the Crimean and Caucasian provinces.
According to documents later published by the Russians, Saracoglu
and Menemencioglu gave the definite impression that a German
victory over Russia was sincerely wished by Turkey and that such
a victory would change her attitude. On the other hand, the Turks

had expressed satisfaction with the Anglo-Russian Treaty of May 1943, and government leaders, Inonu in particular, were careful to foster good relations with Allied diplomats in Ankara. The latter, on the other hand, were doing their utmost to check pro-German tendencies, especially those instigated by Pan-Turanists and army officers. Two incidents regarding these efforts are worthy of mention:

At one time, when Sir Hugh Knatchbull-Hugessen was worried about persistent rumors to the effect that Germany was offering two Asiatic provinces to Turkey, he went directly to Saracoglu to ask him about it: "I was at first slightly disconcerted by the very serious expression which he put on. But I was soon reassured. 'That would not be nearly enough,' he said. 'I must have Scotland as well!' "

One day during 1942, at a time when the Allies' fortunes of war in North Africa seemed to be at a very low ebb, the British Ambassador was at the Ankara hippodrome watching the horse races. Ismet Inonu was also there in his Presidential box. When Inonu saw Sir Hugh, he invited the Ambassador to watch the races from his box. They stood there together until the end of the races. The next day their pictures were in all the Turkish newspapers. "It was not till I got back to the Embassy that I learnt that Tobruk had fallen a few hours before. But the President had been aware of it and his gesture was intentional," says Sir Hugh.

It is quite apparent that during 1942 the Turks were inclined to hope for a German victory because it could further their aspirations. Moreover, they were worried that the pro-Soviet attitude in England and America might result in some secret agreements against them—such as the agreements between Tsarist Russia and England and France before and during World War I. On the other hand, there was the awareness of the German terror, effected chiefly through British and American propaganda, which had begun to offset German propaganda; the realization of the possibility that Germany might be defeated, primarily because of American power; and finally, there were memories of the high-handed attitude of the Germans even toward their allies.

Also working against Germany's chances for a Turkish volte-face was the growing disappointment among Turanists at the end of 1943. It had become quite clear that Turco-German collaboration in the Soviet Turkish provinces under German occupation was quite impossible. The Germans, despite von Papen's hints and his detailed conversations with Turkish leaders, and despite the activities of unofficial Pan Turanist groups were determined to rule the occupied territories by themselves without any outside interference. It also became more and more apparent that they planned to use the old Soviet tactics of segregating various Turkish national groups from each other by giving each of them a separate identity. For example, instead of organizing one large Turkish Legion under German army command, they set up several Turkish Legions without mention of the name *Turk*. There were, as a result, different Azerbaijan, Uzbek, and Tatar legions.

On the other hand, the Turks were extremely worried about the Allied attitude and their pro-Russian policies. Articles in the Allied press concerning the right of the Russians to free passage through the Straits had adverse effects on the Turks. They were convinced that there was a secret agreement between the Allies and the USSR for supplanting the Montreux Convention at the earliest opportunity.

All in all, it might be said that during 1942, when both temptations and military-political pressure from the Axis side had reached its highest point, the Turks stood their ground. As Sir Hugh Knatchbull-Huggesen said: "They did not allow themselves to be overawed" by either Hitler's threats or promises.

The activities of pro-German and Pan-Turanist cliques, and the rather indiscreet conversations of Menemencioglu and Saracoglu notwithstanding, Turkish neutrality on the whole was correct and not detrimental to the Allies. The latter had given some thought to bringing Turkey into the war on their side in 1942 but had finally decided against this. The Turkish army was not prepared, and the Allies were too occupied elsewhere to supply it with sufficient equipment. In any event, as there were then no plans for an offensive, the entry of Turkey would not have been of any positive assistance —on the contrary, the opening of a new front could prove a liability. Turkey, in effect, was acting as a "protective pad" against German penetration into the Middle East and her guardianship of the Straits had so far been proper, without any ill-effects to Soviet Russia.

It was a certainty, however, that despite all threats and pressures Turkey was determined to fight should Germany interfere actively. Von Papen had pointed out: "Any attempt to force the Turks to declare their exact position prematurely would inevitably cause Turkey to pass to the enemy allegiance."

Perhaps the speech of Saracoglu, when he became Prime Minister, (replacing Dr. Refik Saydam) in August 1942, better explains the Turkish attitude prevailing in that year: "But should our independence or territory be attacked, we will fight to the last man . . . Turkey does not and will not pursue adventures beyond her frontiers; has sought means of remaining outside the war and has found them in

conscious and active neutrality . . . The treaty with Great Britain
has continued, the Turco-German Pact has sealed the reciprocal comprehension and friendship of the two countries, and the attitude of
Turkey has been equally loyal and friendly towards all opposing
States."

Stricter Neutrality, Followed by Entry Into the War. If one com-
pares Turkey's attitude to a pendulum, which normally remains at
rest but oscillates from time to time, one might say that its movement had considerably weakened toward the end of 1942. The
victories at Stalingrad and El Alamein, and the Anglo-American
landings in North Africa had impressed public opinion; the government was becoming progressively convinced that a clear cut German
victory would not be possible. In order to meet all diplomatic and
military eventualities, the nation resorted to stricter neutrality from
September, 1942. The effects of this move were readily perceived in
the Turkish press. A system of directives emanating from the
Government Press and Publications Bureau in Ankara ensured that
the newspapers did not indulge in attacking any of the opposing sides
and that they gave equal space to respective war communiques. In
fact, *Vatan*, a pro-Allied Istanbul newspaper, was closed at the end
of 1942 because it published a photograph of Charlie Chaplin as the
"Dictator"; conversely, a pro-Axis newspaper was banned for its
excessive attacks on America. This neutrality was, however, interpreted in another way regarding propaganda efforts in Turkey of
both belligerent groups which were given a free hand. The British
Information Office, the Office of War Information and the Russian
Embassy on the one hand, and the German and Italian press attachés
on the other, were competing to impress public opinion and win over
newspaper editors. Turkish-language picture magazines of the Allies,
the *Cephe* and the Turkish version of the German *Signal*, however,
were not permitted to be circulated in Turkey; both sides were told
to restrict their propaganda to foreign language editions of their
magazines and newsletters.

Certainly one main reason for resorting to a stricter neutrality
was the realization of unpreparedness of the Turkish army—and
Turkish leaders were not even willing to fight on the winning side at
the close of the war. "Even the last two days would be enough for
the Luftwaffe to bomb and destroy our beloved Istanbul," the Turkish
press hinted.

To offset such anxiety and induce Turkey to enter the war, the
Allies, the Americans in particular (through Lend-Lease), and the
British by way of their Middle East Command, stepped up their

efforts to supply and modernize the Turkish army. The Germans were still in principle furnishing some war material and industrial machinery to the Turks, but as has been pointed out already, the German High Command, in spite of demands emanating from von Papen and the German Foreign Office, was reluctant to permit delivery of the equipment, which had been originally ordered from the Krupp firm. This reluctance to a certain extent improved the chances of the Allies.

When the British Ambassador returned to London in December, 1942, he was instructed by Churchill to work in the direction of "persuading Turkey to come into war." This was the result of an idea with which Churchill had been toying since the summer of 1942. He had several times tried to convince President Roosevelt as to the desirability of a joint Anglo-American attack, via Turkey, against what he called the "soft under-belly of the Axis," that is, against the Dodecanese, the Aegean Islands and the Balkans. In addition to various strategic motives, Churchill's plan was probably motivated by his anxiety to get to the Balkans before the Red Army.

As for strategic motives, according to Churchill's reasoning, the scene in the Mediterranean had changed since the Allied occupation of Northwest Africa. A new, forward movement, both for opening a new route to Russia and for striking at Germany's southern flank, had now become possible. As Turkey was the "key" to these plans, "to bring that country into the war on the Allies' side had acquired new hope and urgency."

In retrospect, one cannot refrain from agreeing with von Papen's reasoning, which was apparently shared by Inonu and the Turkish Government, that both from the political and strategic points of view, Churchill was miscalculating.

Even if the Allies were first in occupying Bulgaria, Yugoslavia, and Hungary, the confidence enjoyed by Stalin was such that Russians would be invited to share the task of occupation and perhaps Russia would be allowed to "liberate" Turkey or enter Turkey as an ally, if Turkey had participated in the war. Who could have forced Russia to abandon the Dardanelles then?

As for the strategic point of view, an offensive through Greece, Macedonia, and Yugoslavia would be difficult and would take too long.

In a memorandum to the British Chiefs of Staff on November 18 Churchill suggested that, to bring Turkey into the conflict, Ankara should be offered a Russian-American-British guarantee of territorial integrity and *status quo,* and that a strong Anglo-American military mission should be sent to Turkey to make the necessary preparations to ensure a "ceaseless flow of weapons and equipment" to that country. Although Allied activities for supplying Turkey with modern war materials had been intensified since the beginning of 1942, the Turks were not totally satisfied. As a matter of fact, the equipment given to Turkey by the British Middle East Command consisted mostly of captured Axis material not immediately required by the Command itself—a thing which irked the Turks. There was also a natural resistance to British advisers and methods on the part of German-trained Turkish officers. The British military advisers, in turn, had not been particularly diplomatic in dealing with the Turks.

On November 24 Churchill informed Stalin of his plans for Turkey and especially of the proposed joint British-Soviet-American guarantee of territorial integrity to Turkey. Stalin in his reply expressed full agreement with these views and stated that it would be very desirable to do everything possible to have Turkey enter the war in the Spring on the side of the Allies. This development, he said, would be of great importance in hastening the defeat of Nazi Germany. Yet it was apparent that Soviet Russia, while favoring Turkey's entry into the war, never preferred a joint Anglo-American invasion through Turkey and the Balkans to the opening of a second front in Western Europe.

In January, 1943 Churchill decided to meet President Ismet Inonu personally in order to win the latter over to his plans. Although this idea was opposed by the British Cabinet on the grounds that it might be premature to approach Turkey on the highest level without previous preparation, Churchill managed to obtain the agreement of Roosevelt and Stalin. He therefore suggested to Inonu that they meet in Cyprus; Inonu countered by suggesting a meeting in Ankara; and the two leaders finally compromised on Adana. Arrangements were made in great secrecy. The meeting took place in January in the parlor car of the Turkish Presidential train, switched to a siding of the Adana railroad station.

The conversations held between Churchill and Inonu lasted for two days and explored the "likelihood and desirability" of Turkey's taking an active part in the war during the year. There was also some exchange of views on "distant perspectives," possibly such as Turkey's position vis-à-vis Russia in the post-war period.

Inonu made it quite clear that before any decisive steps were taken Turkey should be adequately prepared, both for any possible enemy attack which might come as a result of too close collaboration with the Allies, and for any eventual entry into the war on her own initiative and "in her own interest." He also understood perfectly well, he said, that it was in Turkey's own interest to place herself in line with the victorious nations. Yet he would do everything possible to retard Turkey's entry into war until it was imperative for post-war considerations to do so, and he would take all the military and political precautions to make this entry as little dangerous for the Turkish army and cities as possible and as advantageous as possible for Turkey's post-war status—especially in connection with Soviet Russia.

Churchill tried to convince Inonu by pointing out that Stalin was most anxious to see a strong Turkey after the war and that both Great Britain and the United States would ensure that Turkey be made a "full partner" at the Peace Conference. He expressed confidence that in the postwar period the USSR would concentrate on reconstruction rather than on expanding its territories, that Communism had been modified, and that good relations between Soviet Russia and the rest of the world were possible if "Great Britain and the United States acted together and maintained a strong air force."

Both Inonu and his Premier, Saracoglu, who had accompanied him to Adana, pointed out that Turkey was obliged to be prudent vis-à-vis Soviet imperialism. Churchill's reply to this was that an international organization, stronger than the League of Nations, would secure peace and security. The Turkish leaders stated in effect that they were looking for something more real and fundamental. "Europe was full of Slavs and Communists," they pointed out, "all the defeated countries would become Bolshevik and Slav if Germany were completely beaten." Inonu also tried to impress Churchill with the need for bringing the war to an end promptly. The complete "unconditional" defeat of Germany would give Russia a chance of becoming a grave danger for Turkey and Europe. His offer to mediate, however, was declined. Churchill insisted that he was not "pessimistic" about Russia's intentions, and even in the event that the USSR attacked Turkey, the whole international organization would act on behalf of Turkey and that the international guarantees after the war would be much more exacting.

After the Adana conversations Churchill wrote a letter to Stalin on February 2 pointing out that the Turks were "apprehensive of their position after the war in view of the great strength of the Soviet Republic." He suggested that a "gesture of friendship" on the part of the Soviet Union would be answered by the Turks. Stalin's reply was somewhat cool. As Churchill has remarked: "Victory did not make the Soviets more genial." Stalin pointed out that the Turks had so far not reacted to the friendly gestures of the Soviet Union, and that their international position "remained delicate" in view of their treaties with the USSR and Great Britain, on the one hand, and on the other their treaty with Germany, signed three days before the German attack against the USSR. "It is not clear to me how in the present circumstances Turkey thinks to combine her obligations vis-à-vis the USSR and Great Britain with her obligations vis-à-vis Germany," he said. But he added that if Turkey wished to make her relations with the USSR more friendly, the Soviet Union would be willing to meet Turkey "half way." British and American efforts to effect a conciliation between Turkey and the USSR were to continue during the Cairo conversations.

During the Adana conversations military talks were conducted between the British and Turkish General Staffs concerning the provision of equipment to Turkey "prior and subsequent to any political move by Turkey." The results of these conversations were embodied in a military agreement, which stipulated, among other things, the setting up at Ankara of a Joint Anglo-Turkish Military Commission "to improve communications for the transit of munitions."

The possibility of Turkey's cutting chrome shipments to Germany was another topic under discussion at Adana. This subject had been the cause of increasing criticism against Turkey in the Allied press. But Turkey was to some extent obliged to continue exporting this important material to Germany. Despite Turkish suggestions the Allies had been reluctant to buy the total chrome output at Turkish prices or to supply Turkey with some essential finished goods. Yet the Turks had, notwithstanding strong objections by Germany, managed to cut down chrome exports to that country to 46,000 tons in 1943, an amount considerably below the figure which had been agreed upon.

German reaction to the Churchill-Inonu conversations was surprisingly mild. Hitler sent a message to Inonu which presumably contained a reassurance that Germany would not attack Turkey. Also, von Papen asked the Turkish Government for assurance that the Non-Aggression Treaty between Turkey and Bulgaria was still in force and that Turkey had no designs on its neighbor. Turkey's answers were diplomatic and non-committal; they pointed out that "Turkey remained faithful to her written engagements."

By May of that year new German pressure which was strongly felt by Turkey began to be applied with several "peace" messages by Hitler. A German architectural exhibition was opened in Istanbul by von Papen—as if to emphasize that Hitler was a man devoted to construction and acts of peace. Before long, however, it was followed by hints from von Papen that if Turkey entered the war on the side of the Allies, or even if her collaboration with the Allies increased, the

Luftwaffe would bomb Istanbul and other principal Turkish cities. It was for this reason that during the spring and summer of 1943, there was a return to "emphasizing Turkey's neutrality" in the Turkish press.

Nevertheless, even though the Prime Minister himself reiterated his country's "neutrality," close military collaboration between Turkey and the Allies, which had been stepped up right after the Adana conversations, continued—with a "zero" hour timed for the autumn. Using a term coined during the Adana conversations, Turkish neutrality was being "stretched" very far towards greater compliance with Allied plans.

It is true that there was a group in Turkish government circles, presumably headed by Marshall Fevzi Cakmak and Menemencioglu, which was opposed to increased collaboration with the Allies. This group argued that the German summer campaign might be directed against Turkey, and that it would be "ill advised" at this point, when the conditions were so vaguely defined, to commit Turkey too far. Yet the group which was prepared to bring about a radical change in Turkey's status, provided that certain conditions, such as adequate preparation of the Turkish army and adequate guarantees for the postwar period, proved the stronger.

There was one serious preoccupation in the minds of all Turks: they were reluctant to enter the war because of the possibility of being liberated later by the Red Army. Perhaps because of a similar preoccupation, Soviet leaders were pressing the British and the Americans to persuade Turkey to enter the war, even if the Anglo-British invasion through the Balkans did not take place. They were in any case opposed to Churchill's plan and wanted to retain all operations in the Balkans and, if possible in Turkey, under their own monopoly.

Toward the end of 1943, Turkish-Allied collaboration was at its peak. The collapse of Italy had removed one more worry from the minds of the Turkish leaders. The Allies were now secretly using certain bases in the Izmir region and the Office of Strategic Services and the British Intelligence Service were actively operating in Turkey with the understanding and help of the Turkish Secret Service.

When, however, operations were launched against the Axis-held Dodecanese Islands, Cos, Leros and Samos, with the intention of "clearing the Aegean, and thus levering Turkey into the war," Turkey did not openly permit the use of Turkish airfields by the R.A.F. in support of ground operations, but she did give a great deal of material assistance by allowing the shipment of supplies to the islands from the Turkish mainland. Turkey also rendered assistance when the operations failed and Allied forces had to be evacuated.

Some Allied observers put the blame of the failure on Turkey's refusing the Allies use of its vital airfields. Others, including Sir Knatchbull-Hugessen, are of the opinion that the Turks gave a great deal of assistance during these operations, at a time when it was quite risky for them. Nor did the official reasons adduced by the Allies for the failure blame the Turks; it was, rather, the failure to capture the Rhodes airport, the surrender of the Italian garrisons to the Germans, and the impossibility of coping with the Luftwaffe which had caused the defeat. The failure in the Aegean at all events had some adverse effects on Turkish public opinion and somewhat revived the fears of a possible Luftwaffe attack on Istanbul.

When Ismet Inonu said in November "We wish the victors of this world war to be civilization and humanity" there was no doubt he meant the Allies, yet he was still trying to find a solution to protect Turkey from "midnight" disasters. The Allies were aware of this preoccupation and they did not confront him with a major proposal concerning Churchill's "soft under-belly" invasion plans.

During Allied conversations in Moscow in October, when the situation was reviewed, one of the decisions taken was the desirability of bringing Turkey into the war "as a hopeful contribution to an early victory." The Turks were rightly worried concerning these conversations and decisions taken "at their back." They were furthermore annoyed by the apparent fact that it was decided "in their absence" to get them into the war as soon as possible—a decision they thought contrary to their understanding with the British. At the request of the Turkish Government, Menemencioglu was invited to Cairo in November 1943 to meet Anthony Eden.

When Mr. Eden most eloquently set forth the reasons in favor of Turkey's entry into the war during these three-day conversations at Cairo, Menemencioglu countered them with the following main objections: The idea of entering the war at the eleventh hour, and according to decisions taken in their absence in Teheran and Moscow, was distasteful to the Turkish government. There were some political and military points to be cleared up before any such decision could be made: the Turkish army should be adequately equipped to cope with every eventuality; the Turkish General Staff should not be merely ordered as to what its tasks, if any, would be; Turkey's entry should not be merely for the purpose of obtaining the use of air and naval bases, but definite tasks should be allotted to the Turkish army. On the political side, Menemencioglu hinted that Great Britain and the

United States should establish adequate safeguards to prevent Turkey's falling into the Soviet sphere of influence after the war.

As a result of these first Cairo conversations between Eden and Menemencioglu, Turkey declared that she had decided "in principle" to enter the war, but on the condition that she first receive adequate defense against a German attack and that a scheme for military cooperation in the Balkans be arranged. These conditions were considered "heavy" by the Allies.

At the end of November Ismet Inonu was invited to Cairo, this time by President Roosevelt and Mr. Churchill. Inonu said in advance that if he was to be confronted at Cairo by decisions already made at Teheran he would not go; he made it clear that Turkey would not accept the position of a pawn. When these fears were allayed Inonu went to the Cairo meeting.

During the Teheran Conference Turkey's entrance into the war had been discussed by Roosevelt, Churchill, and Stalin, as well as the question of a "warm water port" for the Soviet Union. Churchill emphasized the desirability of getting Turkey into the war over and over again. Roosevelt is reported to have said that if he met Inonu he would try to persuade him to enter the war, but that if he were in Inonu's place he "would demand so high a price in supplies, airplanes, tanks, and equipment" that it would be impossible to carry out Operation Overlord. When Hopkins repeated this comment to Molotov he is reported to have said that Stalin would oppose Turkey's entry if it would mean the postponement of Overlord. However, the statesmen conferred and agreed that Turkey would be brought into the war on February 15, 1944.

In *Roosevelt and Hopkins*, Robert E. Sherwood points out that, due to previous conversations with the Turks the results of which had been "somewhat less than negative," both Stalin and Roosevelt were rather skeptical of the outcome; yet Churchill was still toying with his idea of a Balkan invasion and "was never discouraged." He added that the United States chiefs of staff were actively alarmed that Turkey might come into the war and thereby, as General Marshall liked to express it, "burn up our logistics right down the line." At Cairo, Inonu reiterated Menemencioglu's argument. Sherwood states in this connection: "It became clear that they [the Turks] were much influenced by two suspicions, the first that they were being pressed to enter the war as pawns on the general chess-board and in order to realize the decision reached at Teheran, in the general interest no doubt, but with no great regard for the possible consequence to themselves; the second that their acquiescence would only be made the occasion for ourselves

to use Turkish naval and air bases without assigning any special role
to the Turkish forces."

Undoubtedly at the bottom of these suspicions was the Turkish experience of a somewhat subservient alliance with Germany in World
War I. At the end of the second Cairo conversations (Dec. 4, 5 and 6)
which according to Menemencioglu were conducted with "almost
brutal" frankness, it was declared in a joint communique, that Inonu,
Roosevelt, and Churchill had examined the general situation, had
taken into account the "joint and several interests of the three countries," and had indicated that "the closest unity existed between the
United States, Turkey, and Great Britain in their attitude to the
world situation." It was also stated that the identity of interests
and views of the United States and Great Britain with those of the
Soviet Union, and the traditional friendship between the three powers
and Turkey, had been reaffirmed throughout the proceedings at the
Cairo Conference. What actually happened, according to some accounts, was that Inonu promised Turkey would enter the war provided
that his suspicions were allayed and the Turkish army would be
equipped "beyond the possibility of disaster."

Even the date was set. Inonu mentioned April 1 as the date for
entry into war. Roosevelt joked about it being April Fool's day and
another date was chosen. According to the understanding reached,
the Turkish President would return to Ankara, call a Cabinet meeting, get a decision, have it approved by the Turkish National Assembly, and convey the result to Roosevelt and Churchill who were flying
on the Casablanca. Roosevelt's and Churchill's sons had accompanied Inonu and Menemencioglu in their flight back to Ankara; they
were supposed to wait for the final Turkish decision and take it to
their fathers at Casablanca. Since none of the Turkish statesmen involved have written their memoirs what actually transpired can only
be deduced from oral accounts of the three critical days in Ankara.

What transpired in Cairo was described by Inonu in accounts he gave
his Chief of General Staff, Marshall Cakmak, and in Cabinet meetings which continued into the small hours of the morning at Cankaya,
official residence of the President. Inonu himself was apparently of the
opinion that Turkey had no choice but to enter the war, some time in
April. The Ministers had some questions but did not voice any real
opposition. On the second day of Cabinet meetings, however, Marshall Cakmak's eloquent intervention changed the trend. Cakmak,
an extremely honest and patriotic soldier, pointed out to Inonu and
to his Cabinet that the Turkish Army, although courageous and well
disciplined, was sadly lacking in modern equipment. Allied promises

had not been fulfilled and the equipment given then was second-rate, captured German or Italian material. There were not enough tanks, anti-tank guns or anti-aircraft guns. Ammunition supplies were low.

Furthermore, for years the Turkish Army, in keeping with the peaceful precepts of Ataturk, had been geared, trained and fortified for defensive purposes, and mainly against possible aggression from the north east (Russian), or from the Balkans (German or Russian). It would be extremely difficult for it to take the offensive, either in the Balkans or against the German-held islands. He said "the Turkish soldier is brave. He will do his duty. He will even die if ordered ...But let us not have him killed in vain."

The Turkish Government communicated to the Allies that the decision made at Cairo was not changed, but asked for a joint staff meeting to review the military situation prior to the announcement. A few days later a British Military Delegation, consisting of Field Marshal Sir Harold Alexander, Admiral Andrew Cunningham, Field Marshal Henry Maitland Wilson and General Sir Bernard Paget arrived at Ankara and met with Marshall Cakmak and his generals. The Turkish version of the meeting is that the British realized the Turkish Army was indeed incapable of conducting an offensive war with the available equipment, and they felt it was impossible to wait longer because of the necessity of formulating other plans. This proved to be a great disappointment to Churchill. Elliot Roosevelt, in *As He Saw It*, says that this was "Winston's last effort to force an Allied attack from the south, from the Mediterranean."

On the other hand, the Americans had never been too enthusiastic either for a Balkan invasion or for Turkey's entry into the war. At the Cairo Conference Roosevelt had "frequently betrayed a considerable amount of sympathy for the Turkish point of view and even stated on one occasion that it was quite understandable that these distinguished and amiable gentlemen should not want to be caught with their pants down."

A period of some difficulty was to follow the Cairo Conference during which the British and the Russians made no attempt to conceal their disappointment. The Allies had agreed at the end of the Cairo Conference to end Lend-Lease to Turkey, and this decision was put into effect in March with an announcement that it was discontinued due to Turkey's failure to fulfil the military terms of the Anglo-Franco-Turkish agreement. The Turkish Government retorted by pointing out that the main reason for its non-entry into the war was the fact the Allies had not kept their promise of sending 500 tanks and 300 planes. It was specifically during this period, which immediately followed the Cairo Conference, that British-Turkish friendship deteriorated dangerously.

On April 20, after the Allies had officially demanded of the neutral countries that they stop trading with the Germans, the Turkish Government announced that chrome deliveries to Germany were stopped, pointing out that she was not neutral but an "ally of Great Britain." This did not stop Churchill from making a blunt statement in the House of Commons to the effect that no pressure had been brought to bear on Turkey, adding that Turkey would not have the strong position at the peace conference which would "attend entry into the struggle."

By this time the British Prime Minister had given up his Balkan scheme, mainly because of Turkish reluctance, and American opposition which had profited from this reluctance. Although he still believed that Turkey's entry into the war, especially after Italy's surrender, would be helpful, he observed "emphatically" at an Allied conference in North America that he was no longer advocating the sending of an army into the Balkans "now or in the near future" (May 31, 1944).

It has been pointed out by more than one observer that Numan Menemencioglu, Turkey's Foreign Minister, was the person responsible for his country's reluctance to take a definite stand, but on June 15, he was out of office. In the beginning of June there were some difficulties with respect to the passage of certain German ships through the Straits. On June 14, Mr. Eden expressed deep concern in the House of Commons concerning the matter, and on the following day Menemencioglu resigned. From that time on, to the extent that Turkey took action against Germany, her relations with the Allies and especially with the British improved.

On August 2, 1944, Turkey broke off diplomatic and economic relations with Germany. According to Ismet Inonu the Turkish Government even "manifested an inclination to enter the war immediately," but Great Britain made it clear, once this first step had been taken, that when the proper time arrived she would request further action. It is apparent that Turkey's participation at this time constituted a problem for Great Britain, the United States, and Russia.

The winter of 1944-45 ended with deep Turkish anxiety concerning Soviet Russia. Both the Government and the people were becoming increasingly uneasy over Russian advances in the Balkans and Anglo-American appeasement towards them. They fervently hoped for a last-minute compromise between liberal elements in Germany and the Anglo-Americans, that is, a change in the "unconditional surrender" policy which they thought would benefit only the Russians, but Spring came without the fulfilment of these hopes.

During the preceding months there had been conversations between Turkey, Great Britain, and the United States concerning the right of merchant vessels to pass through the Straits into the Black Sea, and by January supplies to the USSR were actually being shipped via the Straits.

On February 23, 1945, at the request of the Allies, Turkey declared war on the Axis. This had been decided, much against the wishes of the USSR, at Yalta. The Turkish Government issued a communique and explained that the war was declared at this juncture "so that Turkey should be able to play a constructive part in the peace." Yet this was not actually "war" for the Turkish people. It was evident that they did not like the idea of this "midnight" declaration of war against Germany, which was still resisting the combined forces of America, Russia, and Great Britain. D Day therefore caused no rejoicing in Turkey; the Turks were much too preoccupied with Soviet Russia.

As a consequence of her declaration of war, however, Turkey was invited to participate at the San Francisco Conference for organization of the United Nations.

* * * *

Turkey has been blamed for not honoring the terms of her treaties with Great Britain, France, and the Balkan countries when Italy declared war against France and Greece and, later, when Germany attacked both Greece and Yugoslavia. She has been accused of flirting with Germany when Axis successes were at a zenith. It has also been charged that she schemed with Germany against Soviet Russia, that she bade her time, wavering and waiting an opportunity to enter the war on the winning side. In the period following Stalingrad and El Alemein, Turkey has been blamed for not entering the war in compliance with the demands of the Allies, thus disrupting the plans for an early victory. Finally, the "midnight" declaration of war against Germany has been considered opportunistic.

These criticisms seem to have lost their importance with the course of events in the post-war period. In retrospect, many objective observers now justify Turkey's "sitting on the fence" and not quixotically joining the war. Such action on Turkey's part might have meant the destruction of Turkey and would have served no useful purpose for the Allies. A. E. Yalman, a pro-Allied Turkish editor, summed up the situation as follows: "We were allies of Great Britain and indirectly allies of the United States and Soviet Russia. We were definitely against aggression and Fascism. Although we were non-belligerents, we kept one million men under arms, to resist the Germans in case they attacked this strategic passage from Europe to Asia, and the Mediterranean Sea. Then we were protecting the flanks of the Russian armies in southern Russia and of Allied Arms in Africa and the Middle East. In defensive war we can always give a good account of ourselves. For offensive action we are not mechanically equipped or trained. We could make our best contribution without actual fighting because we could only be a liability to our allies if they had had to divert materials and forces from other fronts to support us."

To recapitulate, on the eve of World War II Turkey's good intentions and active efforts for permanent world peace, an effective international organization, and for regional collective security arrangements were well known and praised by Great Britain, France, and the United States. Indeed, just before the war, Turkey had shown that her inclination was toward the democracies by declaring her alliance with Great Britain and France at a time, as Churchill said, "when our [Britain's] armaments were weak and our policy pacific." Later, in 1942, he pointed out that Turkey had been almost the only unshakable ally of England in the dark days and could always be relied upon. Furthermore Turkey had hoped to link Soviet Russia with the Western Allies, but as we have seen, these hopes could not be realized because of Soviet Russia's rapprochement with Germany. When Turkey went ahead with plans for an alliance with Great Britain and France—after the Moscow conversations between Saracoglu and Molotov had failed in October 1939—both the Soviet Government and the press warned in no uncertain terms that Turkey would be sorry for this action and they stressed that Soviet Russia would remain a "faithful ally of Germany."

If Turkey did not enter the war in 1940 and 1941 to honor her obligations to France and Greece, it was because of her understanding that the British Government thought it would not be advisable to open a new front, which would certainly be a liability in view of joint German-Italian-Bulgarian strength, and of the lack of modern equipment in the Turkish Army. As a matter of fact Allied promises to equip the Turkish Army with modern arms were never fulfilled.

Up until 1942, when Axis strength was paramount and Turkey was virtually encircled, Turkish statesmen did their best to parry German promises and intrigues to bring them into the war. Specifically, they tried to convince the Russians—a-propos of German intrigues to bring about a Soviet-Turkish misunderstanding from which they could profit in order to bring Turkey into their own sphere of influence—that their policy towards Russia remained correct. During this period the Turks were careful not to provoke the Germans and to give the impression of "playing along" with them. But even during this tense period President Inonu did not hesitate to say: "It is my duty to state that at a time when Great Britain is compelled to struggle gallantly for existence under difficult conditions, the ties of alliance that bind us to her are sound and unshakable."

Turkey had to appease Germany in that difficult period, and her statesmen indeed succeeded in so appeasing without sacrificing either their independence or their ties with Great Britain. It was only by this policy that they could prevent a German attack on their vulnerable cities and on their as yet unprepared army; it was only thus that they could still obtain from Germany the industrial and military materials with which neither Great Britain nor America could supply them; it was thus that they could act as a block of resistance to possible German penetration into Iraq and Syria.

"There were moments," says Sir Knatchbull-Hugessen, "when in reliance on this 'protective pad' we were able to move forces into North Africa which would otherwise have had to be held inactive elsewhere to contain a possible German diversion."

This was also mentioned by Churchill as a Turkish service to the Allies and, before their current anti-Turkish campaign took its present vigor, the Soviet press expressed the same point of view, that Turkish neutrality had played a positive part in favor of the Allies.

Even the German-Turkish Treaty of June, 1942 was by no means an anti-Allies action. The Turks had adamantly refused secret protocols and the passage of German arms and troops to aid Rashid Ali in Iraq. And in fact the text of the treaty, which contained a reservation on the Turkish-French-British treaty, was more favorable to Turkey than it was to Germany.

Following the conclusion of the German-Turkish Treaty, it still remained a fact that any request by the British Ambassador, even if it had to be refused to save appearances, "was quietly fulfilled" later.

It is apparent from Italian criticisms of the German attitude toward Turkey that if it had not been for Turkish diplomacy and resistance the Axis would have penetrated into the Middle Eastern countries. There was no question of Turkey's entering the war on the side of the Axis, either during the difficult years of 1940 and 1941, or during overwhelming German successes in Russia. Possibly one small mark against Turkish actions during the war years might be the attitude of some of her government and military personnel toward the

German-occupied Turkish provinces of Soviet Russia (i.e. ethnic Turkish areas).

Public opinion, which had been quite favorably disposed towards
Soviet Russia until 1935, had steadily grown suspicious of Russia's
subversive activities in Turkey and of her intention in regard to the
Straits. Furthermore, there was a sympathetic attitude toward the
oppressed Turks in Russia. Within this context, and in view of an
imminent Soviet defeat, which seemed very near, the Turkish Government could not be blamed if it sought some arrangements to have a
voice regarding the future of the bordering "Turkish provinces" of
Russia. Yet these negotiations never reached the stage of even preparations for a joint Turkish-German military action across the Caucasus. Moreover, it is a fact that both after the German attack on
the USSR and during the various Axis campaigns in Africa Turkey
"steadfastly refused to give passage to the German and did not allow
an Italian fleet to pass from the Mediterranean to the Black Sea."

Sir Hugh, the British Ambassador to Ankara during the war, has
stated: "Never did such an idea [to join the Axis] enter the mind of
the Turkish Government. Nothing could have brought it about short
of the complete overrunning and control of the country by Germany,
as happened in Romania and Bulgaria. I am quite certain that the
Turks would have died in the last ditch sooner than allow an invader
to cross their frontier."

It is true that Turkey continued to be reluctant to enter the war
after 1943, when the fortunes of war had begun to favor the Allies.
There were several reasons for this reluctance: Turkish statesmen,
as all patriotic statesmen, were determined to do their best to keep
their country out of the war because they knew that Allied efforts to
supply their army had never reached a satisfactory stage, and because
they knew that even if they entered the war when Germany was tired,
their vulnerable cities would be under the threat of the Luftwaffe.
"Turkey could not be expected to risk her whole existence by coming
in." At Adana, Churchill himself had admitted that the British could
not expect an ally to fight without proper weapons. Furthermore, they
did not see any benefits to Turkey in entering the war; they considered
it highly undesirable, as did the Turks in general, to enter merely to
be pawns of the Allied High Command without having any voice as
to the conduct of the war. They also felt that the Allies probably
only wanted to make use of their air and naval bases.

There were other psychological and political factors governing Turkish reluctance: The Turks were never strongly anti-German; on the
contrary, the Germans enjoyed great popularity among the Turkish

people. In view of the traditional suspicion against the Russians and the apparent warm feelings, at the time, between Great Britain, the United States and Soviet Russia, they were rather inclined to hope for a last-minute compromise between Germany, Great Britain and the United States so as to check possible Soviet expansion, rather than an unconditional German surrender which would destroy the balance in Europe in favor of Soviet Russia. Linked with this fear was the reluctance to be "liberated" by the "Allied" Red Army.

Necmeddin Sadak, a prominent Turkish editor and a former Foreign Minister, has pointed out: "Indeed one can readily believe that Russia's greatest regret is that Turkey was not occupied and then 'liberated.' If Turkey had gone to war when she was without arms, completely isolated and without any hope of aid, the German armies would have occupied her territory within a few weeks. Later on, the Red Army would have liberated her, as it liberated Poland, the Baltic countries, Romania, Bulgaria. . . . A lost opportunity!"

In view of the fact that Turkey's chief critic and accuser, insofar as her foreign policy is concerned, is Soviet Russia, one must remember that in 1939 and up to their being attacked by the Germans, the Russians were not only living in peace with the Axis but were calling them their "faithful allies," and were adopting a line of conduct favorable to them. Only after they were actually attacked, did they become "active enemies of Fascism."

CHAPTER V

THE POST-WAR PERIOD

Physically Turkey passed through the hazards of the Second World War unscathed. Yet when the peoples of the victorious, liberated, or even neutral countries were rejoicing on VE Day and were hopefully looking forward to a bright future, Turks looked forward uneasily. With the end of the war, internal unrest and instability, which had been restrained to a considerable degree by the patriotism of the people and by vigorous measures of the Turkish government, came out into the open.

Kemal Ataturk had ruled the country by admittedly authoritarian methods. He sought to lay the foundation of a modern and western Turkish Republic unequivocally with his iron hand; as he himself stated, he wanted to dictate democracy so "firmly that it would be impossible for any of his successors to retreat to totalitarianism." The Turkish people had so much confidence in him that even the intellectuals who had longed for true democracy, tacitly supported him and tolerated his methods. They knew that this was a necessary transitional phase which Turkey had to go through in order to attain ultimate democracy.

When Ataturk died in 1938 and Ismet Inonu, his prime minister from 1926 to 1937, succeeded him many intellectuals looked to him for relaxation of the authoritarian regime and the adoption of the multiparty policy. Indeed Inonu, after his election as president, made several gestures which could be interpreted as such. For instance, he welcomed back to Turkey such opposition leaders as Rauf Orbay, Adnan Adivar and Halide Edip (Adivar) who had gone into exile in the late 20's. But Inonu soon made it clear that relaxation was to stop there. He accepted the title of "National Chief" in the style of Duce, Fuehrer or Caudillo, which was bestowed upon him by the single ruling party, the People's Republican Party, and the same authoritarian regime continued. As one humorous magazine saw it, in the Bath House the bath utensils were all the same—only the personnel had changed.

Inonu found a convenient excuse for his prolonged authoritarianism during the Second World War. "External Dangers" made it imperative that "no internal dissension be allowed." Perhaps he was justified; it would possibly have been unwise in wartime to initiate political reforms which undoubtedly would cause great social and economic upheavals in the country. The Turkish people, patriots first, accepted this. It must be pointed out also that they had some confidence in Inonu's "diplomacy" and comprehension of foreign affairs, and they felt better with him at the helm during the dangerous period. But when the war ended there was no more justification for Inonu's single-party dictatorship. Although the people were grateful that they were spared the war, they could not forget that Inonu and his government had surpassed basic freedoms and rights.

One significant factor in the general discontent was the economic situation. Throughout the war years various People's Party Governments (the only party then in existence) had made chaos of the economic situation by taking contradictory measures and by negating one another's policies. The upward spiral of the cost-of-living was not checked until it reached 400/600 percent of pre-war levels. One cause of this was the severance of trade contracts with Germany, Austria, and Italy. Also there was a serious shortage of foreign exchange, and this was constantly getting worse due to the general maladjustment in relations between the so-called hard and soft currencies.

These two main problems were made worse by the constant depreciation of the currency, and by necessary expenditures for maintaining a large standing army—tying the money to a non-productive purpose. More than half a million men were under arms and for several years at least 40 percent of the national budget had been devoted to military expenditures. Poverty, disease—especially tuberculosis—had increased, both in urban and rural areas, and corruption in government offices had spread.

Thus the relaxation, to some extent, of the external danger brought the people to the realization of their economic plight and of their frustrated desire for a political change—a change towards democratic government.

The intellectuals lost no time in channeling these frustrations, economic deprivations, and the political aspirations of the masses into a strong and organized proposition against Inonu and his party. They pointed out that Turkey, as a member of the United Nations, was obligated to have a really democratic regime.

Stalin must have found the internal discontent in Turkey most opportune for his new move toward that country. He must also have felt that as a powerful and victorious ally of the Western powers he would be given a free hand. Indeed, the honeymoon between Russia and the Allies was still on.

The Turkish government and the Turkish people, on the other hand, were not entirely unprepared for a Russian move against their country. The first hint of changing Soviet attitude towards Turkey had been shown when the Russians showed unwillingness to sign a new treaty of friendship with Saracoglu in 1939. Later, the revelations about secret negotiations concerning Turkey between Molotov and Hitler and Ribbentrop served to sharpen the traditional suspicion of the Turks against Russia. The chief concern which guided the Turkish statesmen during the Second World War had been not to fall an easy prey for a victorious Soviet Russia. Turkey had resisted Allied efforts to persuade her to enter the war in order to provide bases and a passageway for possible joint Russian-Allied moves through the Dardanelles and the Balkans. The Russians, even as allies or liberators, would have been hard to move out. Inonu and other Turkish officials had time and again warned the Allies against postwar dangers of an unchecked Russia. They pointed out that by insisting on an unconditional surrender by Germany and by allowing the Russians to occupy or liberate Europe and the Balkans, the Allies were making a tragic mistake. Now these prophecies were coming true and Turkey was marked as the first target of post-war Russian imperialism.

When Turkey was confronted with the first Soviet Note of March 19, 1945, just before VE Day, she was completely alone against Russia. Both Churchill and Roosevelt were still confident about Stalin and were convinced that any international dispute could be effectively handled and solved by the proposed United Nations Organization. Furthermore, neither the United States nor Great Britain were too enthusiastic about Turkey and her worries.

The Soviet note stated brusquely that the Turkish-Soviet Treaty of Neutrality and Non-Aggression of 1925 was no longer "in accord with the new situation." Molotov told the Turkish Ambassador in Moscow, Selim Sarper, that "great changes have taken place particularly during the Second World War which required a new understanding." On March 21, 1945, *Izvestia*, the organ of the Russian Communist Party, commented: "It is no secret that during the present war Soviet-Turkish relations at specific moments might have been better than they were. It is not in the interest of the two countries automaically to extend the terms of an agreement concluded in a totally different situation. Neither would this be in the interest of the fruitful development of international relations as a whole, now when the democratic countries that have united for the defeat of the German aggressor, are concerned with laying the foundation for a lasting peace among all peace loving peoples. It is clear from what has been said that the Soviet-Turkish agreement calls for serious amendments."

The New York Times of the following day indicated that the improvements Russia wanted in the pact "might resemble the undertakings already reached with Czechoslovakia and Poland." Apparently these undertakings, which were to prove the doom of those countries, were not yet considered alarming in the western world. Only the Turks seemed to have realized what they really meant.

The full significance of Soviet intentions concerning Turkey were made clear several months after the war in Europe ended. A furious propaganda campaign was unleashed by the Soviet press and radio.

Turkey agreed in principle that the 1925 Treaty might require revisions, and instructed her Ambassador to Moscow to approach the Soviet government to learn the conditions under which a new agreement could be concluded. During the interview between Mr. Molotov and the Turkish Ambassador, Selim Sarper, on June 7, 1945 the Soviet Foreign Minister stated that the USSR had two conditions: the eventual rectification of the Turkish-Soviet frontier fixed by the Treaty of 1921, and the granting of bases for Soviet Russia on the Dardanelles. Mr. Sarper rejected these conditions then and there without even requesting instructions from his government.

The revisions of the 1921 frontiers meant the return of the provinces of Kars and Ardahan in Eastern Turkey to Russia. Tsarist Russia had taken these two provinces after the war of 1877-78 and Soviet Russia had returned them in 1921.

Renewed Russian demands on them had become evident after 1939, and in 1941 Stalin had mentioned his desire for Kars and Ardahan to Mr. Eden and had even hinted that in return for them Turkey could be given portions of Northern Syria, including Aleppo. In 1945 these "compensations" were again hinted at. There was perhaps another purpose in this: if Turkey showed any interest, the Soviet propoganda machine could easily convey to the Syrians that Turkey coveted portions of their country. As a matter of fact Syrian and Lebanese Communists did make use of this theme. The semi-official Turkish news agency, the Anatolian Agency, however unequivocally denied any Turkish aspirations on Syrian territory.

The Turkish people read about the Soviet demands in the semi-official Istanbul daily, *Aksam.* On June 29, 1945 the Ankara Radio disclosed that Soviet Russia had proposed a new treaty which would be tantamount to joint control of the Straits by Russia and Turkey. Public reaction to these demands in Turkey was electric. The nation was at once united against an imminent Soviet aggression. Ismet Inonu in his November "state of the republic message" expressed national feeling in these words: "We shall not give up any

Turkish territory or territorial rights. We shall live and die as honorable men."

Hasan Saka, the Turkish Foreign Minister, had stopped in London while returning from the San Francisco Conference in order to sound out British feeling concerning the Russian demand to alter the Montreux Convention bilaterally. In a press conference there, he expressed the official Turkish point of view: Montreux was a multilateral convention and could not be subject to bilateral revision by Turkey and Russia alone.

The Background of the Straits Question. Before going into the details of the post-war negotiations concerning the revisions of the Straits Convention a brief recapitulation of the background of the Straits Question is appropriate.

The Turkish Straits connect the Black Sea with the Mediterranean by way of the Aegean Sea. They command the strategic and economic communications with the Black Sea, Western Russia and the Danube valley. They offer access to the coal of the Donetz Basin, to the oil of Baku and Rumania, and to the iron of the Black Sea coast. Russia, whatever her regime may be and whosoever her rulers, has always wanted to dominate and control this important waterway. She has attempted to do this by force of arms, by diplomacy, by subversion, and even under the guise of cooperation.

The question of the Straits has been the crux of Turkey's relations with the great powers for almost two centuries, and has been a problem ever since the Turks acquired control of both banks of the Dardanelles in the 14th century. By their conquest of Istanbul in 1453 they had also acquired the exclusive control of the Bosphorus leading from the Sea of Marmara to the Black Sea. From 1475 (conquest of the Crimea by the Turks) up to 1774 the Black Sea was a virtual Turkish lake. By unwritten law all foreign ships were excluded from these waters.

Suleyman the Magnificent, however, gave concessions which were known as capitulations to Francis I of France in the Treaty of 1555 which included the right of passage through the Straits and permission to enter the port of Istanbul. These capitulations were later given to other European countries. But none of these concessions allowed the ships of the signatories to enter the Black Sea.

After the Treaty of Kaynarca in 1774, and the subsequent loss of the Crimea to Russia, this monopoly ended. Russia obtained the right of free passage through the Straits and thus the "Question of the Straits" came into being. From then onwards the Russian policy vis-a-vis Turkey and the Straits would be dominated by Catherine's ambition to conquer Istanbul and reach the Mediterranean.

With the Treaty of Yash (or Jassy) in 1792, England entered into the picture as a rival of Russian power and the main struggle for the Straits was between these two powers until Lausanne. By the Treaty of Hunkar Iskelesi in 1833 Russian influence prevailed and the Sultan had to relinquish his ancient rule of keeping the Straits closed to all vessels. A secret protocol stipulated that, while the Straits would be closed to the warships of all other powers, it would nevertheless be open to the Russian war vessels. Under the pressure of England and France this was abrogated and by the Conference of London in 1841 the Straits were once again proclaimed as closed to the war vessels of all foreign nations. Now the ancient rule of the Sultan had become an international law.

The Paris Treaty of 1856, signed after the Crimean War, stipulated that while the Black Sea was neutralized and its waters thrown open to merchant vessels of all nations, the Straits were closed to the war vessels of both the Black Sea powers and the non-riparian powers. "Before the Russian expansion under Peter the Great and Catherine II the Black Sea was a Turkish lake," according to C. Phillipson. "After the Treaty of Hunkar Iskelesi it became a virtual Russian lake. Now the Treaty of Paris made it a European sea and placed it under the express sanction of the powers." Russia took the opportunity afforded by the Franco-Prussian War of 1870 to denounce this provision.

In a conference held in London in 1871, the provisions of the 1856 Treaty were abrogated. The conference maintained the principle of the Treaty of 1841 with regard to closing the Straits to the passage of foreign warships. But it was stipulated that the Sultan would be free to open the Straits in time of peace to warships of "friendly powers."

Only six years later, on April 19, 1877, Russia used a Balkan crisis as an excuse and declared war on Turkey. Her primary aim was to acquire a favorable position on the Straits. This time Turkey was alone against Russia. The Crimean coalition was dissolved and Russia was sure of Austro-Hungarian neutrality. Britain reasserted her intention of maintaining the integrity of the Ottoman Empire, but without a continental ally and bases nearby she could not take any action.

Turks fought valiantly. The defense of the Plevne fortress by Ghazi Osman Pasha was one of the most heroic defenses against superior and advantageously placed forces. Plevne was captured after a long siege but this defense changed the course of history and perhaps gave the Ottoman Empire another forty years of life and thwarted Russian moves towards the Straits.

Due to the defense of the Plevne Russian aggressiveness and Russian demands were checked by a now determined Britain. Austria-Hungary awaked to increasing Tsarist ambitions and sided with Britain. Thus the Treaty of Berlin (July 13, 1878) reaffirmed the *status quo* of 1856-1871 treaties concerning the Straits.

The subsequent secret and open treaties (concluded by Germany, Austro-Hungary and Russia, and later the Triple Alliance, Franco-Russian Entente, etc.) sought the preservation of the *status quo* regarding the Straits. But Russia had by no means given up her ambitions. A Russian memorandum dated 1882 still termed the Russian occupation of the Straits an historical necessity.

During the negotiations leading to the Triple Entente between Russia, England, and France at the beginning of the twentieth century, Russian representatives attempted to introduce the question of the revision of the status of the Straits. But Sir Edward Grey rebuffed these attempts. Russia then attempted to circumvent the Turkish control of the Straits by Pan Slavism. The secret annex of the treaty negotiated between Russia and Bulgaria contained provisions concerning Russian interests in the Straits.

Later, the Russian Foreign Minister, Sergei Sazanov, openly requested British and French approval of the Russian annexation of the Straits together with the Sea of Marmara and the islands of Imbros and Tenedos, as well as territory from the Enos-Midya line in European Turkey to the Izmit peninsula on the Asiatic side.

The British, French, and Italians however had their own claims in the Middle East. An agreement was reached concerning these and Russian claims and a series of secret treaties were signed which were to prove embarrasing for the Allies later. England and France agreed to Russia's annexation of the Dardanelles, Constantinople, and European Turkey up to the Enos-Midya line and the islands of Tenedos and Imbros. In return Russia agreed to certain French and British claims in Asia Minor. Also a free port was to be established in Istanbul.

When they came to power the Bolsheviks denounced all the secret agreements of the Tsarist regime. Thus at the Sèvres Conference France and England, now free from their embarrassing promises to Russia, competed with each other for the control of the Straits. A middle ground was reached in the Sèvres Treaty of August, 1920, by the stipulation that an International Straits Commission would be

established to control the seaways.   Turkey would not be represented
on this Commission.

At the Lausanne Conference Russia entered into the scene again,
and started her attempts to make the Black Sea a *"Mare Clausum"*
(a closed sea).   It is noteworthy that the Turkish delegate at
Lausanne, Ismet Pasha, at once saw what the motives of the Soviet
delegation were, and did not press in the direction of the Soviet point
of view.   As a result, Soviet desires were not fulfilled, but Turkey
got what she could for the time being.

The four main principles of the Lausanne Convention for the
Straits were the following:

(1) Liberty of Passage: the signatories agreed on the principle of
freedom of transit and navigation by sea, as well as by air in the
Straits.

(2) Demilitarization: Turkey managed to lose military rights over
as small an area as possible.

(3) The International Commission: Turkey would be represented on
the body, the duty of which would be to supervise the freedom of
passage and to ensure the proper application of the provisions of the
Convention.   Supervision of the demilitarization was not among the
duties of this Commission.

(4) Measures against the violation of the established statute: Although Turkey had originally wanted, in lieu of fortifying the Straits,
individual and collective undertaking from all signatory powers to
assist Turkey by all means in their power in the event of an aggression in the Straits or Marmora; she had later consented to a general
guarantee under the Article X of the Covenant of the League.

It was precisely the last principle which was featured in Article 18
of the Lausanne Convention that was the cause of subsequent Turkish
worries.   Events soon showed that the League's collective security
system could not have been effective.   Therefore, to rely on this system for the protection of her vital sea-ways seemed to be foolhardy.
The Turkish Government raised the issue of the revision of the
Lausanne Convention and especially of its provisions concerning demilitarization.   Subsequently a revision conference was held in Montreux, beginning June 22, 1936.

At Montreux the British and Soviet points of view clashed once
again.   Litvinov requested a revision which would have closed the
Straits to nonriparian war vessels at all times.   The British, on the
other hand, were in favor of free access through the Straits to all
countries.   However, under the pressure of the overall international
situation, a hasty compromise (which still did not satisfy the Soviets)

was reached. Under the new Convention: (1) Demilitarization clauses of the Lausanne Convention were abrogated. (2) Freedom of navigation in the Straits was maintained. (3) Merchant vessels were allowed passage in war, if Turkey was neutral, and in case Turkey was belligerent the merchant vessels of all non-belligerents could pass freely. (4) Warships: In time of peace, light surface vessels, minor warships and auxiliaries belonging both to riparian and non-riparian powers would have freedom of transit. Black Sea powers could send through ships of more than 15,000 tons if they pass singly. Transit of all warships would be preceded by a notification to the Turkish government. In time of war, *Turkey being neutral*, vessels belonging to belligerents should not pass through the Straits, except in execution of obligations under the Covenant of the League, and in cases of assistance rendered to a state victim of aggression, in virtue of a treaty of mutual assistance binding Turkey. In time of war, *Turkey being belligerent,* or considering herself threatened by imminent danger of war, the passage of warships was to be left to the discretion of the Turkish government. (5) The International Commission was abolished and its functions reverted to Turkey.

The Montreux Convention was a great victory for Turkey. Although it did not make a *"Mare Clausum"* of the Black Sea as the Soviets wished it would, it was more in line with the Soviet proposal for the defense of the Straits exclusively by Turkey. Nevertheless the Convention did not please the Soviet government and the Soviet press complained that "Turkey had yielded to the pressure of the imperialist powers." As Soviet Russia grew stronger its conception of the safety of the Straits and of the Black Sea had evolved into the idea of complete Soviet domination over the Straits. This intention became clear when Soviet Russia denounced her treaty of friendship with Turkey in March 1945 and later when she made known her proposals concerning the revision of the Montreux regime, in August 1946.

It should be noted here that when Turkey was seeking revision of the Lausanne Convention and suggested to the Soviet Union that a conference of Black Sea powers be convened for this purpose, the Soviet government had shown a marked reluctance.

Later, several months after the conclusion of the Montreux Convention, Litvinov proposed to the Turkish Minister for Foreign Affairs in Geneva that the two governments sign a pact for the joint defense of the straits. This proposal, which was made in a most friendly manner, was politely refused by Turkey.

During the war Soviet Russia was apparently quite satisfied with the Turkish guardianship over the straits. On August 10, 1941 she handed a note to Turkey, jointly with Great Britain, reaffirming her fidelity to the Montreux Convention and assuring that she had no aggressive intentions or claims concerning the Dardanelles. This had been iterated once before by Molotov, in November 1939, in spite of his "regret that Turkey had joined Great Britain and France."

In 1945 the centuries-old Russian aspirations for the Straits assumed a new tone. Soviet demands showed that the Russian policy had not really changed since the time of the tsars. As Necmeddin Sadak, a prominent Turkish editor put it: "At the beginning of the war, Soviet Russia had laid down her conditions: the Dardanelles. During the war she had bargained with Hitler: the Dardanelles. After the war, she stated the conditions clearly to Turkey: the Dardanelles."

In fact, since 1921 when the first treaty was signed between Turkey and the Soviet Union the Soviet government had been aiming at a "Closed" Black Sea, under the guise of "the Black Sea for the Black Sea Powers" doctrine, which had some appeal for a nationalist Turkey. The Soviet point of view in 1946 was basically motivated by the same desire which had motivated Chicherin to oppose the Lausanne Convention in 1923 and Litvinov at Montreux in 1936.

Now that the Soviet power was at its zenith there was no longer a need for a disguise and no need to out-Turk the Turks as Chicherin or Litvinov did, by wanting the Straits to be fortified exclusively by the Turks, to keep out "all non-riparian war vessels, even during peace time." The Soviet Government could now profit from the internal upheavals in Turkey and press for a "joint defense" of the Dardanelles and for a revision of the Montreux regime, by a conference to be attended exclusively by the Black Sea powers. Sadak pointed out: "If there had ever been a Turkish government willing to yield to these demands [of 1946] Turkey still could not have reached an agreement with Moscow. For after the occupation of the Dardanelles, the Soviet Union would demand a Communist government in Ankara and would impose one on Turkey. Moscow would ask 'can we have confidence in a Turkish government which is politically linked to the capitalist powers?' "

At Potsdam. The Straits question was discussed at the Potsdam Conference during July, 1945. The Western Allies were extremely conciliatory towards Russia. We learn from Truman's memoirs that Churchill supported the need for the modification of the Montreux Convention. He welcomed the free passage of Russian ships through the Straits. But he also stressed the importance of not alarming Turkey.

Stalin and Molotov tried to minimize the Soviet pressures concerning the Turkish provinces. They contended that Turkey with her "23 divisions" had no reason to be alarmed and that the border rectification had been brought up in connection with the Turkish suggestion for a new alliance. If Turkey had not made this suggestion the question of borders would not have been raised. Regarding the Straits, Churchill pointed out that this question could not be considered bilaterally and that Britain could not push Turkey to accept such proposals.

Stalin regarded the Montreux Convention with contempt. Turkey could, under the provisions of this treaty, block the Straits even if she considered there was a threat of war. The result was that a small state, supported by Great Britain, could conceivably hold a great state (Russia) by the throat and give it no outlet to an open sea. Russia wanted to pass to and from the Straits freely and as Turkey was too weak to guarantee the free passage in case complications arose, Soviet Russia wanted to share its defense.

Truman himself expressed the view that a revision of the Montreux Convention was necessary. He added, however, that the freedom of the Straits should be guaranteed by all. Furthermore, he suggested free access to all seas of the world "by Russia and by all other countries." This meant that the Kiel Canal in Germany, the Rhine-Danube waterway from the North Sea to the Black Sea, the Black Sea Straits, the Suez Canal and the Panama Canal be made free for the passage of ships of all countries.

Although Great Britain had lodged a similar complaint with the Turkish government, in June, 1944, Turkey had immediately complied with the British demands and had prevented the further passage of "camouflaged" Axis vessels through the Straits. Britain praised the attitude of the Turkish government by stating: "The British Government, although it had some difference of opinion with the Turkish Government about the interpretation of the Convention, held that on the whole its [Montreux's] terms had been conscientiously observed."

Another interesting development in connection with the Straits in the period immediately following the Second World War was the increasing interest of the United States Government in the question. By the end of the war, everybody concerned, including Turkey, felt that Montreux required some revisions. The matter was also discussed at Potsdam. Truman's report of August 9, 1945, summarized the position of the United States at the Potsdam Conference:

"One of the most persistent causes of wars in Europe in the last two centuries has been the selfish control of the waterways of Europe. I mean the Danube, the Black Sea Straits, the Rhine, the Kiel Canal and all the inland water ways of Europe which border on two or more states. The United States proposed at Berlin that there be free and unrestricted navigation of these inland waterways. We think this important to the future peace and security of the world. We proposed that regulations for such navigation be provided by international authorities.

"The function of the agencies would be to develop the use of the waterways and assure equal treatment on them for all nations. Membership on the agencies would include the United States, Great Britain, France, and the Soviet Union plus those states which border on the waterways."

At Potsdam, according to British sources, the three governments decided that the Montreux Convention should be revised according to present-day conditions. It was also agreed that the next step would be for each of the three governments to take up the matter in direct conversations with the Turkish government.

In keeping with this agreement the United States government presented a note to Turkey on November 2, 1945, proposing that action for the revision of the Montreux regime proceed on the basis of the following principles: The Straits should be open to merchant ships of all nations, in time of peace or war. The Straits should in all circumstances be open to war vessels of the Black Sea Powers. Passage through the Straits should be forbidden to war vessels belonging to other powers, except with the consent of the Black Sea Powers or in the execution of a mission under the authority of the United Nations. Certain changes to modernize the Montreux Convention, such as the substitution of the United Nations system for that of the League of Nations and the elimination of Japan as a signatory.

The United Kingdom government concurred with these principles and on December 6 the Turkish Government accepted the United States proposals as a basis for discussion. Turkey was willing to approve a revision "enacted at an international conference as long as it did not infringe on her independence, sovereignty and territorial integrity." At this time both the United Kingdom and the United States governments implied that they did not "want Turkey converted into a satellite state."

From December 6, 1945, to August 21, 1946, the Straits Question remained where it was. But there were other, unrelenting facets of Soviet pressure on Turkey. On December 20, 1945 an article by two members of the Soviet Academy of the Georgia Republic appeared simultaneously in *Pravda*, *Izvestia*, and the *Red Star*. These articles claimed the Turkish territories of Ardahan, Artvin, Oltu, Turtum, Bayburt, Gumushane, Giresun, and Trabzond. These reaffirmed and elaborated on Molotov's earlier demands for frontier "rectification." Coinciding with Russian moves in the Azerbaidjan province of Iran at that time these demands were extremely significant and indicative of Russian desire for expansion. In reply to these demands the Turkish Foreign Minister, Hasan Saka, plainly stated that Turkey would continue her "policy of no claims and no surrender."

In January, 1946, Prime Minister Saracoglu expressed Turkey's feeling of isolation with these words: "Even deprived of foreign assistance, Turkey will not hesitate to fight against aggression."

During the negotiations of the 1921 frontier treaty (Kars Treaty), the Russian delegate stated: "We recognize the Turkish rights (to Kars and Ardahan) and invite other nations to recognize them." The Turks now reminded the Russians of this pledge.

Although there was an internal upheaval in the striving for a multiparty regime in Turkey, the Turkish people and the Turkish press were fully behind the government in foreign affairs. Ahmet Emin Yalman wrote in *Vatan*:

"Turkey is not Czechoslovakia . . . Partial Russian occupation first, potential complete occupation, and ultimate death . . . The Russians cannot split our unity with their time-honored methods because we know their game and cannot become dupes.

"If they use force we shall resist, knowing that we connot count on positive help from outside. But the Russians must realize that any shot on the Turkish-Russian frontier may become the first shot of the Third World War because all nations are bound to awaken to the fact the Russian appetite cannot accept Trafalgar Square or Times Square as its final limit. Distance is no protection!"

Such feelings, shared by most Turkish papers, were prophetic in warning the west against an acquiescent policy in regard to Russia.

Alone, Turkey faced and resisted the Soviet war of nerves. While the Russian press and radio attacked Turkey, Russian troops advanced toward Lake Urmia near the Turkish-Iran border, and a Soviet supported "Independent Kurdistan" was established. On Turkey's western frontier Greece was threatened by Communist guerilas.

For only a brief period there was danger of subversion in Turkey: In 1946 important developments had taken place in Turkey. Inonu, under the pressure of public opinion, had acquiesced to the formation of other political parties besides the People's Party.

One of the new narties, the Democratic Party, was formed under the leadership of an ex-prime minister, Celal Bayar. Co-founders, of the party were Adnan Menderes, a brilliant young politician, Refik Koraltan, an ex-governor, and Fuat Koprulu, a distinguished scholar. The Party, formed in the beginning of 1946, had by the summer of the same year become a considerable political force.

The People's Party Government, fearing this growing political power, prematurely announced that general elections would be held before the regular time, and the way they were conducted, especially in the rural areas, caused much dissension in Turkey. It was pointed out by both Turkish and foreign observers that the Democratic Party was confronted with a *fait accompli* before it had even had a chance to complete its organization throughout the country. Furthermore the People's Party organization was widespread and so closely linked with local authorities that it proved to be more than a match for the one-year old Democratic Party. Thus when the elections were conducted with coercion and intimidation in the rural regions, the majority in the Grand National Assembly (396 seats) was easily attained by the People's Party, in contravention to the real sympathies and feelings of the populace. The Democrats won 65 seats in "un-coercible" regions including Izmir and Istanbul.

Leftist elements, although very few in number, attempted to exploit this tense and unsettled situation; first to make use of the new freedom to spread their venom and then, if possible, to infiltrate the bona fide opposition parties.

Several magazines and newspapers (ostensibly Socialist and Liberal, but in reality Communist,) tried to undermine the public confidence in the established authority and also to hint that it was to the best interests of Turkey to seek a reconciliation with Russia. The Government could not reintroduce repressive laws to deal with these publications, but the Turkish university students, possibly with the tacit approval of the authorities, took the matter in their hands. On December 5, 1945 the offices of the pro-Soviet publications *Yeni Dunya* and *Tan* as well as bookstores selling Soviet literature were attacked and destroyed. The ferocity of the Moscow Radio and press in lamenting over the destroyed newspapers helps justify the students' attacks.

American Interest. If the United States was hesitant to come to the unequivocal aid of Turkey during this critical period, it certainly was not the fault of President Truman or of the military leaders.

Truman even during the first few days of his presidency had the courage and foresight to say to the Turkish Ambassador in Washington, and to the new American Ambassador in Ankara, (Edwin C. Wilson) that "the United States would go to the aid of Turkey if she

were attacked." We also read in his memoirs that as early as
January, 1946, he did not doubt that "Russia intends an invasion of
Turkey and the seizure of the Black Sea Straits to the Mediterranean."
He wrote at that time that "Unless Russia is faced with an iron fist
and strong language another war is in the making. Only one language
do they understand 'how many divisions have you.' "

Also it was due to leaders like Forrestal that dispatching of a U.S.
fleet to the Mediterranean was suggested. A gesture of friendship toward Turkey and a show of force in her support were evident in sending
the body of the deceased Turkish Ambassador in Washington to Istanbul aboard the "U.S.S. Missouri."

But there were those in the U.S. government who advocated "refraining from such actions which might provoke Russia." The then
Counselor of the State Department, Mr. Benjamin Cohen, even went
as far as favoring a Russian base on the Straits.

In spite of the restraint and caution of some State Department
officials, the trip of the "Missouri" to Istanbul served its purpose form-
idably. At a time when Turkey felt isolated and neglected, the
battleship's appearance signified America's interest in her welfare
and her determination to resist the Soviet Union. The American
sailors were accorded a tumultuous reception and to the present day
the name "Missouri" remains on Turkish hotels, restaurants, and
movie houses as a reminder of that fateful visit.

Admiral Hewitt, Commander of the U.S. Mediterranean Fleet, (no
doubt at the suggestion of the still hesitant State Department) tried
to minimize the significance of the "Missouri's" visit by pointing out
that it was merely a gesture of goodwill. But the Turks in general
knew that there was more to it than this.

The Fleet Commander paid a visit to Ankara and had a long conversation with President Inonu. The official communique stated that
he had conveyed to the President a message of America's goodwill.
Whatever the contents of the message, or whatever was discussed, the
Turks had the impression that, now that Great Britain was preoccupied with her own internal problems and was no longer as strong as
she had once been, the United States was getting ready to take her
place in the Mediterranean region and that Turkey was, after all,
not as isolated and exposed as they had begun to fear during the past
few months.

While the Turkish press hailed the United States as the defender
of the Near and Middle East, the Soviet press first tried to minimize
the trip of the "Missouri" as "yacht making courtesy calls," but then
began to attack the "meddling" of the United States.

Russia Strikes Again. On August 7 the Soviet Government again took up the question of the Straits with a verbal note, which was handed to Turkey, the United States, and the United Kingdom. This note criticized the Montreux Convention, pointing out that Turkey had violated it and made it redundant in the course of the Second World War. In the note were specified the dates and details of alleged passages of German and Italian war vessels through the Straits in contravention of the provisions of the Montreux Convention.

The Soviet panacea to prevent future complications was contained in the following principles:

"(1) The Straits should always be open to the passage of merchant ships of all countries.

"(2) The Straits should always be open to the passage of warships of the Black Sea Powers.

"(3) Passage through the Straits for warships not belonging to the Black Sea Powers shall not be permitted except in cases specially provided for.

"(4) The establishment of a regime for the Straits, as the sole passage, leading from the Black Sea and to the Black Sea, should come under the competence of Turkey and other Black Sea Powers.

"(5) Turkey and the Soviet Union, as the powers most interested and capable of guaranteeing freedom of commercial navigation and security in the Straits, shall organize joint means of defense of the Straits for the prevention of the utilization of the Straits by other countries for aims hostile to the Black Sea Powers."

These "principles" were a real threat to Turkish sovereignty. They also threatened the delicate balance between the strategic exigencies of Turkey, riparian and non-riparian powers. In case of war Turkey could safeguard her neutrality by prohibiting the passage of all belligerent war vessels. However, if the war vessels of Black Sea powers were to be given free passage in time of war, and entered the Aegean and Mediterranean to engage the enemy and then withdrew through the Turkish Straits to the Black Sea, Turkish neutrality would be threatened.

Obviously Soviet Russia desired ultimate control of the Straits and Turkey "by joint means of defense of the Straits." Sensing this design, President Truman remarked at that time that "to allow Russia to set up bases in the Dardanelles or to bring troops to Turkey, ostensibly for the defense of the Straits, would in the natural course of events result in Greece and the whole Near and Middle East fully under Soviet control."

The Turkish government showed no sign of giving in or of appeasing the Soviet government by any conciliatory gesture. One of the first things the new Prime Minister, Recep Peker, had to say was this: "The new government's attitude in regard to relations with Soviet Russia is exactly the same as that of the former government. This is a dry statement, but I am not issuing a sentimental declaration. Merely, we are going to follow the same policy as previous governments because it is not party politics; it is a national policy."

The Turkish government informed the American, British, and French governments of the Soviet note, and received immediate support. Truman instructed his envoy in Ankara to suggest a reasonable but firm reply.

The United States sent the first reply to Soviet Russia on August 19, pointing out, among other things, the following:

In regard to the fourth proposal: The United States could not accept the establishment of a new regime confined to Turkey and other Black Sea Powers. The regime of the Straits was the concern of other powers including the United States.

In regard to the fifth proposal demanding joint Turkish-Soviet defense of the Straits, the United States was firmly of the opinion that Turkey should continue to be primarily responsible for the defense of the Straits. Should the Straits become the object of attack, or threat of aggression, the resulting situation would constitute a threat to international security and could clearly be a reason for action by the Security Council of the United Nations.

America found it necessary to bring the Straits regime into appropriate relationship with the United States and was willing to participate in a conference to revise the Montreux Convention. The British note of August 21, 1946 was along the same general lines.

The Turkish reply of August 22 contained, first, specific answers to the Soviet charges concerning the Italian and German war vessels which had passed through the Straits during the war. Then, examining the five points proposed by the Soviet government, it accepted the first three points as a basis for discussion, these being, in fact, similar to the first three points in the American note. It refused, however, the fourth and fifth points. Turkey contended that to exclude non-riparian powers from the negotiations for the amendment of the Montreux Regime would "upset the broad basis and general harmony of the regime." As for the proposition that there be a common defense of the Straits, it was pointed out that this was inconceivable since it would limit Turkish sovereignty on the Straits. The Soviet government reiterated the same allegations and proposals in a second note on September 24 and the Turkish government reaffirmed its earlier position in its note of October 18.

In her note of September 24, 1946 Soviet Russia repeated the accusations concerning the passage of German and Italian warships through the Straits during the Second World War, and stated that this had threatened Soviet Russia and caused her strategic worries in the conduct of the war. The Russian note also tried to explain why the Black Sea should be a closed sea and why consequently the Straits differed from such waterways as Gibraltar or the Suez Canal. According to the note, recognition of the special position of the Black Sea powers had precedent in treaties concluded between Turkey, and Soviet Russia, Turkey and Transcaucasia, and Turkey and the Ukraine in 1921 and 1922. They also contended that joint Soviet-Turkish "defense measures" would not jepordize Turkey's security.

The U.S. reply on October 9, 1946, pointed out that the United States did not consider that the direct conversations which might take place between any of the signatories and Turkey, contemplated at the Potsdam Conference should have the effect of prejudicing the participation of the other two signatory powers in the revision of the Straits regime. The note thus reaffirmed the position the United States had taken in the previous note.

Turkey in her reply of October 18, 1946, reaffirmed her earlier point and then replied to Soviet charges concerning the passage of Axis ships during the war. The Turkish government was confident that she had acted in good faith and in loyalty to the provisions of the Straits Convention. The note pointed out that thanks to Turkish vigilance, the USSR was able, during the entire length of the war, to remain in the Black Sea sheltered from every Axis attack coming from the Mediterranean. Commenting on the Soviet view that the Black Sea was essentially a closed sea and that this limited interest in it to those powers which bordered upon it, the Turkish note, first pointed out that Turkey was the first power to recognize the vital interest which free navigation through the Straits had for the maritime countries of the Black Sea, and they reminded Russia that Turkey could not forget, however, that she herself was also a Mediterranean country. Considering the delicate geographic situation which made Turkey a "liaison between the two worlds separated by the restricted space of the Straits," she could not consider the question of the Black Sea and of the Straits as a problem interesting the maritime powers exclusively.

Turkey did not accept the Soviet reasoning based on the 1921-1922 treaties as they were clearly superseded by the Turkish-Soviet participation in the subsequent Montreux negotiations. They also recalled that it was Litvinov who had said at Montreux that "All those who have participated in the conference will go away satisfied, there will be no one dissatisfied." Again in 1936 both governments had accepted that the Straits Conference would not be limited to Black Sea Powers exclusively.

The Turkish note repeated point five of the August 7 Note and pointed out that "acceptance by Turkey of Soviet defense of the Straits would mean no less than her sharing her sovereignty with a foreign power."

The Russians were reminded that Chicherin, the Russian delegate at the Lausanne Conference, had protested against a proposal to take control of the Straits away from Turkey and had considered it "a flagrant violation of the sovereignty and independence of Turkey."

Inonu elaborated Turkey's stand in his state of the republic speech of 1946: "We agree that it is necessary to improve the Montreux Convention in a manner conforming to new conditions, in keeping with the methods and within the limits clearly foreseen by Montreux. We are considering with good-will that the Convention in question should become the subject of conversations at an international conference. We shall welcome wholeheartedly any modifications which take into consideration the legitimate interests of each of the interested parties on the basis of ensuring the territorial integrity and sovereign rights of Turkey. We are convinced with a perfectly clear conscience that, during the Second World War, the Montreux Convention was applied by us with the greatest attention; and the allegation to the effect that the Montreux Convention was applied with a bias in favor of the Axis Powers is manifestly unjust. We have nothing to fear from submitting our actions to examination and decision by arbitration. Inasmuch as concerns the question of the Straits, too, we perceive in the United Nations Charter every possible guarantee for ourselves and for every other nation concerned. So long as the clauses of the United Nations Charter concerning territorial integrity and sovereign rights are respected, no obstacle should exist to prevent the adjustment of relations between ourselves and the Soviet Union."

Thus Turkey stood firm—prepared to fight in case Russia pressed any further. But the Russians did not make any formal moves, either on the Straits question or on the question of the Eastern Provinces. The time-tested Turkish belief that if, in dealing with the Russians, one shows determination and courage, nine times out of ten the Russians will not attack.

One important result of Turkish resistance was that it served as a warning to the free world of the true intentions of Soviet Russia. Turkey was no longer to be alone in the struggle—her struggle had become the struggle of the whole free world against a system which threatened it.

CHAPTER VI

THE U.S. AND TURKEY: THE HONEYMOON PERIOD

"We did not join the West—the West joined us!" This was the answer of a Turkish statesman to a question put to him by a journalist on Turkey's foreign policy. There is more truth than pride in this answer. It was perhaps inevitable that Turkey would be caught in the middle of the power struggle which started after the second World War. It was also inevitable that she would be one of the first objectives of post-war Stalinist imperialism. Due to her special geographic position, Turkey was constantly involved in power struggles and stood in the path of conquests and imperialistic ventures. She was the main obstacle to Russia's ambition to reach the open sea of the Mediterranean, and in modern times her importance as a bulwark, or passage or base, (depending on which way you look at it) on the route or air-corridor to oil fields in the Middle East had increased tremendously. But the Turkish people and statesmen, especially since the founding of the Republic, did not merely accept this precarious situation as "Kismet" and assume a passive attitude toward the struggle raging across their country. In fact, Turkey tended to use its special geographical position as an advantage in the conduct of her foreign affairs.

In *The Middle East* Dr. Halford L. Hoskins points out that "the prominent place assigned to Turkey in the contemporary power alignment is by no means due to geographical position alone. The part Turkey has come to play in international affairs is no more due to strategic location than the remarkable character and outlook of its people." He points out that Turkey's foreign relations record since 1920 "clearly discounts any theory that the survival and progress of the State has been mainly due to luck. Indeed it seems clearly to show that survival and growth in national strength have been due to conscious and unwavering purpose on the part of the Turkish nation. This purpose has appeared in two principal manifestations: The first has been a universal willingness to place all life and property at stake; and to direct all foreign policy to the end of becoming and remaining a free people."

The purpose and manifestations mentioned by Dr. Hoskins were evident in a firm Turkish "No" to the Soviet demands on the Straits and on the Eastern provinces. In a way it would be correct to say that it was following this first "No" that the development of the Containment Policy of the United States and the West began to take shape. It was also this first "No" which marked the beginning of close United States-Turkish relations.

Nightmare in Greece. The dangerous situation in Greece was another important factor which forced the hand of the then reluctant United States to develop a containment policy.

After the liberation of Greece in October 1944, Communist and Leftist elements, which had played a very important part in the resistance movement, were threatening to take over the control of the country. In fact a civil war had actually started. While Winston Churchill, whose troops had liberated the country and were still occupying it pending the establishment of a permanent regime, realized this danger and showed determination "to guarantee that the Greek people will have the opportunity to chose their own form of government" freely and in law and order, the United States was showing considerable indifference. The secretary of state of the time, Mr. Stettinius, more or less washed his hands of getting involved in a Greek civil war.

The British managed to compel the armed forces of the communists to disarm in 1945, and thus the way to a plebiscite to select the form of government (Monarchy or Republic) and elections for a constituent assembly was prepared. However, much communist agitation preceded and accompanied the elections. The communists in conjunction with the Soviet Union started a campaign to force the immediate departure of the British troops and Soviet Russia even brought this issue to the United Nations. Communist guerilla bands became active, especially in Macedonia. In spite of all this, the elections were held in April, 1946 under the eyes of Allied observers, and the Populists won 231 seats out of 354 in the constituent assembly. Subsequently a plebiscite was held on September 1, 1946 to decide the form of government, and of the 1,700,000 voters, 70 per cent voted for the return of the monarchy. Among those who voted thus were many Republicans who feared that a Republic at that time might strengthen the communists.

Upon the return of the King on September 27, 1947, communist guerilla activity which was openly encouraged by Albania, Bulgaria, and Yugoslavia, increased. The Greek government brought charges to that effect against these countries in the Security Council of the United Nations.

Greece, suffering from the after-effects of a tragic occupation and in the throes of an economic crisis, was now being confronted by the first "indirect aggression" which was to become the pattern of communist imperialism. Britain, who had been acting as caretaker and guardian, was in economic difficulties herself, and it was evident that she could no longer support Greece or defend her after the termination of the formal commitments on March 31, 1947.

Turkey was greatly worried by the course of events in Greece. A communist Greece would make the already precarious position of Turkey even more dangerous—she would become "an island in a sea of communism" as a Turkish editorial put it.

Reason in Washington. It was at this time that reason in the persons of President Truman, and Secretaries Marshall and Forrestal overrode the escapist tendencies of those in Washington who wanted to avoid involvement in the Greek civil war. It became increasingly evident that the United States was ready to assume the role which was being relinquished by Britain, not only in Greece but in the whole Middle East.

The United States ambassadors in Greece and Turkey were pouring alarming messages into Washington. On February 26, 1947 General Marshall, then Secretary of State and Dean Acheson, his Assistant Secretary of State, informed President Truman of a recommendation by the State-War-Navy Coordinating Board: Greece was in need of aid and failure to act immediately would lead to her collapse, with grave consequences for the neighboring countries, as well as for the entire Western world.

There was no doubt of the wisdom and courage of those in the United States government who overrode the isolationism then prevalent in some sections of the country and the so-called "liberal" opinion prevalent in some sections of the government—opinion which would remain indifferent to the fate of free nations in order to appease the Russians.

President Truman deserves much of the credit for choosing without hesitation the new course of American foreign policy for it required common sense, courage, and boldness. He explains his decision in his memoirs in the following words: "If we were to turn our backs to the world, areas such as Greece, weakened and divided as a result of war, would fall into the Soviet orbit without much effort on the part of the Russians. The success of Russia in such areas and our avowed lack of interest would lead to the growth of domestic communist parties in such European countries as France and Italy, where they were already significant threats."

Containment the New Password. Containment, which was to become the password of United States foreign policy for several years

to come, was first outlined by George F. Kennan, in an article in
Foreign Affairs. This article pointed out bluntly that there could
not be any reconciliation or intimacy between the United States and
the USSR. It was evident that the two countries were now rivals and
not partners in the political arena. Therefore it was necessary for
the United States to "contain" her rival. The article presented a
brilliant analysis of Soviet strategy and tactics and demonstrated that
whatever the day-to-day tactics of Russia, the main strategy and
main aims did not change.

The containment policy was to be implemented by economic aid,
military readiness, and atomic retaliation capability. Greece and
Turkey became the proving grounds for this new United States policy.
Truman made his dramatic announcement of what was to become
known as the Truman Doctrine at a joint session of the Congress on
March 12, 1947, after first securing the approval of the Congressional
leaders.

Evolution of the Truman Doctrine. At one point, when Soviet pressure was at its peak, Turkey felt completely alone. Nevertheless she
did not fail to make it clear that she would fight if necessary. But
Turkey was not deserted. The United States and the United Kingdom
replies to the Soviet notes of August and September, 1946, were the
first indications of the reactions of the other big powers to Soviet demands. As evidence of her determination to support Turkey against
Soviet demands, the United States reinforced its fleet in the Mediterranean.

In March, 1947, United States reaction to the aggressive attitude
of the Soviet Union evolved into the Truman Doctrine. In announcing his doctrine President Truman declared: "The gravity of the situation which confronts the world today necessitates my appearance
before a joint session of Congress. The foreign policy and the national security of the country are involved.

"One aspect of the present situation which I wish to present to you
concerns Greece and Turkey .... The circumstances in which Turkey finds herself are considerably different from those of Greece.
Turkey has been spared the disasters that have beset Greece, and
during the war the United States and Great Britain furnished Greece
with material aid.

"Since the war Turkey has sought financial assistance from Great
Britain and the United States for the purpose of effecting the modern-
ization necessary for the maintenance of her national integrity. That
integrity is essential to the preservation of order in the Middle East. . .
As in the case of Greece, if Turkey is to have the assistance she needs,

the United States must supply it. We are the only country able to provide that help."

The President unequivocally warned the Congress of the consequences of a possible refusal to help the two countries: "If Greece should fall under the control of an armed minority, the effects upon its neighbor, Turkey, would be immediate and serious. Disorder and confusion might well spread throughout the entire Middle East."

As requested by the President, Congress voted $400,000,000 for aid to Greece and Turkey ($250,000,000 to Greece and $150,000,000 to Turkey), over a period ending June 30, 1948. Congress also authorized sending a group of American military and civilian personnel to Greece and Turkey "to assist in the tasks of reconstruction and for the purpose of supervising the use of financial and material assistance," and also to instruct and train selected Turkish and Greek personnel.

Opposition Growth. There was, of course, considerable opposition to the Truman Doctrine in the United States. Distinctly vocal was Henry A. Wallace, who accused Truman of "betraying America." Senator Pepper of Florida charged the administration with "sabotaging the United Nations in honest but misguided zeal."

Soviet and satellite press and radio announcements started a vehement attack against the U.S. and Truman. Andrei A. Gromyko, the Soviet Deputy Foreign Minister, officially charged that U.S. aid constituted intervention in Greece's internal affairs and added that "The measures taken by the United States Government in respect to Greece and Turkey seriously undermines the authority of the United Nations Organization and invariably produces distrust in relations among the State members of the United Nations."

In Turkey and Greece, however, the Truman Doctrine was warmly hailed and welcomed. Recep Peker, then Premier of Turkey, declared that "by advocating aid for Greece and Turkey President Truman did not confine himself to understanding of world-wide strategy, but also had been inspired by a point of view both realistic and fully humanitarian." He continued:

"The deep influence of the ideas asserted in these words [announcement of the Doctrine] will reach beyond the Mediterranean, the Middle East, and the Near East. The ideas of the President, which have been applauded by both Houses, represent a complete awakening of American public opinion and a complete realization of the difficulties which surround the world."

Following the announcement of the Truman Doctrine an American Mission headed by General L. E. Oliver, consisting of twelve Army, six Navy, three Air Force officers, and two State Department economists, visited Turkey in May, 1947 to determine the needs of Turkey and the allocation of the funds authorized by Congress. A United States-Turkish agreement for carrying out the aid program was signed in Ankara on July 12, 1947. This was unanimously approved on September 1, 1947 by the Turkish Grand National Assembly. An auspicious phase—a honeymoon period—in Turkish-American relations had started.

The Roots of Turkish-United States Relations. Although formal relations between Turkey and the United States date back to 1830, and although there was considerable intercourse in the cultural and commercial fields, neither of the countries regarded the other as of much importance in its own foreign affairs. In fact there was never a war between them, nor were they ever allies.[1] During the First World War, America broke off diplomatic relations with Turkey but never formally declared war.

Commercial relations between America and Turkey date back to at least the colonial days. There are records of Turkish goods being received in America, as well as goods from the East which must have passed in transit through Turkey.

However, most important in Turkish-American relations is no doubt the field of culture and philanthropy. American Protestant missionaries have been active in Turkey since 1830. Most of these missionaries, who were dedicated idealists, realized that it would be unwise, and in fact would be quite impossible, to try to convert Moslem Turks to Christianity. Therefore they turned their efforts either to non-Moslem communities, such as the Armenians and Greeks, or embarked on humanitarian or cultural projects such as the establishment of medical centers, orphanages and schools.

It is interesting to note that most of the reaction to the work of such missionaries came not from Moslem Turks but from the dignitaries of the established Armenian and Greek Churches, who contended that Protestant proselytizing was an encroachment on their "Millet" autonomy granted by the Ottoman Sultan. It is also interesting to note that Turkish authorities promptly took steps to preserve the "religious autonomy" of their Armenian and Greek subjects.

The works of the American missionaries who chose the educational or humanitarian fields have endured to this day, and the medical centers and orphanages established by them have done much for the Turks as well as for the Christian communities. In the field of education the foresightedness of a missionary named Cyrus Hamlin continues to pay dividends in American culture and goodwill in Turkey. Hamlin, seeing the real need of the country, resigned from his Mission and established a college in Istanbul—a Christian college but not a missionary institution—in which he invested all his money (which he made baking bread and laundering uniforms for the Allied troops during the Crimean Campaign). When his own money was insufficient, he got financial backing from other American philanthropists. The college was named Robert College in honor of Christopher Robert, one of his chief supporters.

At the beginning, Robert College students were exclusively non-Moslem. The social order of those days would have made it impossible for Moslem Turks to attend. But after the Revolution of 1908, Turks began to attend both the Robert College and its sister institution, the American College for Girls. Other American schools were established at Istanbul, Talas, Adana and Izmir. After the establishment of the Republic large numbers of Turkish students attended them.

As a graduate of Robert College, the author can personally vouch for the vital and positive part played by the college in the formation of several generations of his countrymen. These institutions not only provided a well-rounded modern education but also prepared the cadres which would be receptive to American methods and way of life. This was to prove invaluable when Turkish-American relations became closer. It would be safe to say that until recently Turkish-American relations were more or less confined to the work of institutions like Robert College.

But, in spite of these efforts, Turkish-American relations were not perfect. The majority of Turks were antagonized by the activities of the missionaries who, they thought, were seeking to "hunt the souls" of Moslems. Stories about Turks who had been converted increased this antagonism. Obliquely, the support given to Armenian, Arab, and Greek nationalists within the country by missionaries irked the Turks also.

Immediately after the First World War, the unqualified support of American public opinion and the Congress for the Armenians embittered the Turks further. It was also disappointing to see that American relief agencies concentrated their efforts on non-Moslems and even played political roles against the Turkish independence movement. However, there were some Turks who believed that a United States mandate would be preferable to British-French domination, or to a division of the country. These people were especially shocked to see that Wilson's idealistic Fourteen Points were being used to prevent the survival of Turkey.

Kemal Ataturk, the leader if the Independence movement, although opposing vehemently the idea of any mandate, had confidence in the basically good intentions of the Americans. He expressed this opinion to several visiting American journalists and tried to rally the support of American public opinion for the Turkish cause. He was encouraged by the attitude of the American representative then in Istanbul, Admiral Mark L. Bristol, who supported Ataturk's cause against the instructions of the State Department. He and his representative in Ankara, Captain Robert Imbrie, deserve much credit for establishing the basis of Turkish-American understanding.

Despite Admiral Bristol's efforts, public opinion in the United States, prodded by propaganda for the "poor starving Armenians," continued to remain anti-Turkish. The U.S. Congress refused to ratify the Treaty of Lausanne or the American-Turkish Treaty of Friendship and Commerce in 1923, due to the efforts of the Armenian lobby. The Congressional Records pertaining to those debates are full of anti-Turkish attacks. Of course, these in turn caused anger against America in Turkey.

After 1925 there was an increase in Turkish-American trade. In 1925 year exports to the United States (chiefly tobacco, cotton, dried fruits) constituted 13 per cent of total Turkish exports. In 1927 Congress finally approved the appointment of an American Ambassador to Turkey; Joseph Grew became the first Ambassador, while Muhtar Bey became the first Ambassador of the Turkish Republic to Washington. Subsequently Turkish antagonism and suspicion against America and Americans diminished, evolving into a feeling of friendliness and admiration. An increasing number of Turks sent their children to American schools, without fearing, as formerly, that they would be converted to Christianity. The number of Turkish students studying in the United States increased considerably.

By 1937 Turkish exports to the U.S. amounted to approximately 19 million Turkish liras—7% of her total export. The imports from the U.S., low up to that time, had risen to about 15% of the total Turkish imports. In 1939, a commercial treaty was signed between Turkey and the United States.

By 1937 the social as well as the economic goodwill in the United States had changed, and the ill-feeling against Turkey had considerably diminished. It is true that the bulk of Americans did not really know the Turks and remembered them by cliches such as "Terrible Turk," "Armenian Massacres," "Fez and Harem," but there was no more an active antipathy. Even the "poor starving Armenians" were to a degree forgotten, and when the Truman Doctrine was announced there was relatively little public opposition. The protests of the individual Armenians writing letters to the editors, or of the National Armenian Council of America, went undeeded.

In Turkey a new era in Turkish-American relations had already started with the visit of the battleship U.S.S. Missouri in 1945. When the Truman Doctrine was announced the good feeling for America and Americans was limitless. A Turkish journalist's observation that "the country in which Americans are most popular in the world is Turkey" went unchallenged.

A new American Ambassador in Ankara, Edwin C. Wilson, played a very important part in the cementing of Turkish-American relations, both by his realistic reports to Washington and by his refreshing attitude with the Turkish leaders.

Problems in Turkey. In spite of Soviet threats and misrepresentations, the Turkish people and the Turkish Government were extremely enthusiastic and receptive to American aid.

The economic problem of Turkey had two main aspects. In the pre-Truman Doctrine days, the basically agrarian economy of Turkey relied on primitive methods and tools of production and transportation. There were very few modern agricultural implements and certainly no adequate storage facilities. The country was minerally rich but had not enough equipment for working the existing mineral resources or for exploring new ones. There were only a few thousand kilometers of serviceable roads, and almost no modern ports. The industries, which have been virtually started by the State only after the founding of the Republic, were unable to meet the basic needs of the country. These conditions reflected on the health and culture of the country, as well as on its army. Although Turkey, confronted by the Russian threat, spent more than half her budget on national defense, the armed forces had very little modern equipment, little training in modern warfare for a serious campaign, and relied on their traditional courage and discipline and on their famous bayonets.

The basic need therefore was not only to equip and strengthen the army, but to infuse new blood, new methods, and new tools into the economy in order to bring about a development which would offset the load of national defense in the budget, and also support the defense effort by a healthy economy.

Although the Truman Doctrine aid appeared to be stopgap aid, it was due to the farsightedness of some Turkish and American officials that at least five percent of the $100,000,000 appropriation was earmarked for improving the transportation system—the roads of Turkey. The efforts in this direction of Herbert J. Cummings, one of the two civilians in the first Exploratory Mission under General Oliver, should not go unmentioned here.

While modern weapons for the Turkish Army, Air Force, and Navy started to flow, a new spirit and a new system were injected into the Turkish armed forces. It must be admitted that the top echelons of these services, while extremely brave and valiant, were still geared to the cavalry and bayonet concept of warfare. They were not receptive to new ideas and new concepts which were required for the conduct of modern armies and modern warfare. A silent struggle took place between these conservatives and the young Turkish officers— the latter winning—and the result was that a new mentality was introduced into the Turkish armed forces, first, by the American instructors and later by the Turkish officers trained in the United States.

The road program was later incorporated into a long-range highway program stipulated in an agreement between the Turkish and American Governments. Under this agreement Turkey, aided technically and materially by the U.S. Bureau of Public Works, established a bureau of highways which undertook an initial program of 20,000 kilometers of a national highway system, 25,000 kilometers of provincial roads, and approximately 150,000 kilometers of country roads. The Truman Doctrine, though limited in scope and objectives, primed the pump of Turkish development. It was also evident that the United States aid and interests in Turkey would inevitably become a long-range undertaking.

The Truman Doctrine, according to Foreign Minister Necmeddin Sadak, "was a great comfort to the people of Turkey, for it made them feel that they were no longer isolated. They saw that a great nation, the most powerful in the world, was interested in their independence and integrity. The aid in military equipment which the Congress granted as a logical consequence of the Truman Doctrine was vital for Turkey. The strengthening of the Turkish army by the most modern of weapons will serve the cause of peace in our part of the world, for it will strengthen our power of resistance to any aggression. The Turkish people and army know how precious this aid is, and they know very well that no matter what sacrifices their country was willing to make, it could not have procured this equipment in any other way."

Successors of the Truman Doctrine. The economic aspects of the Truman Doctrine of aid to Greece and Turkey were later absorbed by the Marshall Plan Aid which was established by the Economic Cooperation Act which founded the Economic Cooperation Administration in June, **1948.**

Turkey became a member of the Organization of European Economic Cooperation and was thus eligible for Marshall Plan aid. An agreement entitling her to this aid was signed between the U.S. and the Turkish Government on July 4, 1948. Four days later the Turkish Grand National Assembly ratified the agreement. The aid was administered through the newly established Economic Cooperation Administration and its Mission in Turkey.

Under different laws passed by the U.S. Congress, three successive agencies—the Mutual Security Agency (MSA), Foreign Operations Administration (FOA), and the International Cooperation Administration (ICA)—implemented the economic aid to Turkey. Under these various organizations Turkey received different kinds of aid of both direct and indirect nature (such as long-term credits, grants) amounting to $839,329,000 up to June, 1958. Military assistance, which had been administered through the Defense Department channels and by the U. S. Military Missions in Ankara, are not included in this figure. The exact amount of such aid is secret, but it has been estimated that over one billion dollars worth of military assistance has been given to Turkey since 1947.

The Military Assistance Program to Turkey has equipped the Turkish Armed Forces with modern weapons and equipment, and improved their training and maintenance facilities. It also made the training cadre of instructor officers possible. These officers in turn have trained many other officers and the Turkish Army, Navy, and Air Force have been completely modernized. The Turkish Armed Forces are today considered the strongest, best equipped, and best trained in the Middle East; the army, with its twenty-two divisions, constitute the largest land force in NATO. It must be pointed out, however, that Turkey still allocates approximately half of its budget to national defense.

Perhaps as important as these tangible results in the military field are the changed trends in economic development and standards in Turkish society since 1950. The peasant, whose standard of living and consumption has risen, has perhaps for the first time realized his importance and the value of his toil in terms of the country's economy. Industrialization has created a movement toward urbanization and in urban centers private enterprise has gained the ascendancy.

The close relations between the U.S. and Turkey and the new economic climate in Turkey have had important by-products; these in turn have been instrumental in furthering economic development. Trade between the two countries, already considerable, increased interest of many American private investors who established businesses in Turkey. New Turkish laws facilitate and guarantee their investments.

Turkish statesmen have repeatedly expressed their gratitude for American aid. Certain difficulties and misunderstandings in economic relations have never diminished this gratitude nor effected Turkey's political ties with America.

Since 1947 Turkish foreign policy has been based mainly on friendship and alliance with the United States. President Celal Bayar in a speech to the Grand National Assembly on November 1, 1950, stated: "There is almost daily strengthening in our close political, economic, and cultural relations and friendship with the United States—a friend of peace, a respector of equal rights, attached to democratic traditions sincerely desiring that international disputes shall be resolved within the framework of the United Nations. We attach great value and importance to even greater increase in this close friendship which finds expression in the relations between our two countries and in international cooperation."

His speech to the Grand National Assembly in 1957 included the same thoughts: "I am happy to witness and state that our relations and cooperation with our great friend and ally, the United States of America are constantly developing. We are tackling all our problems with all sincerity and in a manner that becomes friends with full confidence in each other."

These words should not be construed as mere lip-service for the assistance received. The proud words of the Turkish statesman who said: "We did not join the West—the West joined us" carry much truth. Turkish leaders have steadfastly maintained that their full cooperation with the United States in international affairs stems from a realistic understanding of mutual interest and mutual aims vis-a-vis mutual dangers.

In a significant recent speech Prime Minister Adnan Menderes declared:

"We are receiving very extensive aid from the United States in the military field. The beneficial influence of technical, material, and monetary aid from the United States is to be seen in the existence of the modern and technologically-advanced Turkish army, of which our nation is justly proud. It can be said that it is almost impossible for countries such as ours to maintain by their own means a modern army that would conform to today's requirements.

"The primary aim of our efforts for the speedy realization of Turkey's economic development is to attain in the shortest possible time a level where we can defend our frontiers with our own resources, without recourse to aid from any other country.

"We have also received a great deal of economic aid from the United States, but it is obvious that, situated in a delicate and critical geographic location, the needs of a country like Turkey are very extensive. This point too should be taken into account. Turkey stands like an island of peace and stability in the midst of a stormy ocean. Many are the waves of disorder and instability that crash upon and are stopped by the firm rocks around these shores. In view of its importance and capacity, it is only natural that Turkey is a weighty component of primary value in the common front of the peace-loving nations that choose to make such great sacrifices for the preservation of peace."

In another recent speech, Mr. Menderes stated: "Not only does this aid indicate the importance of the contributing share assumed by the United States in support of Turkey's efforts aiming at reconstruction, but it constitutes also an excellent manifestation of the large-scale cooperation between our two countries which are sincerely united in the cause of defending the peace and security of the free world."

The visit of President Celal Bayar and Prime Minister Adnan Menderes to the U. S. on invitations from President Eisenhower in January and June of 1954, constituted the climax of the "honeymoon period." They were welcomed enthusiastically by officials and the press as representatives of the "staunchest ally" of the U. S.

Bayar said in his speech to the joint session of the U.S. Congress on January 29: "I assure you and the people of the United States that the memory of your noble deeds will live forever in the heart of every Turk." The same evening, addressing President Eisenhower, he elaborated: "The American people, who in perilous days have set the whole world an example of idealism and magnanimity, may rest assured that, in this hazardous path that mankind must tread they have found in the Turkish nation a firm companion on whom they can rely in every way."

The Turkish press supported these sentiments in their editorials, and in Turkey there was a general atmosphere of gratification due to the hospitality shown to the President in his visit to the United States. When Adnan Menderes visited the U.S. a few months later Turkey had begun to feel growing pains and was confronted by economic difficulties. The U. S. attitude continued to be lauditory and sympathetic, and there were reports that a $300,000,000 long-term loan to Turkey was being considered.

But in the beginning of 1955, the difficulties started. The Associated Press carried a report, that a "responsible administration" official in Washington had pointed out that the United States would not continue to support the ambitious programs of the Turkish Government. These remarks caused serious repercussions in official Turkish circles and in the Turkish press.

When the mission of Fatin Rustü Zorlu, then Minister of State, went to Washington to discuss the possibility of a long-term loan with government officials and it proved fruitless, there was great disappointment in Turkey.

In spite of the failure over the loan, Prime Minister Menderes pointed out that Turkey would remain an ally of the U. S., emphasizing that her friendship was not a prerequisite for aid. But these words were practically unnoticed in official circles in Washington. Turkish officials began to get the impression that the U.S. government was deliberately avoiding Turkey's political and stategic importance, and was, rather, emphasizing her economic difficulties. The American press also followed the same line of thought.

Wonderful as the developments of the honeymoon period were, by the beginning of 1955 the realization that it had ended, or it was to end, was beginning to dawn upon some observers.

It is difficult to pin-point the reason or reasons for this. Perhaps it was the result of complex factors. The first enthusiasm felt in the U.S. for Turkey was soon shadowed by the rush of other events. The change of administration in Washington brought in a new group of administrators and some new conceptions. Perhaps the short-lived Geneva spirit obliterated the need for a loyal ally. Perhaps Turkey's earnest struggle for a better economic and political society was not well understood by the American people. On the Turkish side there was deep disappointment regarding what was termed "being taken for granted" and Washington's failure to understand Turkey's social and economic goals and problems.

It is no secret that Turkish-American relations at the personal level in Turkey had lost the spirit of cooperation. The large numbers of Americans living in their prosperous suburbia were bound to be irksome, especially if they did not bother to mingle with or try to understand their hosts, as their predecessors of a few years before had done. When Turkish industrialists or farmers could not find parts for the equipment which had been obtained through American aid, these irritations increased. By 1955, the honeymoon was definitely over and officials in Washington openly said so.

CHAPTER VII

KOREA AND AFTER: MOVES AND COUNTER MOVES

On June 25, 1950, North Korea invaded the Republic of South Korea. The United Nations Security Council immediately met at the request of the United States and, appraising the situation as a breach of peace, called for cessation of hostilities and withdrawal of the North Korean forces to the north of the 38th Parallel. This had no effect. On June 27th, in the absence of the Soviet Delegate, then boycotting the Council on the issue of Chinese representation, the Council recommended that "Members of the United Nations furnish such assistance to the Republic of Korea as may be necessary to repel the armed attack and restore international peace and security in the area." This was indeed a momentous decision. In spite of the shortcomings of its Charter, the UN was standing up to the challenge and taking action such as it might not be able to take again when the Russians were seated and could use the veto.

The Korean aggression was a new step in Stalin's postwar strategy to achieve world domination. He had failed in his attempted encroachments on Greece and Turkey, but was alarmingly successful in the global struggle elsewhere. He had seized control of East European countries; his Cominform was dangerously active in many Western countries. He was blocking the completion of peace treaties and was maintaining large forces in Eastern Europe, Germany, and Austria. Now in Korea he was attempting a new pattern: local aggression through a satellite. If he were to be successful in Korea, his ambition would know no bounds and he would attempt new coups elsewhere. Most Western diplomats and statesmen interpreted the situation realistically: Stalin had to be stopped.

The Turkish Government was one of the first UN members to support the Security Council resolution. The Turkish press almost unanimously praised the prompt action of the Council. In Turkish minds—official and unofficial—support or non-support of the Republic of Korea by the United Nations, and especially by the United States, would be the acid test of the free world's determination to resist aggression in line with commitments to the small nations. The question was, especially, "Will the United States stand up to this challenge?"

On July 26, 1950, the Turkish government followed up its initial

resolution to "comply with any decision taken by the Security Council
on Korea" by offering to send 4,500 men to Korea; it was one of the
first countries to guarantee troops to the United Nations Command
there. Prime Minister Adnan Menderes explained this step in these
words: "If the United Nations were to fail to take action against an
aggression in no matter what part of the world, this would pave the
way to further aggressions and would constitute a sort of premium
for them . . . Turkey has always proclaimed her attachment to the
United Nations Charter. Our Government is convinced that the
strongest guarantee for the safeguarding of peace, which is an indivisible whole, lies in the faithful implementation of the Charter.
We therefore consider it essential that each member State of the United
Nations should discharge its obligations without hesitation."

A few days later he added: "The best way to guard against danger
is to be ready and determined to meet aggression. Besides, there is
a kind of peace that is as bad as war. We have no use for the kind
of peace that leads nations into slavery and humiliation. Much more
noble is the kind of struggle that is undertaken to ensure the continuation of national independence and honor."

Some members of the opposition contested the constitutionality of
Menderes' decision, but in principle they approved it. Ex-Foreign
Minister Necmeddin Sadak stated in his newspaper AKSAM: "Turkish foreign policy is that of the nation as a whole and is completely
bi-partisan and every party is solidly behind the Government in its
foreign policy which is in the hands of able, farsighted, and patriotic
men."

The most interesting and remarkable aspect of this dramatic
decision was that it was made by a government which had come to
power only a few weeks previously, following the general elections of
May 14th which had resulted in a landslide victory for the newly
formed Democratic Party. The People's Republican Party of Ismet
Inonu was swept from the power it had held for more than twenty-
five years and was reduced to a small minority in the Grand National
Assembly. New leaders took over the helm of government: Celal
Bayar, who had been Prime Minister during the last year of Ataturk's
Presidency, was elected President. Adnan Menderes, a co-founder of
the Democratic Party, was appointed Prime Minister; in his new
Cabinet he gave the Foreign Ministry to Fuat Koprulu, a scholar of
Oriental Literature.

The Korean situation and the appeal of the United Nations was
quite a challenge for these new leaders and their decisions would call
for courage and foresight. By meeting the challenge as it did, the

new government took a bold and unprecedented step. Up to this
time Turkey had stubbornly avoided military action or intervention
outside its own territory, so the sending of troops to Korea was a
courageous action.

In theory, Turkey's approval of United Nations intervention and
subsequent action by the major powers was quite logical and in
keeping with Turkey's "world outlook" and foreign policy, because,
since the days of Ataturk the country was always in favor of collective security arrangements and collective action against aggression
anywhere. However, actual participation in a collective security
undertaking which involved sending Turkish troops into action was a
radical, new step—a step indicative of the new approach and new
concepts concerning foreign policy on the part of the newly elected
leaders.

Ismet Inonu, the former President, who led the Turkish government
during the Second World War, had adopted a cautious and almost
passive attitude; he had reiterated the principles of Ataturk but had
avoided foreign entanglements.[1] There are those who say that this
attitude kept Turkey out of the war; there are others who criticize
Inonu's extreme caution and contend that Turkey could have derived
more benefits from a more dynamic foreign policy. Although the
debate is now academic and cannot possibly be resolved, it was
apparent in the post-war era that Inonu's too cautious attitude was
not bringing any rewards. For example, the Turkish government's
attempts to join the North Atlantic Treaty Alliance were unsuccessful
until 1952.

The leaders of the new government had no quarrel whatsoever with
the basic precepts of Turkey's traditional foreign policy, such as a
determined stand against Russia, friendship with the West, the shun-
ning of irredentism and foreign adventures. They realized, however,
that the post-war situation and its realities called for a dynamic approach and new methods very different from those of nineteenth-cen-
tury diplomacy. Turkey had to assert herself and by demonstrating
her geographic importance, her basic strength, and her dependability,
acquire the guarantees she sought.

The Korean War was an opportunity to give the world a demon-
stration of the new Turkey. In Korea the Turkish soldier fought
bravely and fought well. Moreover he knew how to resist the Communist brain-washing in prisoner-of-war camps. Turkish casualties
were the second highest among the United Nations troops; Americans
incurred the highest casualties. Out of the 29,882 Turks who participated in three years of combat, there were 717 dead and 2,246 wounded.

with 16 missing, and 219 known to be prisoners. Among these prisoners there was not one who yielded to Communist pressures or enticement.

In the summer of 1953 Adlai Stevenson wrote: "The Turks are the world's best fighting men and America's most dependable ally . . ." A U.S. newspaperman wrote: "Meet Mehmetcik, ally of the West, unbelievably tough and fearless . . . the fighter who enjoys soldiering at twenty-one cents a month . . . Mehmetcik's bravery is now legendary." General Douglas MacArthur, admirer of ruggedness, christened him, "bravest of the brave."

Throughout the Korean War there were continuous reports of the bravery of Mehmetcik and the toughness of the Turkish troops. The Turkish soldier, at the price of his blood, had reminded the world of Turkey's determination and value to the West. The Korean War had considerably altered the connotation of the word "Turk" in the minds of the average American. "Turk" no longer was synonymous with the word "terrible" or "unspeakable" but connoted dependability and valor.

Seeds of European Unity. The Truman Doctrine saved Greece and Turkey from immediate Communist aggression; the Marshall Plan provided the basis for economic cooperation in Europe, and, in conjunction with American economic aid, economic defenses against Communist subversion were established on the European continent. Yet the danger of Stalin's imperialism had not been averted. In 1948 the free government of Czechoslovakia was overthrown by a Communist coup d'etat, and Jan Masaryk, the Foreign Minister, who had thought it would be possible to co-exist with Russia and the Communists, committed suicide in despair. Later that year, in June, Russia stopped traffic between Berlin and the Western occupation zones in Germany in order to put pressure on the Western Powers. The United States met this challenge with determination and did not yield to pressure, and a gigantic Western airlift defeated the Russian move. But it was becoming more and more evident that the countries of Western Europe should bring unity and cooperation into their policies and defense efforts.

There were other foundation stones besides the Marshall Plan for the establishment of a Regional Defense System of Europe. In 1947 France and Britain signed the Dunkirk Treaty of Alliance and Mutual Assistance. On March 17, 1948 Great Britain, France, Belgium, the Netherlands, and Luxembourg joined in signing the Brussels Treaty for closer economic cooperation and for mutual aid in case of an attack on Europe.

The United States government, in addition to the Marshall Plan, was supporting European attempts to establish a regional security system. President Truman in a speech to the Congress on March 17, 1948 expressed his Government's support for the Brussels Treaty. He also pointed out that the security interests of the United States and Canada were identical . . . the concept of a North Atlantic Alliance was rapidly developing. On June 11, 1948, Senator Vandenberg proposed a resolution urging the progressive development of "regional and other collective security arrangements." This was passed by the Congress and the U.S., on this basis, could consult with Brussels Treaty members and Canada for the purpose of creating the NATO. The original North Atlantic Treaty was signed on April 4, 1948 by Belgium, Canada, Denmark, France, Great Britain, Iceland, Italy, Luxembourg, the Netherlands, Norway, Portugal, and the United States. The Treaty came into force after ratification by the legislative bodies of the signatories in August, 1949. Military assistance was provided for members, on the principle of the Mutual Security Act of the United States.

Turkey Seeks Guarantees. After the rejection of Soviet demands on the Straits, there had been no new developments in Soviet-Turkish relations. The Soviet press and radio unceasingly attacked Turkey and her leaders. Since the beginning of American aid and the Marshall Plan, the appeal of Russian propaganda was more and more to "the misguided Turkish people" who had been drawn into the sphere of influence of "the imperialist war-mongers by lackeys of the United States and Wall Street, in contravention of the legacy of Ataturk."

In the face of these attacks and threats, Turkey did not feel really secure. Since 1947 she had received more than $250,000,000 in military aid under the Truman Doctrine, and approximately $103,000,000 in aid from the Economic Cooperation Administration. Although their army, navy, and air force were equipped with modern weapons, the Turks felt that they lacked the full protection of formal guarantees and a formal alliance. Turkish foreign policy was now aimed mainly at seeking these guarantees and, specifically, an alliance with the United States and the West. In July 1948 Foreign Minister Sadak declared: "Turkey, already more than an ally of the United States, is looking forward to a crystallization of this relationship in an alliance." The following April he explained this aspiration by saying: "Peace and security cannot be made to depend indefinitely upon mobilization and armament, above all for countries which are not rich.

All the peaceful countries must, as soon as possible, organize a defensive security system capable of halting in advance any war of aggression. Until the United Nations carries out this task the European countries, in association with the most powerful idealist of peace, the United States, must assume it, needless to say, within the United Nation's framework. Thus alone can war be avoided, thousands of human lives spared, the modern civilization saved from collapse."

However, Secretary of State Marshall made it quite clear to Turkish leaders that the United States could not sign an alliance with Turkey or make bilateral commitments to her, because such a move would necessitate the revaluation of American relations with practically every country. This refusal was interpreted by the Russians as a "coolness of the United States' attitude towards Turkey" and they immediately changed their tactics. A new Ambassador, Anton Lavrischev, was appointed to Ankara. (Since the departure of Serge Vinogradov, Russia had kept only a chargé d'affaires in Ankara.) Lavrischev made overtures to Turkey in an attempt to draw her away from the United States, hinting that Turkey could benefit more by friendship with the USSR. The same approach and tone were used in the Turkish language broadcasts of Radio Moscow. But neither the Turkish government nor the people responded to these attempts.

In September, 1958, during initial phases of the North Atlantic Treaty negotiations, the Turkish Ambassador to the U.S., Feridun C. Erkin, informally suggested to the Department of State that Turkey be included among the initiators of the Treaty, but the Department pointed out that it was a Pact regional in character only. However, in February, 1949, when it was reported in the press that Italian and French possessions in North Africa would be included within the scope of the Pact, the Turkish government drew the attention of the U.S. government to the apparent contradiction.

In the face of insistent Turkish demands, Secretary of State Dean Acheson expressed sympathy with the Turkish desire, but requested that the demands be withdrawn pending "friendly and careful consideration" of Turkey's security problem after the North Atlantic Treaty came into effect. Nevertheless disappointment in Turkey— and in Greece—increased. The Turks argued that by leaving Turkey and Greece out of this Alliance the Western Powers relegated them both to the status of secondary countries and expendable military outposts. Turkish commentators pointed out that by not including these countries in NATO a dangerous gap was left in the security system; containment was incomplete at the south eastern flank; Turkey was a country with internal stability and a strong army; she was the key to the defense of the Middle East and therefore had every right and reason to be part of NATO. A military analyst commented: "This is a stategy beyond reason—to leave the door open and try to defend the territories beyond it." Sadak, the Foreign Minister said publicly: "The Atlantic Pact is incomplete because it fails to cover the Eastern Mediterranean—potentially one of the most dangerous areas in the world."

There were also many supporters of the Turkish-Greek case in Europe and in the United States. Senator Mundt of South Dakota declared: "If the Atlantic Pact is to operate successfully it must be so implemented, so revised, and so remodelled as to bring over to our side of the ideological warfare all the areas and all the countries and all the peoples who share our desire to oppose the Communist menace."

Senator Cain of Washington pointed out that "with the exclusion of Greece and Turkey we have left our right flank or eastern flank open, and in the event of total war in that area I am afraid that exclusion would cause us to run a better than a calculated risk of losing the war before we had any more than become involved in it. . . ." But all these arguments and all the diplomatic efforts of the Turkish and Greek Governments were making no apparent headway.

General Dwight D. Eisenhower, Supreme Commander of NATO, stated that "the struggle against the threat of dictatorial aggression has no geographical bounds; it is all one." And, indeed, there was nothing in the letter or spirit of the Alliance to prevent the widening of its scope, as the Pact denoted a concept and not a limitation to the Atlantic region. If this had been the case, the inclusion of Italy, and later the Algerian Department of France, would not have been possible. Also the reference in the Treaty text, which deals with regional arrangements, was not to Articles 52, 53, 54 of the Charter, but to Article 51 which mentions the inherent right of individual or collective self-defense. More explicitly, there was no mention of geographical conditions of membership in the Treaty. Obviously there were other reasons for the objections to Greek and Turkish membership. The principal objectors were the small Scandinavian and Benelux countries who said they did not want to extend NATO to include Turkey and Greece because the "geography would be too great." But there were other, perhaps more practical objections:

The inclusion of Turkey and Greece would add to the rearmament burden and divide United States aid further. Also the NATO alliance meant "automatic action by all in case of an attack against one of the members." The smaller countries were afraid that the inclusion of Turkey and Greece would increase the danger of war and their own involvement; hence their reluctance to pledge themselves to take immediate action involving an attack far away from their frontiers. Although Turkey herself might be a military asset, her inclusion might encourage requests from weaker nations which could cause embarrassment. What was less understandable, however, was that even Great Britain and France were against the inclusion of Greece and Turkey. Admittedly they were afraid of spreading NATO too thin and they argued that both Greece and Turkey were military liabilities rather than assets. They told Turkish diplomats that through their treaty of alliance of 1939 with Britain and France they already had all the advantages of Atlantic membership. The real concern of the British and French actually was to preserve their influential position in the southern Mediterranean, and a formal alliance between Turkey, Greece, the United States, and the West would presumably interfere with that dominant position. The British advocated that Turkey and Greece instead be parties to a separate Middle East defense system which would be linked to but separate from NATO. But an objection, which was perhaps at the root of all the other objections, worried the Turks most. Some British commentators defined it in the following words: ". . .If there is ever to be a real European community it must possess natural homogeneity. The inclusion of a Moslem state like Turkey would weaken the ideal of a Christian, democratic community of free states." The Turks resented these remarks which, they said, were reminiscent of "the spirit of the Crusades."

The Korean war added to the anxieties of Turkey and Greece. Foreign Minister Koprulu pointed out that the event "proved that geographical areas not under contractual agreement permit free play to international greed and this may open the way to aggression." However, the Korean conflict, and Turkish participation in it, also increased her chances of membership in NATO.

Thus, with the coming into power of a new government in Turkey and with the Korean War, a new phase in the diplomatic struggle for membership in NATO had started. The *New York Times* correspondent in Turkey noted this change in a dispatch on August 14, 1950. "During the twelve years of General Ismet Inonu's Presidency," he wrote, "the approach to problems of foreign policy was extremely cautious. Firmness under severe pressure was shown on many occasions, but initiative was rarely shown. Since the voters changed leadership three months ago the foreign objectives remain the same—peace if possible—but it is already clear that the style has changed. Premier Adnan Menderes' Cabinet acted boldly and suddenly on the question of troops for Korea when a wait-and-see attitude would have been perfectly understandable. Similarly, the Atlantic Pact application was revived with a minimum of diplomatic preparation."

In one of his first statements to the foreign press Prime Minister Menderes pointed out bluntly that the "close, mutual friendship between the United States and Turkey" had not "marched hand in hand with the ever increasing seriousness of the world situation." It was his opinion that "closer relations and formal agreements with the U.S. were required . . . The way the Korean affair has developed and the decision taken by our government in reference to Korea have underlined the urgency of the problems facing us." Remarking on the rejection of the Turkish application for NATO membership, he added: "This may well be construed as encouragement of any contemplated aggression on Turkey."

He concluded his remarks with the following words: "It is our fervent wish that a third world war may never take place. But if it comes, Turkey's important and critical position in such a world catastrophe cannot be overlooked. There are those important key positions in the world where if weak, and without guarantees, aggression would be facilitated, or even provoked. We believe the reality of this situation will be recognized and serious measures will be taken not to leave doors ajar to aggression. Further, the entry of Turkey, whose military strength is known, into the Atlantic Treaty under present-day conditions would reinforce the security and defense system as constituted by this Treaty."

In line with these views the Turkish government intensified its diplomatic efforts and approached the governments of the twelve member nations regarding NATO membership. Mr. Acheson met the Turkish Ambassador's request with sympathy. In May, 1950, the U. S. government announced that it was ready to propose Turkey's membership in the North Atlantic Alliance and promised to discuss it with the other members of NATO. This decision was undoubtedly influenced by the deteriorating situation in the Middle East, especially in Iran and Egypt. When the matter was discussed in the September meeting of the NATO Council of Foreign Ministers, there was a general recognition that the participation of Turkey and Greece in the collective defense system was in the interest of all the members, but full membership was not deemed feasible; instead the Council decided to permit the association of Turkey and Greece with such phases of the NATO military planning work as was concerned with the defense of the Mediterranean.

There was great disillusionment in Turkey over this decision. Although Ankara officials accepted what they termed a "shirt tail arrangement," they did not hesitate to express their feelings through diplomatic channels. A Turkish newspaperman, in a letter to the *New York Herald Tribune*, wrote that Turkey "wanted to be a real and contributing part of the Western family, and not merely a well-behaved stepchild." He complained of the "They-are-already-in-the-bag" attitude which seemed to be prevalent at the time in the U.S. . . . "I cannot help but note that the weak card in our hands is the fact that Americans know very well that Turks will resist any Soviet aggression at all costs, with or without foreign assistance, and whether Turks are included in an alliance or not. They will never go as far as to say: 'Either comply with our demands, give us more aid and take us into the North Atlantic Alliance or sign some other treaty with us; or else we will make a deal with the other side.' "

In October, 1950, the Turks were further disturbed when they read an article by General Omar Bradley in the *Reader's Digest* in which he described Turkey, with Siam, Burma, Afghanistan, Iran, and Iraq as potential "local war" areas. He wrote: "We will refuse absolutely to allow local wars to divert us unduly from our central task. They must not be allowed to consume so much of our manpower and resources as to destroy our strength and imperil our victory in a world way." This seemed to be an official re-affirmation on the part of the United States of a plan to consider Turkey as an expendable "local" outpost.

In January Turkish Foreign Minister Fuat Koprulu made a new démarche; he suggested that since Turkey was not accepted as a full NATO member, the U. S. should establish direct contractual ties with Turkey—that is, sign an alliance to guarantee Turkey's independence and integrity. The Secretary of State informed the Turkish government that this was impossible. The Turkish government then suggested a new formula: adherence of the U. S. to the Treaty of Mutual Assistance of 1939 between Turkey, France, and England. Since only the U.S. and Turkey were concerned, it should not be necessary to consider the objections, if any, of the other powers.

The U.S. government took this proposal under consideration, but finally turned it down on the grounds that Congress would not endorse new commitments and that it would be easier to convince the Senate to approve of the adherence of the two countries to the Atlantic Defense System. Consequently the U.S. government adopted the policy of trying to get NATO membership for Greece and Turkey, rather than having bilateral agreements with them. A third suggestion by the Turkish government for an eastern Mediterranean Pact,

based on the Atlantic Pact and including France, Great Britain, and
the United States, was also turned down by Washington. (At this
point the British government had changed her reluctant attitude and
was supporting NATO membership for Greece and Turkey.)

Membership at Last. Finally, through the efforts of the United
States and the United Kingdom at the Ottawa Conference of NATO,
held from September 15 to 20, 1951, it was agreed to recommend to
the member governments the admission of Turkey and Greece to the
North Atlantic Treaty Organization, which recommendation was approved. On September 21, 1951, President Truman sent a message
to President Bayar expressing his gratification: "I am particularly
pleased with this decision because I know that it represents the fulfilment of a deep desire on the part of the Turkish government and
people and a recognition of the valiant efforts Turkey has made in
the postwar period to maintain her independence and integrity in the
face of present threats and pressures." In his reply President Bayar
said: "It is an added pleasure for me to affirm that Turkey will never
hesitate to carry out the obligations that will devolve upon her within
the Atlantic community which she is about to join."

The protocol prepared to carry out the decision of the NATO Council was ratified by the legislative bodies of all member governments[2],
and when the notifications to this effect were completed on February
15, 1952, Turkey and Greece formally became members of NATO.
At the Lisbon meeting of the NATO Council, February 20 to 25, 1952,
the Turkish ground and air forces were assigned to cooperate under
the command of the Supreme Allied Commander in Europe. Admiral
Robert B. Carney recommended Izmir, in Turkey, as the headquarters
of the Allied Land Forces, Southeast Europe.

The Turks were jubilant. "A great victory," wrote a Turkish editor, "not only from the standpoint of protecting Turkey's security
but for the world's peace. . . .Today's Turkey is a might for peace, not
a liability." It was indeed a great diplomatic victory for the new
Turkish government. Its dynamic diplomacy had achieved for Turkey the prestige and security of membership in a Western alliance.
This meant her recognition at last as a first-rate Western power with
equal obligations and equal rights. She was no longer an "outsider,"
and had won in her struggle to join NATO, which was so important to
her, not only for security reasons but because she wanted to be an
integral part of the West.

Turkey's ardent desire for close association with the West stemmed
back to the days of Fatih Sultan Mehmed and Suleyman the Magnificent. The latter (perhaps the greatest of the Ottoman Emperors)

seriously hoped he could become a part of the West and to that end worked for a rapprochement. This would not have been a mere diplomatic alliance, but would also entail the complete orientation of Turkish society and culture towards the Western world. The fatalism and apathy of the East had never really appealed to the dynamic Turkish mind and soul, which were in search of new horizons. Suleyman personally symbolized this new spirit.

Harold Lamb in his excellent biography dramatizes Suleyman's feelings vividly: "The realization seemed to grow upon him that he would never find the friendship he had sought in the West. Francis who had appealed to him tried to use him as a weapon against Charles, to be discarded when not needed. For the nearest of them, Ferdinand of Austria, he had gained only contempt. He had been willing to meet the Western princes more than halfway—they had never understood how far he had gone to meet them. In their society he would find no place. He would be alone, a Turk!" Modern Turks were filled with almost the same feelings when their repeated requests to join NATO were turned down, and their inclusion finally in the organization filled Turkish hearts with pride and exaltation. They were no longer "outsiders"—they were at last a part of the West!

Subsequent events proved that Turkey did not become a liability to NATO. On the contrary, with her determination and twenty-two divisions, she bolstered the organization morally and physically. In retrospect, one cannot help wondering why such formidable objections were first raised and why so much valuable time was lost in joint planning, preparation, and training!

Life and Death of a Balkan Alliance. The new Turkish government of Adnan Menderes had been exerting diplomatic initiative in another but related direction. Starting from the premise that peace is indivisible, the new leaders of Turkey aimed at supplementary defense arrangements which would support the Western Defense system. One basis for such an arrangement in the Balkans was Turkish-Greek friendship. The alliance and friendship between these traditionally inimical countries had been achieved in the 1930's by Ataturk and Venezolos and served as the foundation for the Balkan Entente of 1934, but had failed because this Entente (just *like* the Little Entente) did not see and prepare for the real danger ahead—i.e., possible aggression by powerful nations.

Now Menderes hoped to revive Turkish-Greek friendship and use it as a lever for a new Balkan Pact, realistically designed against Soviet aggression. In his second month in office as Foreign Minister, in June, 1950, Fuad Koprulu made a point of meeting the Greek Prime

Minister, General Plastiras, in Paris to review Greek-Turkish relations. A joint communique issued after this meeting pledged the in-
itiation of "effective and close cooperation in all spheres."

The Greek civil war ended on October 16, 1949 as a result of a combination of United States military aid and the determination of the
Greek Commander-in-Chief, Marshall Papagos; also the rift between
Tito and Stalin, which resulted in Yugoslavia's expulsion from the
Cominform, eliminated that country as a base of operations for the
Greek rebels. Greece now had freedom of action in the diplomatic
field, and her leaders, together with the Turkish leaders, sought new
avenues of cooperation such as membership in NATO and other regional arrangements. A new potential member, namely Yugoslavia,
was now also in the picture. The end of the Greek civil war, and
Tito's renunciation of the Greek rebels, made better relations possible
between Yugoslavia and Greece and between Turkey and Yugoslavia.
Various trade and cultural agreements were signed.[3] Delegations of
statesmen, members of Parliament, military officials, and newspaper-
men all exchanged visits. Tito, who at the time of his break with
the Soviet bloc stressed independence and non-alignment, was now
definitely veering toward the West; he particularly wanted closer
ties with Greece and Turkey. On August 7, 1952 he told a visiting
Turkish delegation: "During the last few years we have shown in
practice that cooperation is possible between countries which have
identical interests, although the internal systems are not the same."

The Western powers, especially the U.S., supported these trends.
In fact the U.S. Government extended very extensive aid to Yugoslavia after the Tito-Stalin rift. Either independent, or linked with
the West, Yugoslavia was considered very important to the NATO
defense system. The U.S. and the United Kingdom therefore en-
dorsed the Turkish-Greek-Yugoslavia cooperation efforts and hoped
that it would extend to include Italy also. By January, 1953, the
preparatory talks among the three Governments had progressed considerably. The Turkish Foreign Minister spoke of "an identity of
views, especially in the field of joint security." In February military
negotiations were held in Ankara between the general staffs of the
three countries, and on the 28th of that month a five-year Treaty of
Friendship and collaboration was signed in Ankara. This Treaty
called for combined efforts of the three countries against all outside
aggression and for consultation and cooperation on matters pertaining
to their common interests, "particularly concerning defense." The
Treaty did not contain a clause of automatic involvement for other
members in case of attack against one of the members because Greece

and Turkey, as NATO members, could not very well enter into such a commitment with a non-NATO member—Yugoslavia.

In November a supplement to the Treaty of Ankara was signed in Belgrade setting up a permanent Secrerariat to work out a military agreement for the defense of the Balkans against aggression. Later that month military representatives of the three countries signed another agreement defining their mutual obligations in their joint defense effort. These obligations were still short of automatic involvement, however.

In April, 1954, on the occasion of Tito's visit to Turkey a joint communique stressed "the need for the perfection and development of defense organizations whose purpose is the maintenance of peace and security." There was considerable delay, however, before the Balkan Defense Pact was signed. Italy, because of her dispute over Trieste with Tito was not in favor of her two NATO allies joining Yugoslavia in a military pact. Also, some of the NATO powers had some misgivings as they were not clear as to their own responsibilities in the event that Greece and Turkey called on them for help in carrying out their obligations under the Balkan Pact. But these misgivings were finally overcome. On August 9, 1954, the Balkan Defense Pact was signed at Bled, Yugoslavia; it contained the following provisions:

"The contracting parties have agreed that any armed aggression against one, or several of them, on any part of their territories, shall be considered as an aggression against all the contracting parties, which in consequence, exercising the right of legitimate individual or collective self-defense, recognized by Article 51 of the United Nations Charter, shall individually or collectively render assistance to the party or parties attacked, undertaking in common accord and immediately all measures, including the use of armed force, which they shall deem necessary for efficacious defense . . .

"The contracting parties have undertaken the obligation to extend to each other mutual assistance in order to maintain and strengthen their defensive capacity.

"With the purpose of insuring an efficacious application of the present treaty, the following has been decided:

"To establish a Permanent Council composed of the Foreign Ministers and of such other members of the governments of the contracting parties. . .

"Decisions on essential questions will be passed in unanimity by the permanent council.

"The General Staffs of the contracting parties shall continue their joint work started in conformity with the Articles 2 and 3 of the Ankara agreement. . .

"The present treaty has been concluded for a period of twenty years. If none of the contracting parties should cancel it one year before its term has expired, the treaty shall be considered as tacitly prolonged for another year, and so forth, until cancelled by one of the contracting parties."

In spite of its excellent purpose and in spite of the long preparations which went into it, the Balkan Pact was stillborn. Its permanent Council has not met for over three years and the "joint work" of the General Staffs has not been continued. One factor in this was Tito's reconciliation with Kruschev's Russia.

The visit of Bulganin and Kruschev to Belgrade in 1957 greatly enhanced Tito's prestige in the Communist world. After the visit he began to stress his neutralism and the fact that he was "not joining any of the blocs." As early as December, 1954, he had said: "Many people affirm: 'Yes, you are in favor of normalizing relations with the Soviet Union, and this means the breakdown of the Balkan Alliance.' And I say that they are mistaken. The Balkan Alliance has not failed! The Balkan Alliance was not created for any aggressive purpose. If we had created it for aggressive purposes against the Soviet Union, this Pact would of course have broken down with the normalization of relations. But since the Alliance was created on a purely defensive basis with a view to strengthening our independence, it has not failed as far as Yugoslavia, Greece and Turkey are concerned."

Late in 1955 Tito added:

"The Balkan Pact was set up at a time when we and our partners were in danger. We did not set it up for military purposes only. Of course, we had this in mind, but we hoped it would develop into an organization which would guarantee peaceful cooperation between us and those Balkan countries with which our relations were formerly very tense. In short, The Balkan Pact was set up in order to prevent an explosive situation in the Balkans. We decided to form a Balkan consultative assembly so that the military aspect of this Pact would be of a temporary nature, and in order to emphasize the necessity of further developing our economic, cultural and other relations. . .

"If we were to strengthen the military aspect of the Balkan Pact, we would thereby deviate from our foreign policy principles. . .

"The danger of war has been removed; we are not threatened by war from the Soviet Union. I am deeply convinced of this. Then why should we brandish arms?"

Although it was evident that the moving spirit behind the Balkan Pact was the necessity for military cooperation, Tito was now relegating this to the background. On the other hand, the economic aspects of the pact were not functioning as well as was hoped originally.

Yugoslavia's reconciliation with Russia was short-lived. With Kruschev's renunciation of Tito in the Spring of 1958 a new spark of life could have been ignited in the Balkan Pact. Indeed, since the second Russian-Yugoslavian rift, there are evidences of a Greek-Yugoslav rapprochement. The visit paid by Greek Foreign Minister Averof to Brioni in June of this year was a case in point. The new meetings suggest a new direction—perhaps a neutralist Balkan-Middle East bloc rather than revival of Turkish-Greek-Yugoslav cooperation. The factors encouraging such a grouping are varied. There are those who contend that Yugoslavia entered an alliance with Turkey and Greece merely as a temporary gesture of defiance and independence towards Moscow and as a means of getting United States aid to tide her over a difficult period. Her need for the Pact ended with her brief reconciliation with Moscow, and even though that reconciliation is now over she still does not need the Balkan Alliance as an instrument of diplomacy. Tito has found that his neutral and independent course carries considerable prestige and does not seem to affect the continuation of Western support.

It was chiefly Turkish initiative which prepared the ground for Turkish-Greek-Yugoslav cooperation in the first instance and it could be argued that it was the realistic and person-to-person approach of the Turkish leaders which originally persuaded Tito to abandon his neutralism in 1952. On that same premise, one can theorize that if the Turkish-Greek rift over Cyprus had not happened, the same Turkish initiative would have succeeded in keeping Tito in the Western camp. A Balkan alliance thus preserved would perhaps mean little from the military point of view, but would be a good psychological asset in today's world where the balance of power can be influenced by intangible and sometimes subtle things. Conjectures such as these are, of course, all academic speculations in retrospect!

The Cyprus Problem. The real cause of the breakdown of the Balkan Pact was the Cyprus problem. An island of 3,572 square miles, forty miles south of Turkey, and some seven hundred miles distant from Greece, it became the focal point of a new eruption of deep-rooted Turkish-Greek antagonism.

Acting as the spokesman for the Greek-speaking Cypriots, Greece demanded self-determination for them, this being at once

synonymous with a demand for Enosis or annexation of the island to
Greece. Although official Greek spokesmen are careful to stress self-
determination and not to mention Enosis, it was apparent that the
granting of self-determination to the Greek-speaking population would
immediately lead to annexation. In fact the password of the Greek
Cypriots has been 'Enosis' (union); self-determination has merely
served as the external propaganda instrument. In opposition to the
idea of annexation of Cyprus to Greece, Turkish arguments are based
on geographic, strategic, and humane considerations. But what made
the problem almost insoluble were the deep-rooted complexities of
Turkish-Greek relations.

Since their independence from Ottoman rule in 1823, the Greeks
have frequently been motivated by a combination of animosity
towards the Turks and a desire for territorial aggrandizement. They
have kept alive this antagonism and "Megali Idea," or the revival of
the old Byzantine Empire, has been the guiding light for Greek intellectuals and statesmen. Between 1890 and 1922 six aggressions
against Turkey were admittedly motivated by these factors.

Two great statesmen, Kemal Ataturk and Elefteros Venizelos,
achieved what was almost the impossible in the early 1930's by burying
intense animosity and bitter memories. Immediate problems between
the two countries were solved by bold and decisive measures, and the
new Turkish-Greek friendship served as the basis for the Balkan
Entente. The subsequent failure of the Entente was certainly no re-
flection in any way on the relations between the two countries. After
the Second World War, the new leaders of Turkey were ready to
follow up the achievements of Venizelos and Ataturk by once again
making an alliance between Turkey and Greece the foundation for a
more realistic Balkan Pact, even at the price of some concessions to
the Greek "philotimo" or vanity.

The new Foreign Minister of the Democratic government, Professor
Köprülü, advocated the passage of a bill giving fishing rights to
Greeks in Turkish territorial waters in the face of strong opposition in
the Turkish Parliament. Again, on the occasion of the 500th anni-
versary of the Conquest of Istanbul, the celebrations were toned down
by the government in order not to offend the feelings of the Greek
people.

But even by 1950 and 1951, the Greek government's conduct on the
Cyprus question was causing concern in Turkey. Agitation in Cyprus and demonstrations in Greece caused Mumtaz Faik Fenik, then
editor of the semi-official *Zafer* to write: "If there is any question of
changing the status quo of Cyprus and transferring the island to any

other country, the first such country that comes to mind is Turkey which has incontestable geographic and ethnic rights. Turkey wishes to cooperate with Greece in performing duties within the framework of the Mediterranean defense system, we do not desire to make an issue of the matter of Cyprus and hope that Greece will show the same spirit of understanding."

Although Köprülü, who was still striving to strengthen the Balkan cooperation during the early 1950's, had been insisting "there is no Cyprus issue," it was quite apparent by the beginning of 1954 that the Greek government had found an alternative to its internal troubles in the Cyprus question and was determined to bring it to an international head, notwithstanding NATO, and the Balkan Alliance of Friendship with Turkey. In May, 1954 Marshal Papagos, Premier of Greece, asked Britain to cede Cyprus by August 22nd or he would take the matter to the United Nations Assembly. In private, Turkey begged Greece to refrain from such action.

Reaction in Turkey stiffened in view of public demonstrations in Greece for Enosis, and the intention of the Greek government to take the issue to the UN. Editorially, *Zafer* again warned Greece to "act with foresight and prudence" with the reminder that "up to the present Turkey has been scrupulously careful and has remained faithful to its friendship and has retained its self-possession. . ." It went on to say: "The truth of the matter is this: preservation of peace and the prevention of friction in the Mediterranean will ensure Greece on matters of greater and more vital interest than Cyprus. But if this peace is disturbed and faith is shaken, no one can foretell what course events may take!"

Meanwhile the Turkish government was subjected to pressure by the public to allow public meetings and to adopt strong diplomatic measures. But on September 30, 1954, the Prime Minister, in explaining his resistance to these pressures, said: "There is no doubt that this sensitivity has been provoked by certain rashly made ostentatious moves and tumultuous meetings in Greece, our closest neighbor, friend and ally. It would be impossible to maintain that the attempts to hold meetings in Turkey are not fully justified from the viewpoint of retaliation, but if such moves in the friendly and allied country are deemed to be wrong, then it would be equally wrong to consider ourselves bound to commit the same errors. In the matter of Cyprus, we are convinced that the friendly and allied country of Greece will realize sooner or later the true significance of these moves that are cloaked in the mantle of religion and endeavor to make it appear that the aim is the reaction of national aspirations."

The Turkish government was acting with considerable restraint and was asking for the same degree of restraint from Greece and from her own worried people. This restraint on the part of the Turkish leaders, however, was later to be interpreted as lack of interest in the future of Cyprus.

It soon became evident that the Greek government would not heed the cautious advice of Turkish leaders; perhaps it was not its own master. The Greek representative at the UN presented a formal request on August 20, 1954 for inclusion in the General Assembly Agenda of an item entitled "Application Under the Auspices of the UN of the Principle of Equal Rights and Self-determination of the People in the Case of the Population of the Island of Cyprus." Despite the opposition of the British and Turkish representatives, the item was included in the agenda.

At the First Committee meeting (the Political and Security Committee), and later at the plenary session, a resolution was adopted to the effect that "for the time being it does not appear appropriate to adopt a resolution on the question of Cyprus." On June 30, 1955, Sir Anthony Eden invited Turkey and Greece to attend a tripartite conference in London on "political and defense questions which effect the Eastern Mediterranean, including Cyprus." The meeting opened on August 29th and was suspended on September 7th without having reached a solution on Cyprus.

In the meantime, on September 6th and 7th, grave incidents took place in Istanbul and Izmir. A false report to the effect that Ataturk's birthplace in Salonika was destroyed by a bomb transformed a peaceful meeting in Istanbul on the Cyprus question into a mob rioting against the Greek minority both in that city and in Izmir. This incident in effect marked the end of Turkish-Greek friendship and the Balkan Pact. Although the Turkish government apologized for the "deplorable" incidents and took immediate measures to pay compensation, Greece was reluctant to accept a rapprochement. These happenings, however, showed that the Turkish people were indeed vitally and seriously concerned with the fate of Cyprus.

The Greeks assert historical claims to Cyprus by mentioning the "birth of Venus" on this island, and quotations from Aeschylus's *Suppliant Women* and *Homer*. They also allude to the conquests of the Byzantines as a basis for their claims. The Turks, however, argue that these historical ties, if any, are too remote and too romantic, whereas their own historical connection is more recent and still very much in evidence.

After three hundred years of rule, the Ottoman Empire entrusted the *administration* of the island to Great Britain by a treaty signed in Istanbul in 1878. This was done as a measure of common defense against probable aggression by the Tsarist Empire.[4] By the Lausanne Treaty of 1923, however, *sovereignty* of the island was transferred to Great Britain and Cyprus became a Crown Colony.

An official memorandum of the Turkish government states that "even in the most remote times Cyprus never belonged to Greece . . ." but that, "by going back a reasonable time in the past we see that Turkey was the only power to which Cyprus belonged."

Pan-Hellenic agitation motivated by "Megali Idea" started in the late nineteenth century in Cyprus. Behind this agitation, as behind all the Pan-Hellenic movement, was the Greek Orthodox Church and the Ethnarch of the time, Archbishop Cyprianus. The Archbishop, making full use of his position as the titular head of the autonomous "Greek Millet," was like his successor, several times removed, Makarios, fostering in the minds of the Cypriots, Enosis or Union with Greece.

In 1912 and again in 1915, the British Government offered Cyprus to Greece as an inducement to join the Allies. The offer was refused by the Greek Government of Premier Zaimis (and subsequently in October 25, 1915 cancelled by the British). But that offer has been one of the main arguments of the Enosis movement ever since.

The first serious uprisings by the Enosis movement took place in 1931, but it was not until the election of Makarios in 1950 as the new archbishop, to replace Cyril III, that organized and calculated agitation started against British rule. The Orthodox Church conducted a "plebiscite" and announced that 211,000 of the 215,000 voters had voted for union with Greece. Makarios also visited the United Nations at New York in 1950 to agitate for Enosis. In the meantime, the Greek government and its propaganda organs intensified their campaign for Enosis. A terrorist organization known as EOKA under a retired Greek colonel, Grivas, increased its activities against the "collaborationist" Greeks and security forces. The main aim of the EOKA at the time seemed to be to intimidate the Greek population into adhering to the cause of Enosis.

Communists on the island (who are numerous and influential in local government) were supporting actively the Enosis movement, and the Soviet radio and press were endorsing them. It was an excellent opportunity for the Communists to disrupt the cooperation between Greece and Turkey and Britain. While the Greek appeal for self-determination is emotional, and sentimental, the Turkish appeal is to reason and their arguments are based on strategy, survival, and security for all those most closely concerned.

Turkey tried to avoid making an issue of the Cyprus question, but when it became apparent that the Greek leaders could not and would not listen to reason, Turkey pointed out that she would never accept a change in the status quo of the Island which was inimical to her interests. If Cyprus were to change hands, it should revert back to its previous owner—Turkey. Notwithstanding this strong feeling Turkey was, however, always willing to use tripartite negotiations in an effort to reach a solution—even after the government announced that partition[5] of the island was the only answer to a far from simple problem.

Turkey's reasoning regarding the Cyprus situation has always been the same; primarily, she draws attention to its geographical proximity to Turkey. As it is only forty-three miles from her southern coast, it is of vital strategic importance for her defense. In addition, this proximity makes the island almost an integral part of Anatolia. On the other hand, Greece is 683 miles from Cyprus.

In September 1955, Turkish Foreign Minister Zorlu explained the importance of Cyprus in the defense of Turkey:

"I would like to add here that Cyprus must of necessity, from the military point of view, belong to Turkey or to a country which is as closely interested as Turkey in the fate of Eastern countries in the vicinity of Turkey. That is to say, if Turkey, or one of the countries of the Middle East which is bound to Turkey by military commitments, should be involved in a war Cyprus too should be at war as an ally. The defense and the logistics of this area cannot be conceived otherwise. In case of war, outside assistance to the war potential of Turkey can only come through her western and southern ports in the Mediterranean. The western ports of Turkey are unfortunately within the effective operations area of the potential enemy and Turkey at war can only be supplied through her southern ports. The Second World War made this situation quite clear.

"It is with that in mind that the whole system of infrastructure which will supply Turkey has been given its bases in Turkish ports like Antalya, Mersin and Iskenderun; even the fuel supply of Istanbul is provided by a pipeline starting in the southern ports. And all these southwestern ports are under cover of the Island of Cyprus. Whoever controls this island is in a position to control these Turkish ports."

This concern over encirclement has even deeper roots. Since 1829, the Turks had been wary of Greek imperialism, and their ambitions to recreate Byzantium. The Greek Orthodox Church, in inciting the

Greek Revolution of 1829, used the symbols of Byzantium and the recreation of the Byzantine Empire as the ultimate ideal of Greek revolution and nationalism. And, indeed Greece had taken many other steps toward this ideal.

In 1864 Greece took over the Ionian Islands. In 1878, they seized the opportunity of the Russo-Turkish war to take Epirus. In 1913, after the Balkan War she annexed Southern Macedonia and most of the islands in the Aegean Sea. Also in 1913, she assumed sovereignty over Crete. In 1919, Greece attempted to reach the ultimate goal by occupying Anatolia. In 1945, after the Second World War, the Dodecanese Islands were given to Greece.

In August 1955 Turkish Prime Minister Menderes was forced, after it had become clear that Greek ambitions could not be restrained, to point out the extent of their ambitions: "Was it the principle of majority rights which took them to the gates of Ankara in 1922?" he asked. "Greek irredentism is at the root of our present troubles. . ."

Turks wondered whether it was not conceivable that Greece might not one day go Communist, or at least neutralist, in view of the recent rise of leftist parties in the last Greek general elections. A Cyprus in the hands of a Revisionist or Communist, leftist or neutralist Greece would greatly jeopardize Turkey's security. Zorlu has said, "No country should be allowed to leave her entire security at the mercy of any one country, no matter how great a friend and ally that country may be at the time."

Self Determination. The Turks have countered the main argument of the Greeks—namely, self-determination in Cyprus—with several arguments of their own. First, they point out that this is "a transparent guise for Enosis and Megali Idea." They contended that lofty and noble as the ideal of self-determination may be, there were cases where it is "naturally limited or outweighed by other important factors such as geography, history or strategy." They recall that the Aaland Islands, where the majority of the population is Swedish, were awarded to Finland by the League of Nations, due to strategic considerations. Also, Western Thrace was awarded to Greece, although the majority there was Turkish.

Moreover, they argued that the principle of self-determination is applicable to nations as a whole and not to "pocket majorities" such as in Cyprus. If it were to be applied to such majorities, abuses would result. They also maintain that if self-determination for the majority should result in the oppression of the minority, as would be the case in Cyprus where it would not mean liberty for the Turkish population but subservience, they would disapprove highly.

The Turkish delegate to the UN, Ambassador Seyfullah Esin, has elaborated this point of view:

"The Greek contention is well known: relying on their present greater number on the island, they are asking for the application of self-determination to Cyprus as a single unit. In return, we point out that the principle of self-determination cannot be applied to a *territory* but only to *peoples* living there. After all, self-determination is one of the most fundamental *human* rights, and its equal application to the two peoples of Cyprus as separate units would be wholly in conformity with the letter and spirit of the Charter of the United Nations, which enumerates among its purposes the following: 'To develop friendly relations among nations based on respect for the principle of *equal rights* and self-determination of peoples.'

"Just as the Greek Cypriots desire to be liberated from foreign rule in order to live under the Greek flag, so do the Turks of Cyprus wish to be freed of alien rule and live under the Turkish flag."

Turkish Population on Cyprus. One of the major factors in the Cyprus question has been the fate of the Turkish population on the island. The ratio of Turkish population on the island, which was fifty percent of the total in the nineteenth century, has declined due to emigration to Anatolia, whereas Greek immigration to Cyprus took place. Today the ratio is about eighteen percent Turkish to eighty Greek, with two percent peoples of other nationality or origin.

Turks contend that the Turkish minorities in Greece, or under Greek domination, have always suffered from open or subtle oppression. They point out that the Turkish population on Crete, which once amounted to 200,000 compared to 60,000 Greeks in 1760, had been decimated by 1913. They also argue that the Turkish population in western Thrace and in the Dodecanese are constantly being subjected to subtle but evident pressures and are being forced to emigrate. They were therefore afraid that annexation of Cyprus to Greece, or even a Greek self-government on the Island, would oppress the Turkish population there.

Lausanne Treaty and Cyprus. Greece contended that by signing the Lausanne Treaty in 1923, which among other things established the status of Cyprus as a British Colony, Turkey relinquished all her rights to the island.

The Turks point out that it was Turkey who relinquished her rights on Cyprus—not unequivocally but with certain conditions and in return for certain implied and written guarantees within the context of the Treaty, which was also signed by Greece. Basically, Turkey was then agreeing to give up Cyprus with the knowledge and guarantee that the Island would remain under British rule as a guarantee against possible Russian aggression (a threat which existed in 1923 as it is today for Turkey). In fact it was for this same reason that Cyprus was first turned over to Britain in 1876. Any change in the status of Cyprus would be tantamount, according to Turkey, to an Amendment of the Lausanne Treaty, and to disregard any portion of that Treaty (on a unilateral basis) would disrupt the delicate balance it established between Turkey and Great Britain and Turkey and Greece, and would create new revisionist problems.

An official Turkish publication pointed out that "tampering with the Lausanne Treaty would entitle Turkey not only to insist that Cyprus revert to the status it held prior to the date when she waived her rights in favor of Great Britain, but also to put forward certain other demands which in obedience to the Lausanne Treaty, she has hitherto refrained from making." Turkey maintained that any change in the treaty, including any change concerning Cyprus, can only be effected through negotiations and agreement between the signatories of the Treaty.

Greece refused direct negotiations with Turkey or Great Britain, or NATO's good offices. After the London Conference of 1955 it brought the matter to UN attention at each General Assembly session.

At the London Conference the British Government, taking into consideration the "close interest of the governments of Greece and Turkey, naturally took in the welfare of the Greek and Turkish communities in Cyprus," proposed several constitutional reforms: A new and liberal constitution leading to the fullest measure of internal self-government "compatable with the strategical requirements of the present international situation" was to be introduced. An assembly with an elected majority and proportional quota of seats reserved for the Turkish community would be established. Defense, foreign affairs, and security would be in the government's hands but other departments of government would be transferred to a Cypriot minister. Unfortunately, however, the London Conference was suspended without an agreement.

At a United Nations session in 1957 an Indian draft resolution called for negotiations among interested parties, but Greece maintained that Turkey, by virtue of the Lausanne Treaty, is not an interested party and refused tripartite negotiations.

In the meantime, the terrorism and Archbishop Makarios' reluctance to condemn and help stop the tragedy led to the banishment of the prelate to the Seychelles on March 12, 1956.

EOKA terrorism was at first aimed against the Greek "collaborators" and the members of the security forces. But later many of the attacks were made on civilian Turks. In the three years up to June 1958, ninety-six British, fourteen Turks, and one hundred and fifty-one Greeks were killed. In the month of July 1958 forty-four Turks were murdered. This provoked retaliations and counter-attacks by the Turks against the Greeks, and tension between the two communities reached a climax. This situation strengthened Turkish belief that the co-existance of the two communities is impossible. They maintained that the only lasting solution would be partition of the Island.

The Macmillan Plan was the major constitutional project since the abandonment of the Radcliffe proposals.[6]

This plan, which Mr. Macmillan termed as an "Adventure in Partnership," called for two legislatures to govern the community affairs in Cyprus, one Greek and the other Turkish. Internal affairs beyond the scope of the community level would be under the authority of a council composed of the British governor, one representative each from the Greek and Turkish Government, four members of the Greek Legislature and two members of the Turkish Legislature.

External affairs would be the province of the British governor acting in collaboration with representatives of the Greek and Turkish Governments. Cypriots would be given dual citizenship, either British and Greek, or British and Turkish.

The proposal implied that eventually Britain, Greece, and Turkey would share the sovereignty over the island.

The plan would be for seven years, during which time there would be no change in the international status of the Island. At the end of seven years, a final settlement of the status would be made, if partnership had not worked satisfactorily.

After the disclosure of the British plan, Turkey made these points:

"1. The British Plan, by acknowledging the necessity of the presence of Turkish and Greek representatives in the administration of the Island, has correctly evaluated the present realities and has reaffirmed Turkey's right to an interest in Cyprus.

"2. The British Plan does not purport to contain a final solution and therefore does not bar the principle of partition (which was actually first suggested by Sir Lennox Boyd in December, 1956) as the ultimate solution.

"Turkey believes that partition is the only possible permanent solution, but she also maintains that fusion of the principle of partition with the principle of partnership advanced by the British is quite possible through patient, serious, and sincere negotiations.

"3. The Turkish government, with the maximum of conciliatory spirit, believes it is necessary, with the shortest possible delay, to hold a conference at the highest level among the three parties concerned with a view to finding a solution to the Cyprus problem and to accept the British plan as a conference paper."

In his letter to the British Prime Minister after the announcement of the British plan, Mr. Menderes said: "The solution is becoming increasingly grave. We are therefore convinced that it is now time to find a final solution to this problem by generally adopting the ideas of partition which is the most equitable, just, moderate, and practical solution. It is also certain that the various other solutions which have been put forward are not such that they would cause less disturbance on the Island, or bring about peace, calm and stability in Cyprus more speedily.'

Solution? In the beginning of August, 1958, the British Prime Minister appealed to the heads of the Turkish and Greek governments and to the Turkish and Greek communities on Cyprus to use their influence to end the terrorism.

The Turkish Prime Minister immediately responded to this appeal and expressed his government's opposition to violence. But he pointed out that the Turks on Cyprus had endured for several years a situation where their lives and property were in danger. The Turks had used their "legitimate right of self defense" only in the recent months, because terrorism had increased and was now mainly aimed at the Turks.

At the beginning of August 1958, British Prime Minister Macmillan unexpectedly visited Athenes, Ankara and Nicosia in order to pursuade the Greek and Turkish governments and the Cypriot leaders, to go along with his plan. Both the Greek government and Archbishop Makarios were adamant in their refusal. The Turkish government continued its insistence on the principle of partition and again pointed out that the "idea of partition was not irreconcilable with the principle of partnership." It was ready, however, to enter into tripartite negotiations.

After his trip, Macmillan announced that the British government would go ahead with its plan. The Turkish government announced its decision to participate in this "partnership" arrangement, without, however, prejudicing her determination on "partition." Mr. Zorlu explained that, according to his government, the British plan did not constitute an "ideal solution," but that it offered the advantage of at least "preparing the ground for cooperation among the communities and the governments which are concerned with the Cyprus question." The plan went into effect on October 1, 1958 and a Turkish representative appointed by Ankara assumed his duties under the arrangement, in Nicosia. But Greek opposition and terrorism continued: both the Athens government and Greek Cypriots were determined to sabotage the "partnership plan."

While acts of violence continued on the once peaceful island, the matter was brought to the Permanent council of the NATO, by the General Secretary of the organization, Paul Henri Spaak. Council discussions and consulations throughout October once again gave rise to hopes in the western press that a solution acceptable to all the interested parties might yet be reached.

But these mediation efforts within the N.A.T.O. were not successful; nor was a solution reached during the 12th Session of the United Nations General Assembly in 1958. A resolution adopted by that body merely called for the continuation of the negotiations between the interested parties.

There was, however, a *tour de force* in the situation at the beginning of 1959, which a journalist aptly termed as 'miraculous.' It became increasingly apparent to the leaders of Turkey and Greece that a solution could never be reached if public emotions in both countries and on Cyprus were allowed to dominate the scene. Developments in world affairs, especially in the Middle East, were daily emphasizing the extent of communist threat. Both this threat and economic and financial polarization in Western Europe made it imperative that Greece and Turkey hold together and enter once again into vigorous economic and political cooperation. What Ataturk and Venizelos had realized decades ago had now become a stark necessity.

The main gap between the two countries was, of course, the Cyprus dispute. Although it was true that since 1954 the gap had considerably widened and that the progress made in cooperation and friendship since the 1930's was virtually lost, the statesmen of the two countries showed the courage and imaginativeness of trying once again. As important as the Cyprus question was to the two countries both emotionally and practically, mutual interests and potential benefits of closer cooperation transcended them and statesmen of these countries realized this. In effect, close cooperation would provide for both Turkey and Greece the benefits they sought by their respective positions and would eliminate the dangers they believed an unfavorable solution would bring about.

All along Turkish leaders had taken this broad view and had urged it on their Greek counterparts until the matter lost all its perspective in a wave of emotionalism and terror. Not until the beginning of 1959 was there a "miraculous" return to reason.

Away from the propaganda rostrum of the United Nations and aroused crowds, Turkish and Greek statesmen resorted to the methods of sober diplomacy. Talks between Turkish Foreign Minister Zorlu and the Greek Ambassador to Ankara led to meetings between Zorlu and Greek Foreign Minister Averoff-Tozitsaz in Paris early in 1959. These in turn led unexpectedly to a meeting in Zurich between Turkish Prime Minister Adnan Menderes and Greek Prime Minister Karamanlis during the first week of February.

It was announced at the end of these meetings that an agreement for the future of Cyprus was reached. The Island would become an independent Republic with constitutional and military guarantees barring union with Greece on the one hand and partition on the other and securing the rights of the Greek and Turkish communities. Moreover, a joint Greek-Turkish military garrison would insure Turkey against any threats which might develop toward her southern approaches and preservation of British bases would be an additional guarantee for the NATO defense system. Details of a formal agreement concerning these matters as of the new Constitution of the island were to be worked out in a conference of representatives of Turkey, Greece, and Great Britain with the participation of leaders of Cypriot communities.

Although this solution of the Cyprus problem does not involve any basic sacrifice for Greece or Turkey, its benefits and potentials are enormous. These countries can now devote their efforts to mutual interests and cooperation, and, as an American writer has pointed out, "the accord on the future of Cyprus may well be the crucial first step toward an eventual political union of Greece and Turkey."

CHAPTER VIII

TURKEY IN THE MIDDLE EAST

After the failure of his post-war gambles in Greece, Turkey and Iran Stalin did not attempt a direct encroachment in the area during the remainder of his lifetime. Until his death in 1953 Soviet-Turkish relations remained basically unchanged, but there were, nevertheless, strong protest notes, with implied threats, from time to time. The Soviet press and radio continued their denunciations of the Turkish government and on several occasions indirect pressure was brought to bear on Ankara. In August 1950 Bulgaria's government coerced 250,-000 persons of Turkish origin into a mass exodus into Turkey. This was in contravention to the 1925 agreement between Bulgaria and Turkey to regulate immigration. There is little doubt that this Moscow-engineered move was designed to disrupt the Turkish economy and to distract the attention of the nation's leaders at a crucial time when Turkey was seeking to enter the N.A.T.O. and when Ankara had decided to send troops to Korea.

Protesting strongly against Bulgaria, Turkey appealed to the United Nations. On October 7, 1950, she was obliged to close her frontier adjoining Bulgaria; Communist agents were being infiltrated into Turkey among the refugees and there was no way of screening them. By the time a new agreement established quotas of emigration in late 1951 hundreds of thousands of refugees had suffered from forced expropriation, exposure and hunger. Only resolute measures by the government alleviated these sufferings to some degree and prevented large scale economic havoc.

Along with threatening notes, moves of indirect pressure and press and radio denunciations, the Soviet government also attempted some thinly disguised peace offensives. These were feeble and half-hearted when Stalin was alive: they were designed mainly to pressure the status quo in the Middle East while he was busy elsewhere in the world. After his death one of the first actions of the new leaders was to withdraw the demands made in 1945 in an official note sent to Ankara in July 1953. It was openly hinted that the Turkish-Soviet "misunderstandings" were all the fault of Stalin and now that he was dead and gone, a profitable new era of relations could be initiated. Knowing that Turkey was going through difficulties and that there was a shortage of capital goods, they offered their economic cooperation and urged Turkey to take a course "similar to the one during the War of Independence." They made several proposals—either directly or through Poland, Hungary and Czechoslovakia—for technical and financial aid for establishment of new industrial plants and offered long-term credits with "no strings attached."

Since Turkey was having considerable difficulty in obtaining such aid and credits from her Western allies, these offers were very tempting. Some newspapers even suggested that these offers should be accepted since the West was indifferent to Turkey's troubles. But the nation's leaders knew what kind of influence Russia's seemingly "stringless" offers would ultimately entail. They realized that the "New Look" of Soviet policy towards Turkey and the Middle East was in reality a new tactic that could not obliterate the permanent objectives of Russia in that region. They therefore concentrated their efforts on warning their allies and neighbors of the imminent dangers and on forging a collective security chain in that area.

Russian Interest in the Middle East. Russian aspirations in the Middle East and in the Mediterranean are not new. From the days of the Tsars, the Russians have considered the Balkans, as well as the "area to the South of Baku and Batum in the general direction of the Persian Gulf," their sphere of influence, or as they put it, "as the center of their aspirations." Their constant struggle for the control of the Turkish Straits and for "reaching the Mediterranean" was a part of these aspirations. Control of the Middle East and free access to the open sea would have given the Tsars definite advantages in the world balance of power. With the beginning of the oil era, however, Middle East assumed a greater and more vital importance in the world affairs. As the Western Powers became more and more dependent on the oil wells, pipe-lines of the region and the Suez Canal Communist leaders in the Kremlin realized that if they controlled the Middle East or gained influence there, they would have a stronghold on the West. Furthermore, although Russia had adequate oil resources and reserves to satisfy her present needs of fuel, it was conceivable in the long-run, that she might in the future require the Middle East oil for the growing needs of her industry and armed forces.

Parallel to these "offensive" aspirations, Russia has also certain defensive motives and calculations in the area. After the Revolution new leaders have been extremely suspicious of Western attempts of encirclement of Russia; they have consequently tried to prevent the formation of "hostile" blocs and establishment of foreign bases in the Middle East.

But whatever the motivations—offensive or defensive—and what-

ever the time—pre-oil or post-oil—the reality of Russian aspirations
in the Middle East has remained constant.

Changes in Tactics. Both the Tsarist and communist governments
have used a variety of tactics in their Middle Eastern policies. Immediate aim has been, of course, to control or dominate the Ottoman
or Turkish governments and, through this, control the Straits. They
attempted several times to make alliances which would put them in
the role of the "protector" of Turkey. They used subversive methods.
The Tsars tried to provoke the minorities against the Ottoman Empire and acted as the self-appointed champions of Christian minorities and especially of the Armenians and of the Greek Orthodox
Church.[1] Their various interventions for the protection of these minorities and of the Holy Places in Palestine, for example, were all parts
of the general plan to get a foothold in the Middle East. These intrigues, however, were frustrated by Ottoman statesmen and by the
British who did not want Russia to threaten their Empire's life-lines.

As we have already pointed out elsewhere in this book Tsarist Russia came very close to her aspirations when the Allies, in an unex-
plicable move immediately before the First World War, signed secret
protocols agreeing to Russian occupation of the Straits. The leaders
of the Soviet Revolution were quick to renounce and denounce these
secret agreements and all other expansionist schemes. Nevertheless
Russia's active interest in the area remained; to the factors motivat-
ing this interest was now added the phobia of encirclement, and oil.

In the Communist era Middle East tactics changed from time to
time and there were discrepancies between doctrinaire Communist
thinking about the area and Government actions and declarations.
While Lenin's Foreign Affairs Commisar Chicherin was negotiating
treaties with the national governments in Turkey, Iran and Afghanistan, Zinoniev's Comintern was organizing the 1920 Baku Conference
to urge the peoples of the East to wage prolaterian war against Western imperialists and bourgeois governments. The Comintern and the
Communist Party Congresses had reached a "doctrinaire decision"
that although temporary collaboration between Russia and national
"bourgeois" governments and movements was possible and feasible, the
main aim would be to prepare the revolutionary prolaterian movements in all countries and especially in the Middle East. So while
the Soviet Government made friendly declarations and extended aid
to Turkey, Iran and Afghanistan, GPU agents and the agents of the
Comintern were attempting to infiltrate and subvert these countries.

When Stalin consolidated his power after the death of Lenin, he
rejected the "world revolution" thesis of Trotsky. His aim would be

the fulfilment of socialism in Russia first as a base for Russian nationalism and imperialism. Thus, until he prepared this base, Stalin resorted to "peaceful co-existence" especially with his neighbors. He and his Foreign Affairs Commissar Litvinov pursued a policy of strengthening the collective security arrangements. But Stalin was careful to retain his influence on neighboring Middle Eastern countries by signing treaties with them and by preventing treaties which might be against his interests. Russia allowed the signing of Balkan and Saadabad Pacts in 1934 and 1937 because the signatories, mindful of Stalin's suspicions, were careful to make it clear that the alliances were in no way intended against Soviet Russia. But throughout the period preceding the Second World War, Stalin's agents remained active in the Middle East preparing the apparatus of subversion which he aimed to use when the time came.

Tactics again changed when Stalin realized that the collective security arrangements and "co-existence" treaties in Europe and in the Middle East were not enough to check the Nazi expansion. In order to defend Soviet Russia and in order to attain his objectives, Stalin felt it was necessary for him to come to terms with Hitler and divide spheres of influence with him. Litvinov went out and with the appointment of Molotov as the new Minister of Foreign Affairs this new line of thinking was ushered in. The Soviet-German Pact of 1939 was the result.

Hitler was ready to accept, at least for a time, the "Area south of Soviet Russia in the general direction of Persian Gulf" as the Soviet sphere of influence but wanted to control the Balkans and Turkey. Stalin, realized that without the control of the Balkans, Turkey and the Straits, his sphere of influence would be in constant jeopardy. He insisted on also having the Balkans and the Straits. This was the breaking point of Nazi-Soviet "friendship."

After the German attack in 1941, Stalin sought to gain Western acceptance for her sphere of influence in Turkey and the Middle East. He had already taken over the Balkans by default and he diplomatically did not mention the rest of the Middle East in order not to arouse western suspicions. He would be satisfied with the control of Turkey for the time being. In the meanwhile the seeds of Soviet influence were being sown throughout Middle East. While Soviet Russia established diplomatic relations with Egypt and some other countries in the Middle East; her agents were covertly working full time.

Stalin's Offensive and Failure. Stalin's open offensive in the Middle East started soon after the War, in conjunction with his thrusts into Southeastern Europe, Balkans and Eastern Europe. Elsewhere in this book we have attempted to show how this offensive failed in face of Turkish, Greek and United States determination. In Iran, the seperatist movement which had been prepared in the northern part of the country by the Soviet occupation forces during the War, was crushed by a combination of Iranian determination and Western indignancy.

Then, for a time, Stalin was surprisingly indifferent towards the Middle East. Although he quickly recognized the new state of Israel, he did not take any great interest in the Arab-Israeli struggle. One theory is that he did not want to invite further American interest and intervention in the area. Continuation of British influence with its colonial or semi-colonial character or at least memories, would hasten an Arab erruption and possible Russian interference.

Stalin realized that in failing in his attempts he had not only lost the chance of getting a foothold in the Middle East but had invited Western alliances and Western military power to her own doorstep. A thing which he had tried to prevent before the War was now a reality due to his miscalculations. He did not want to take a new chance, thereby causing a tightening of the Western grip on the Middle East.

His successors were confronted by a formidable challenge of the Middle Eastern legacy of Stalin. They realized that it was imperative to eliminate the growth of alliances designed against Russia and also to seek a foothold in the Middle East. The perpetuating mistakes and wrong policies of the Western Powers in the region and the rampant Arab Nationalism gave them an excellent new opportunity. To step into the smoldering Middle Eastern arena as the champions of wronged Arabs would be the new look in the age-old Russian aspirations in the region.

The Arab Nationalism. Arab nationalism is by no means a new movement, nor can it be traced to a single root. There was a patriotic movement in Syria towards the end of the nineteenth century which sought autonomy for the Arabs within the Ottoman Empire. A nationalistic movement with religious overtones had started in Egypt during the same period.

In other Arab countries too patriotic intellegentsia movements seeking autonomy or complete independence flourished by the beginning of the present century. Contact with the West, American missionaries, Western educational institutions as well as British and French agents played an important role in inspiring and encouraging these early Arab nationalists.

But although there was a sense of kinship among the higher strata of various Arab countries, a deep and broad national consciousness did not develop—and it could not very well develop because there was no cultural and even ethnic homogeneity among Arabs, for example between the Lebanese and the Egyptian or the Palestinian Arab and the Saudi Arabian.

Thus in the beginning the Arab Nationalism or rather *nationalisms* were in a nebulous, undefined and unorientated stage. *Nationalisms* involved hatred of foreigners (especially of the Ottoman Turks) ;[2] a desire for liberation and perhaps an undefined, vague aspiration for Arab unity.

The Arab Revolt during the First World War, although sparked by these nebulous ideas of Arab nationalism was not a movement of Arab national consciousness and it, by no stretch of imagination, involved the Arab masses. Many Arabs in Egypt, Palestine and North Africa opposed this revolt which they considered as a collusion of Hashemite interests and British Gold provided by Lawrence of Arabia.

Britain inspired and supported this "Arab Revolt" of the Hashemite family of Hidjaz, because it would hasten the defeat of the Ottoman Empire and because she thought that the newly created Arab Kingdom might serve as a basis for British interests and influence after the disintegration of the Ottoman Empire. And indeed for a short-while after the end of the war, a Great Arab Kingdom comprising of Palestine, Syria, Jordan and Mesopotamia was established. However, this was very short lived; Britain had to sacrifice it for the sake of Western unity. During the war, she had signed the Sykes-Picot agreement promising Syria to France. France, in accordance with this agreement marched into Syria and drove the new King Faisal of the Kingdom of Damascus from his throne. Faisal was later given the Kingdom of Iraq as a consolation prize. In the meantime Ibn Saud, leader of the Vahabi sect and enemy of Hashemites, had gained control of most of the Arab Peninsula.

Thus instead of the Great Arab State, various small states were formed, mostly under British or French protectorate or mandate. Many of the leaders of the Arab Revolt were reconciled to this new situation and lost their Pan-Arabic aspirations. Their nationalism took a rather particularistic character, and they collaborated with their new French or British overlords. Arab liberation had not been achieved; Ottoman domination was simply replaced by Western domination. Why had the Arab patriots and nationalists accepted this new situation? Some of them saw no other way out and sought to make the best out of a temporary accomodation of the West until they

were strong enough to assert their independence.   Others became outright opportunists.   The whole system however proved to be the hot-
bed of the new Arab nationalism.

During the period between the two World Wars, dynastic and personal rivalries between the leaders of the Arab World made any hope
of Arab unity impossible.   Revival of the old idea of the Great Arab
State—the Kingdom of Syria—met with a strong opposition from Ibn
Saud and from Egypt.   Also, the ruling families of Lebanon and
Syria opposed it because it would be the end of their power.   The
creation in 1945 of the Arab League—a loose association of separate
national entities and not a Union—was pioneered by Egypt in order to
prevent the Greater Syria Scheme.

Britain realized, after the Second World War, that Arab Nationalism was rampant.   She was not ready to pull out her influence or her
troops but she sought to placate the nationalistic aspirations by supporting the unity schemes.   First she backed Nuri Said Pasha's and
Prince Abdul Illah's Greater Syria idea.   When she saw the opposition to it, she switched her support to the Arab League.   But the real
Arab Nationalism was developing outside the Arab League and outside the ruling circles.

There are many and complex factors involved in the development
of this new Arab nationalism.   The ideas and writings of early Arab
nationalists were certainly influential.   Islam was also a common factor in the movements in various countries and many nationalists were
religious fanatics but religion was not the guiding principle and one
cannot correctly term the Arab nationalism as an Islamic movement.
Islam has rather "provided much of the setting and scenery" as a
British author has observed.

At the source of the nationalism—or *nationalisms*—one main common factor was the attitude of the British and the French.   Though
there were shades of difference between their benevolence and exploitation they were unmistakably the dominating powers.   The Arab
Countries were outwardly free or autonomus but in reality they were
politically and economically controlled by leaders trusted by the foreign powers.[3]   And of course there were foreign troops, bases and
enclaves.   It is not difficult to see how young Nassers and Kassems
were humiliated and enraged by this situation and by the corruption
and opportunism of their leaders, who were supported by the Western
powers.

As the administration was formally in the hands of indigenous
leaders and as the British and French did very little to improve the
civil service and other public services, nationalism was barren and

negative; the nationalists would have no experience or foundation to build better systems of their own when and if they tore down the old corrupt administrations. In India, for instance, the British regime had provided these services and had trained excellent civil servants; consequently the nationalists had strong and sure grounds to build their own administration on. The hatred there against the British did not last very long after independence. Today even the most extremist nationalists in India and Pakistan are still thankful for the excellent administrative basis the British have left behind. But the Arab nationalists while hating their own rulers, nurtured a stronger hate for the "colonial" powers which supported and collaborated with these rulers—and this hate would continue as long as the shaky administrations remained. In these countries and in Iran, where British oil interests resorted to the same practices, it had become a habit to blame everything on the British and on the British agents.

The British and French persisted in these practices and evidently did not realize the growing inner tension of dangerous nationalism. For even after the war, the French were stubborn in not letting their hold on the Levant—Syria and Lebanon. Britain realized that refusal to give independence to the Arab countries would be dangerous and together with the United States forced De Gaulle to abandon the Levant, but she herself persisted in keeping her bases and troops and in dealing with corrupt semi-feudal regimes.

On top of all these ingredients of dangerous nationalism was added the State of Israel. No objective person can oppose the centuries-old aspirations of Jews to establish an independent and sovereign state, but it is also not difficult to see that such a state imposed amidst the Arabs by the Western powers would increase the hatred against the West.

Later, the humiliation of their defeat in the "first round" of their struggle with the new born state would further increase the bitterness against the West, and against their corrupt leaders who had mismanaged the war.

But Arab nationalism yearned for a hero and leader which would furnish a symbol and a direction. This role was foisted on Gamel Abdel Nasser, who captivated the Arab imagination by ousting a corrupt regime, by initiating social and economical reforms and by standing up against the British and the West. Perhaps, if it had not been for these pressures, Nasser could very well remain simply as an Egyptian nationalist and his movement would not assume a Pan-Arabic character and destination. However, the situation was beyond his control. As he puts it "a role wandering in search of a hero"—that is, Arab nationalism—had found a hero in him and was "beckoning to him, to move, to take up its line and to put on its costume. . ."

Arab nationalism, with all its volatility and extremism offered Communist Russia an excellent chance to get a foothold in the Middle East and choke the life-lines of the West. With its identification with Nasser, the Russian leaders found one single representative to deal with. For them there was no need for an immediate communist revolution in the Arab countries. Though this was never entirely barred out it was yet a long range operation. If there were to be open moves in that direction now, a sober nationalist resistance against communism could develop and benefit the West. Therefore the Soviet Leaders wisely relegated this to the far background (or to deep underground) and stressed cooperation with the Nationalists. They now profited from their experiences and mistakes in dealing with Turkish Nationalists in 1920's and 1930's; they were careful not to make the same mistakes and arouse suspicions. They could afford to wait until the West was completely pushed out and they were entrenched in a most favorable position Then the extremism and unstability of negative nationalism would by itself usher in the communist revolution.

Russians had several advantages in dealing with the Arabs. They had never been identified with the West even in the pre-revolution era. Arabs had never been confronted with the Russians and did not have bitter experiences concerning them. To the poor Arab, in spite of his Islamic religion, communism did not imply the negative connotations it implies even to the poorest Turk.

Russians, in spite of their suppression of Islam and bitter doctrinaire campaigns against it, were careful to utilize agents with Islamic background to influence the Arabs. They sent many pilgrims to Mecca every year from Turkestan, Kazan and Azerbeidjan, who by their mere presence and airs of prosperity, spoke well of the Soviet regime.

Turkish leaders saw all these dangers very clearly. Soviet influence in the Middle East was a danger threatening West's oil resources and supplies but for Turkey it meant encirclement and isolation. Turkey, therefore, was anxious to take the necessary psychological and military measures.

The Vacuum. Western Powers were anxious, especially since 1950 to create a barrier in the Middle East against a possible Soviet advance. But at that time they saw the problem exclusively as a military one. Strategists had certainly the defense of the vital oil sources in mind but they mainly considered the existing bases, especially the

Suez Canal Zone, as the hub of the defense system extending from the Balkans to Persia and even to India. Along with the Suez Canal Base which was the center of the hub, the bases on Cyprus and in Iraq and Jordan had to be occupied by their troops.

But Arab Nationalism was uncompromisingly opposed to the presence of foreign troops under old or new treaties. Even the old regimes which had so far accomodated the West, were finding it impossible to resist this growing public opposition. The bases in Iraq and Suez were clearly in danger. The Wafd government in Egypt, which had usually collaborated with the West started organizing guerilla activities against the British forces in the canal zone. In Iraq the government served notice that it would not renew her treaty with Britain.

With United States yet not quite involved with the problems of the area, Britain conceived the Middle East Defense Organization plan as a substitute for the old system of a network of British bases and bilateral arrangements. The organization would be sponsored by the United States, Great Britain, France and Turkey; the Middle Eastern countries would be invited to participate and offer their facilities in a "voluntary command cooperation." British originators of the plan thought that such a plan of voluntary cooperation would eliminate the stigma of foreign occupation and thus end the nationalist opposition to the bases. Turkey was included among the sponsors, because her strength, determination and geographical location would be essential to any such defense organization and also because, as a Moslem nation, her sponsorship might eliminate some of the suspicions.

The idea was first advanced in early 1950. At the time the British opposed Turkey's membership in the N.A.T.O.; they prefered to link Turkey to the Alliance through a similar Middle Eastern Alliance.

Turkey herself was opposed to this substitute for her membership in the Western Alliance. She considered herself an integral part of the West and not a mere outpost or tool in the Middle East. Furthermore, Turkish leaders had misgivings about the British plan which they though was ill conceived and ill timed. They knew that the mere label of "voluntary cooperation" did not change the fact that the scheme was Western sponsored and that foreign bases would remain. As long as the facts remained Arab Nationalism could never be reconciled to the idea.

But in spite of these misgivings, when Turkey was accepted into N.A.T.O. and the reason for the basic Turkish opposition was eliminated, Turkish leaders accepted to go along with the sponsorship. This was rather a gesture of "noblesse oblige" a Turkish writer remarked.

The proposal was officially made on October 13, 1951 by the sponsors to the governments of Egypt, Iraq, Israel, Lebanon, Saudi Arabia, Syria, Trans Jordan and Yemen. Egypt was invited to participate as a founding member on equal basis with the original sponsors. If she accepted Britain would agree to the abrogation of the 1936 treaty and to withdraw her forces "which would not come under the Allied Command." Egypt would contribute to the defense of the area with her physical facilities and would receive aid.

The Egyptian government, however, took only two days to reject the proposal. She not only rejected it, but the Egyptian Parliament adopted decrees denouncing the Treaties on Suez and Sudan.

Egypt's refusal made it difficult for countries like Iraq, Lebanon, Jordan and Saudi Arabia, whose rulers were inclined to accept a substitute for bilateral arrangements with Britain. But now that Egypt had openly branded the scheme as "imperialism" they did not dare adhere to the M.E.D.O.

The M.E.D.O. proposal served as a new excuse for the nationalists to increase their "Hate the West" campaign.

As the Turkish leaders had warned, the British plan proved to be based on a wrong and incomplete evaluation of the character and purposes of Arab Nationalism and its failure was to be expected. No Arab government could have accepted the proposals in face of this nationalism. The Soviet danger did not mean very much to the Arab world which was primarily concerned with the existence of foreign troops and with Israel. To the Arabs these were the real dangers.

It was now clear that a more subtle approach and more groundwork within the region itself was necessary before a realization of the Soviet danger and possible benefits of a common defense pact was impressed on the Arabs. More specifically it was necessary to allow the Arab leaders or the Middle East leaders to develop their own justifications for such a defense pact and their own line of reasoning for appeasing the nationalism. Evidently it could not be done overnight by Western sponsored proposals. This is where Turkey came in. Her leaders, with a deeper knowledge and understanding of the ways and feelings of their neighbors, were in a better position to devise and implement a new approach.

When the officers' plot of July 1952 brought a new set of leaders to the top in Egypt, both Britain and the United States entertained some hope that these officers (most were British trained) would see the necessity of a Middle East defense scheme. But General Naguib, who preceded Nasser, rejected the scheme because "it implied lack of confidence in Egypt." His explanatory remarks are perhaps responsible for continued hope in Egypt's adherence to a Western alliance: "We realize that nowadays no country can stand alone in the world. There are only three possible courses for free Egypt: to remain neutral and this is, at the very least, extremely difficult, if not impossible; to joint the Eastern bloc, which is out of question as we are not Communists; or join the West. It is our natural inclination to work with the West whose people we know."

When Nasser came to power, Western hopes continued and perhaps increased. Eden's chief object in wanting to conclude a treaty with Egypt for the evacuation of Suez Canal zone was to win Nasser over to the West. The U.S. government was quite enthusiastic about Nasser and, in fact it is not a secret that the American Ambassador in Cairo, Jefferson Cafferey, assumed the role of mediator during the Suez negotiations and urged the British to make concessions to Egyptian nationalism. But neither the Americans nor the British in urging these concessions or accepting them thought of tying Nasser to a specific commitment to join a Western alliance system.

There are those who argue that such an insistence would have made Suez agreement impossible. There are others, however, who maintain that United States missed the chance by not seeking at least a bilateral arrangement with Egypt. But even if Egypt, under duress, had agreed to join the West or sign an agreement with the United States, it would be in form only, without any intention of abiding by it. The spirit which would be necessary to make such arrangements work would not be there because Arab Nationalism was not capable of such a "spirit" where the West was concerned. The efforts of U.S. Ambassador Henry Byroade to win over Nasser and Dulles' visit to Cairo could not change the realities.

The Baghdad Pact. When U.S. Secretary of State John Foster Dulles first mentioned the concept of a "Northern Tier Alliance" during his visit to Ankara in May 1951 it was enthusiastically received by Turkish leaders. They had not favored the M.E.D.O. concept because of its outright Western sponsorship, but they had not stopped seeking for an effective, spontaneous collective security system covering their eastern flank. This would be the nucleus of an alliance which would grow and also bring in stronger United States commitments and more United States aid to the region.

Dulles reasoned that, rather than a Western imposed alliance to bring together countries which are far and oblivious to the Russian danger, and alliance of "Northern Tier" countries—Turkey, Iraq, Iran, and Pakistan—would be more practicable and feasible. He outlined his new approach in the following words:

"A Middle East Defense Organization is a future rather than an immediate possibility. Many of the Arab countries are so engrossed with their quarrels that they pay little heed to the menace of Soviet Communism. However there is more concern where the Soviet Union is near. In general, the Northern tier of nations shows awareness of this danger.

"There is a vague desire to have a collective security system, but no such system can be imposed from without. It should be designed and grow from within, out of sense of common destiny and common danger. While awaiting the formal creation of a security association, the United States can usefully help strengthen the interrelated defense of those countries which want strength, not as against each other or the West, but to resist the common threat of all free peoples. ."

As the new defense concept had to "grow from within" the main effort obviously was to be made by Turkey and the Turkish leaders lost no time in embarking on a new course in the Middle East.

The Beginnings. The first seed of the Alliance had already been sown by the signing of the Turkish-Pakistan Treaty of Friendship on 26 July 1951. This was followed, on April 2nd 1954, by a new Turkish-Pakistan treaty of Friendship and Cooperation for Security. This was not exactly a military alliance but it provided the foundation for closer military cooperation and planning between the two countries.[4] But obviously, without Iraq, a link in the chain was very much missing.

Turkey's active efforts to win over Iraq and the other Arab countries to the West, marked an important change in her attitude in the Middle East. The modern Turkish Republic had literally turned its back to the East, in its zeal for Westernization. While this was a cultural and psychological attitude, it had reflected heavily on Turkey's foreign relations with her Eastern neighbors.

Turks, desirous of becoming a Western nation and remembering their disappointments concerning especially the Arab countries, repeated their old proverb "Neither all the candy from Damascus, nor the face of the Arab" and stayed aloof from the region. This irked the Arabs and Iranians.

The Mousul and Hatay problems in 1929 and 1937 did not stem from any irredentist tendencies on the part of Turkey, as we have already tried to point out in an earlier chapter. Turkey claimed these areas because of their predominant Turkish populations and because of strategic and economic considerations; she certainly did not have any intention of reviving the Ottoman Empire. But the Arabs became suspicious and it is unfortunate that Britain and

France provoked the suspicions and sought to divert the Arab nationalistic furor against Turkey.

Saadabad Pact of 1937 was born chiefly of Ataturk's realization that Turkey could not forever remain indifferent towards her Eastern neighbors and should pioneer an alliance to link them to the West. But his successor Ismet Inönü wanted no entanglements in the Middle East and throughout his leadership Turkey kept aloof from the momentous developments in the Middle East.

The Inonu governments, emphasizing that Turkey was a Western nation and perhaps neglecting the geographic and strategic realities, made no effort to prepare the ground culturally and psychologically for a better understanding and cooperation with the Arabs and Iranians.

Turkey voted against the partition of Palestine but once Israel was established she became the first country in the Middle East to recognize the new state on March 29, 1949 as if to emphasize her Westerness and objective attitude in the area.[5]

Even when pro-Western and pro-Turkish Colonel Husnu Zaim came to power in Syria and openly sought closer relations with Turkey, the Turkish government remained more or less indifferent. A Turkish Military Mission under General Kazim Orbay was sent to Damascus, to modernize the Syrian Army, but the effort was half-hearted and Zaim's fall could not be prevented.

The new leaders were aware of all this back-log in Turkish-Middle East relations but were also convinced that Turkey could no longer avoid her role in creating a Middle Eastern defensive alliance and in linking the Middle East with the West. They well knew the popular feelings in especially the Arab countries; they realized also that even the leaders with pro-Western inclinations could not buck these extremist aspirations and that their positions were shaky. There was also a basic difference between the outlooks of these leaders and of the Turks. To them, the Soviet danger was of secondary importance. They were inclined towards a Western alliance primarily because of its potential material benefits—because of military and economic aid it might entail and because it might bring strong United States commitments into the area.

The Turkish leaders, however, reasoned that if a start was made and the foundations laid, the evident benefits of a pact might be realized by the public and by the other peoples of the area. It might thus eventually gain a wider public support and attract additional members. Especially if an Arab country was to join the Alliance this would be a crack in the anti-Western Arab unity and might, in time, start a pro-Western shift among the Arabs.

Iraq offered the best possibilities. There too was a strong nationalist movement which had risen against the British-Iraq treaty of 1930 and even against the revisions. But two essentially pro-Western leaders were able to hold the reins of government and of the army. One of them was the Crown-Prince Abdulillah, who sought personal, power and glory in his collaboration with the West and the British. The other, Nuri Said Pasha, the perrenial Prime Minister who ruled the country directly or indirectly ever since the creation of Iraq, was also an opportunist, but earnestly desired the greatness of his country. He was admittedly not the idealist he was during the Arab Revolt and openly boasted that he was a practical man.

The two men ruled the country by harsh, dictatorial methods and prevented nationalistic uprisings by a network of spies and of trusted people in key administrative and military positions. Nuri Said did not earnestly believe in democracy; he thought that he could bring greatness and prosperity to Iraq by authoritatian methods. He also believed that Iraq could benefit from an alliance with the West and could perhaps in this way realize the dream of the Kingdom of Syria.[6] Nuri Said, however, also realized the Soviet danger- especially a threat of a Communist inspired Kurdish uprising was something very close to Iraq's borders.

The ground for a Turkish-Iraqi alliance was laid in early 1954 and in October of that year there were strong hints in the press that Nuri Said Pasha actually favored signing a pact with Turkey. On January 6, 1954, Prime Minister Menderes of Turkey visited Iraq, Syria and Lebanon. On the 13th there was a formal announcement from Baghdad that the two countries had agreed to sign an alliance.

Nasser immediately launched a violent campaign against the Pact and against Iraq. He pressured the members of the Arab League to denounce the Iraqi government for breaking the Arab unity. He was not successful in creating a popular uprising in Iraq, however, and the Pact was signed on February 24, 1955 in Baghdad. The two signatories pledged to "cooperate for their security and defense" and undertook to refrain from any interference, whatsoever in each other's internal affairs." But there were no strong clauses, and no specific pledges of automatic aid in case of an attack on one of the parties. Furthermore, technical details of military cooperation were not enumerated. One article simply stipulated that "measures for defense cooperation would be determined" as soon as the pact entered into effect.

The signatories sought to placate the Egyptians and Arab national-ism by mentioning that the Pact was consistent with Article 51 of the UN charter and by pointing out that it was not in contradiction with any of the international obligations contracted previously by either of them. Also the Pact was declared open to any member of the Arab League "or any state actively concerned with the security and peace in this region." Furthermore, letters were exchanged in support of the UN resolutions on Palestine.[7]

Britain had at first opposed the Northern Tier idea, presumably because it would weaken its prestige and influence in the area. But more important consideration led the British to change this attitude: The British-Iraqi Treaty for bases was due to expire in 1956. A re-vision of the original Treaty which had been negotiated in 1948 in Portsmouth was never ratified by Iraq, because of the popular opposi-tion. Now Britain could keep her bases in Iraq through joining the Baghdad Pact. Her accession took effect from April 5, 1955. Bri-tain and Iraq also signed an agreement for mutual defense and coop-eration to replace the Treaty of 1930.

Pakistan's Prime Minister Muhammed Ali announced his govern-ment's decision to join the Pact on July 1, 1955 and Pakistan's accession took effect on September 23, 1955. The Turkish-Pakis-tan agreement of 1954 was thus merged with the Baghdad Pact.[8]

The most remarkable adherent to the Pact was Iran. Now free from Mossadegh's extremist nationalism, Shahinshah Muhammed Riza Pehlevi pointed out that "traditional neutralism" had not saved Iran from foreign occupation in the past and could not be relied upon to save it in the future." Iran consequently decided to join the Baghdad Pact and her formal membership took effect from November 3, 1955.

The cooperation within the Pact developed smoothly in three years. The Permanent Council met four times.[9] A Secretariat was set up with headquarters in Baghdad. Four Committees (Military, Eco-nomic, Counter-subversion and Liaison) prepared the ground work of cooperation between the member countries in the various sectors. A special effort was made to strengthen the military structure of de-fense by embarking upon joint planning and training. At the Karachi meeting, it was also decided to establish a Military Planning Organi-zation. Also it was at this meeting that a joint Communique an-nounced that the Pact had "emerged as a constructive force for re-gional cooperation and as an important element promoting the world peace and security." But there were also weaknesses.

It it no secret that the signatories had, from the beginning, believed that the United States would join the Pact as a full member. Although she participated as an observer since the first Council meeting, joined the Economic, Counter-subversion Committees and later the Military Committee, and shared the secretariat expenses and furnished aid through the pact, America's reluctance to become a full member created apprehension and even irritation among the members. This strengthened the hand of the Middle Eastern opponents of the pact.

The United States apparently was not willing to become a full member, because she still wanted to retain her freedom of action in working with Egypt and Saudi Arabia and did not want to provoke any Soviet move into the Middle East. There was also the desire to not to antagonize Israel, and, possibly, considerations of internal politics.

Nasser and the Pact. Both Iraq and Turkey had extended an invitation to Egypt to join the pact.[10] Nasser not only refused to join but started a violent campaign against Iraq. He wanted to eliminate the Nuri Said Government and also intimidate Syria, Lebanon and Jordan from joining the Pact. Thus a struggle within the Arab League, between Nasser and Nuri Said ensued.

Nasser was too far committed in his nationalism and aspirations of Arab Leadership to either join a Western Alliance or to allow such a Middle Eastern alliance to develop under the leadership of Iraq. His popularity now depended on the perpetuation of Anti-Westernism. The Pact now offered a new excuse for furthering his Pan Arab ambitions.

King Saud, bitter enemy of Hashemite's and opponent of their Great Syria plan, joined Nasser in his attacks against Iraq. The combination of Nasser's agents and Saudi gold was very effective in Syria, Lebanon and Jordan.

Mr. Menderes visited Syria and Lebanon but failed to get them to join the Pact. Although the Governments were willing the public opposition was too great, for them to cope with.

In fact, the activities of the leftist elements and Nasser's agents prepared the way to power for a Leftist Government in Syria. Both the Soviet press and Egyptians provoked the Syrian suspicions about a joint Turkish-Iraqi move to realize the Great Syria. Although Turkey assured Syria that she in no way supported the Greater Syria Plan, Syrian movement towards the left and towards Nasser could not be checked. An Egyptian-Syrian treaty was signed in Damascus on October 20, 1955[11] and soon Syria was receiving Soviet arms.

The efforts in Jordan were also frustrated by Nasser's pressure and subversion. During the visit of the Turkish President Celal Bayar to Amman in November 1955, Turkish observers were led to believe that Jordan was about to enter the Pact. Then Britain overplayed its hand; possibly in its anxiety to retain its influential position in Jordan, she sent General Templar to Jordan to convince the young King. This gave a chance to the propagandists and agents of Nasser to mention a specific example of "Western pressure." It was then easy for them to incite the mobs in Amman to riot. Jordan, an anachronistic state, with its internal order and economy taxed to the limit by thousands of Palestine refugees, proved an ideal ground for subversion. A pro-Egyptian government came to power as a result of the riots and Hüsseyin was forced to dismiss Glubb Pasha and to join the Egyptian bloc.

A dangerous climate had developed throughout the Middle East and was seriously threatening the Baghdad Pact and Western interests. Two developments aggravated the situation and intensified the Arab Nationalism against the West. The first was the Soviet-Egyptian arms deal. Nasser worried about Israel; the Gazza Raid of 1955 had increased his fears. He requested arms from the United States. But negotiations dragged on and on: obviously the American government was in no position to give arms to Nasser unconditionally or in any great quantities. In a dramatic move Soviet Russia stepped in to the breach and into the Middle East arena: the Soviet-Egyptian Arms Deal was announced.

The second development was the withdrawal by the United States and Britain of an earlier promise to aid the building of the Aswan High Dam. The promise was originally made in December of 1955, while some hope was still entertained that Egypt might be induced to join the West. Another but parallel reasoning might have been that such a large aid to a major development project would both favorably impress Egyptian and Arab masses concerning the West's good intentions and also would offset the Communist economic influence which had started with the arms deal. But United States government had serious afterthoughts about the offer. Violent propaganda and subversion campaigns against the West and against the Baghdad Pact left little doubt as to the real course of Nasser's ambitions. Events in Jordan and Syria demonstrated the dangers of his nationalism. To top all this Egypt's recognition of the Chinese Communist regime created an extremely unfavorable atmosphere against Nasser especially in Washington.

There was also the growing resentment among the members of the Baghdad Pact. These countries, while still irritated at United States reluctance to join the pact, were very much irked with the coddling of

Nasser. They openly hinted that "Egypt was getting more by being
naughty than they did by being good!" [12]   In July 1956 the State Department announced that the offer had been withdrawn.[13]

The American Ambassador in Cairo, Henry Byroade was a pro-
ponent of friendship with Nasser, believing that he could be won over.
He symbolized the "flirtation period" between the United States and
Egypt. With his recall and with the withdrawal of the Aswan High
Dam offer a new period of strictness with Nasser started in United
States' Middle East policy.

Nasser's reaction was the unleashing of a furious anti-Western
campaign which now unmistakably included the United States. Then,
on July 26, 1956, he announced in a speech that Egypt was nationalizing the Suez Canal Company in order to use its revenues for the
building of the Aswan Dam. Extreme nationalism had struck at one
of the most important life-lines of Europe. Suez Canal Zone could
have been replaced as a military base but as a passage way for West's
oil supplies and trade with the East it was invaluable.

Tension mounted while the West had a foretaste of economic hard-
ships resulting from Nasser's control of the Suez Canal. Two con-
ferences held in London (without the participation of Egypt) and the
Security Council of the United Nations were unable to find a solu-
tion to the problem. Meanwhile, there was increased apprehension in
Israel due to the stockpiling of the Soviet and Czechoslovak arms in
Egypt and Syria. Frequent forrays into Israeli territory by the
Fedayin groups (semi-military guerillas trained in Egypt) led the
Israel military experts to believe that they should strike first before
Egypt gathered strength for her imminent "Second Round." These
tensions and apprehensions precipitated in the Sinai and Suez hos-
tilities in October 1956, when Israel on the one hand, and Britain and
France on the other, attacked Egypt.

The rapid crystallization of the world opinion against the attacks
prevented the three governments from reaching their objectives and
presumably from causing the downfall of Nasser. They were forced
to obey the cease fire resolution of the United Nations General
Assembly.[14] Nevertheless the hostilities served to increase the Soviet
influence and intervention in the Middle East. Khrushchev talked
about sending "volunteers" to Egypt and the Soviet note mentioned
"the rockets which might begin to fly." Russia had clearly endeared
herself to the Arabs, as the champion of their liberty and independence
at a crucial time.

The Suez Hostilities seriously strained the Baghdad Pact. Britain was a member of the Pact and Turkey had diplomatic relations with Israel.

The Nationalist propaganda stressed these facts to provoke the Arab masses, especially the Iraqis, against the Alliance. For a while the Pact meetings were held without the participation of Britain and decisions condemning the attacks were adopted and announced. Turkey, in order to placate Arab sensitivities, was forced to recall her envoy in Telaviv. Mr. Etem Menderes, then Foreign Minister explained this move in the following words: "Turkey had hoped that retention of the greatest possible contacts with both Israel and the Arab States might make it possible for us to retain a means of some day performing a constructive and useful service between the parties. . . Not only did the turn of events make it impossible to realize this aim, but Israel's attack on Egypt put mutual Turkish-Israeli relations on even more delicate footing. Faced with this situation we recalled our Minister in Telaviv, not as a measure to stall the Palestine Problem, but as an appropriate measure compatible with out ability to influence the march of events. We believe that this measure will serve to ameliorate the general situation by taking some of the ugly and shameful propaganda directed against us."

These dramatic developments had served to show that it fell upon the United States to check both the aggressive Nasser nationalism and the increasing Soviet influence and intervention. Her allies in the area, were pressing her to a review of her policy and to a dramatic decision, joining the Baghdad Pact. United States had participated through an observer in all the Pact Council meetings, was underwriting many of its activities, was giving aid through bilateral agreements to all its members, but the Northern tier countries did not consider this enough. By becoming a full member, United States would bring its full weight and determination against both Russia and Egypt and would bolster the prestige of the member governments against internal opposition and against Nasser's subversion. But the United States remained unprepared to do this, mainly for the reasons mentioned earlier in this chapter.

Instead, Washington sought to placate the apprehensions of her allies by sounding warnings to Moscow and Cairo and by formally announcing on November 29, 1956 that "any encroachments on or threats to the territory of Turkey, Pakistan, Iraq or Iran will be considered with utmost concern."

Then on January 5, 1957, President Eisenhower made specific proposals concerning the Middle East in a special message to the Congress. The main intention was to associate the Administration and

the Congress in a solemn declaration concerning United States' determination in the Middle East. Such a declaration would evidently
not imply or involve radically new policies, but would at a crucial time
reaffirm America's position. The association of the Congress was
essential because the new program, termed "Eisenhower Doctrine"
required authority as concerns the use of the armed forces and money.

Eisenhower's proposals which were adopted with some changes by
the Congress, authorized the President to employ the armed forces
as he deems necessary to secure and protect the integrity and security
of any nation or group of nations in the general area of the Middle
East requesting such aid against overt armed aggression from any
nation controlled by international communism. Furthermore, it authorized him to undertake programs of military assistance to any nation or group of nations in that area desiring such aid and to cooperate
with any nation or group of nations in the development of economic
strength in the maintainance of national independence. The President would spend $200,000,000 dollars for these purposes.

The Eisenhower Doctrine did not bring anything radically new
except an additional $200,000,000 dollars, to be used perhaps less
rigidly than the aid funds previously appropriated. It also did not
cover all possible contingencies. But although it fell short of their
hopes, the Baghdad Pact members welcomed the new United States
program with some enthusiasm.

Terming it as a "very firm step," Prime Minister Adnan Menderes
declared that "Turkey will occupy an important position in the
application of President Eisenhower's program in the Middle East,"
and added: "The Turkish Government considers that the close interest taken by the United States in the Middle East, and the recognition by the peace-loving nations of the importance which this area
deserves, constitute a truly important event."

Turkey's endorsement of the Doctrine was confirmed when Ambassador James P. Richards, President's Special Envoy visited Ankara
in March to explain the program.

In the meantime Syria was more and more becoming the focal point
of Turkish apprehensions. A combination of leftist and extreme
nationalist politicians and officers were gaining control of the country.
Since November of 1956, Turkish press reported with some alarm the
stockpiling of Soviet arms and activities of Communist technicians
in Syria. In December, the Turkish Foreign Minister in a statement
in the Turkish Grand National Assembly said that Syria had definitely
"received more arms from Russia than she can use given her present
capabilities." Already exerting a great effort to defend her long

frontiers exposed to Soviet Russia and her satellites, Turkey was now confronted with a danger from the south.

"Syria has commenced to present a picture that threatens first its immediate neighbors and then the whole of the Middle East" declared Adnan Menderes in an official statement in September 1957. He pointed out that it would be impossible to consider Syria's behaviour as a plausible case of rearmament—the situation was "merely the implementation of the desire to turn the country into a stockpile of arms that will be used in case of need by others. "In short," he added, "Syria, inspired by subversive aims, is on the way to establishing a bridgehead for aggressive ambitions."

Pointedly Turkish army started maneuvers near the Southern borders and deployed several armoured divisions in this area in order to fortify her defenses. Up to that time, the long and difficult to defend Syrian border was only guarded by the gendarmerie and revenue agents against smuggling activities. Soviet, Egyptian and Syrian propaganda organs and officials were quick to interpret these measures as preparations for a Turkish-Syrian offensive against Syria. Soviet Russia increased the tension by sending threatening notes to Turkey, warning her not to attack Syria. This was a new opportunity for Khruschev and Bulganin to show themselves as champions and defenders of Arabs. The "Turkish-Syrian crisis" which was thus inflated by propaganda and diplomatic notes, was brought to the United Nations.

One indication of the fact that Soviet Russia was acting "More pro-King than the King himself" in this "crisis" was pointed out by Mr. Menderes in his reply to a letter of "warning" from Bulganin: "Is it not noteworthy that in view of the present condition of Syria we have received no communication of complaint from her?" he asked. "But as a proof of the Soviet Union's assumption of responsibility of Syria and Syrian problems we received this message from you . . ."

Another indication that Syria's government was not its own master in this matter was the fact that while the government in Damascus was presenting a note to the Turkish Minister on October 8, expressing satisfaction over Turkish Prime Minister's affirmations that Turkey had no aggressive intentions against Syria, that same evening the Syrian delegation at the United Nations was complaining about Turkish troop concentrations in a letter to the Secretary General.

Although there were border clashes and complaints and counter-complaints about violations and although bitter accusations were made during the United Nations debate, at the end the Syrian government was obliged to drop its complaint. Somehow the world public opinion had realized that the crisis was artificial.[15]

But the real crisis and danger in the Middle East was growing. It is quite possible that the Syrian "crisis" was provoked by Russia to provide a new opportunity of intervention and that it camouflaged the imminent Egyptian-Syrian union. During the "crisis" Egypt dispatched troops to Syria under its bilateral agreement of defense with Syria and later, when the Syrian-Egyptian union and the establishment of the United Arab Republic were announced, it did not create much stir.

From then on events progressed rapidly while the West watched. The Turkish government kept warning her Western allies and especially the United States about the ominous developments in the Middle East and about the potential dangers. At the NATO meeting in Paris in December, 1957, Adnan Menderes was quite blunt and rather prophetic about the probable course of events. If aggressive Nasserism and Soviet influence were not to be checked with determined actions, the northern tier countries themselves and Western interests were clearly in danger, he warned. He pointed out that it would be a dangerous delusion to imagine that Iraq, Jordan, Lebanon, Saudi Arabia and even Iran and Turkey could show a prolonged resistance to the immense Soviet pressure and subversive activities. Menderes' proposed remedy was the reinforcement of the Baghdad Pact "which could serve as support for measures to be adopted in the Middle East."

In May 1958 the pro-Western government in Lebanon was threatened by a strange rebellion. This was chiefly caused by a multitude of complex factors and by the peculiar composition of Lebanon; there is also no doubt, however, that Nasser's agents and subversive propaganda were the catalystic agents. Turkey again urged Western action, but there was apathy in the West and United States was not ready or willing to take the initiative.

In June 1958, a well-planned coup toppled the pro-Western regime of Iraq. Young officers and mobs were inspired, if not provoked, by Nasser. For all practical purposes Iraq was out of the Western camp and closer than ever to the United Arab Republic.

The events in Iraq forced the U.S. and Britain to send troops to Lebanon and Jordan, in response to the appeals of the two governments. But these were limited and necessarily temporary measures which dealt with the symptomatic results of Nasser's rampant nationalism. Neither such stop-gap measures nor the Baghdad Pact and the Eisenhower Doctrine could, over a long period, check this movement.

At the time of this writing there is a lull in the Middle East. The Arab-sponsored resolution adopted by the General Assembly in its emergency session provided a needed "breathing-spell" in the dramatic rush of events in the troubled area. But the basic facts and realities have not been altered or eliminated. Soviet influence in the region is unfortunately a reality which cannot be denied. Moreover, expansionist nature of Nasser's nationalism is another reality. Collusion between these two facts is an additional reality.

Abdel Nasser might take great satisfaction from the recognition of his leadership in the Middle East by the United Nations. But unless he can evade the fate of Dr. Faustus and be able to divorce Arab destiny from the clutches of Kremlin and unless he can transform extremism into sober, productive patriotism, his victory will be a hollow one.

Recent Communist intrigues which have for all practical purposes alienated General Kassem's regime in Iraq from Nasser and the cause of Pan-Arabism should by now be obvious to the Egyptian leader. Moreover, the veering of Iraq toward the left should be watched carefully both by him and leaders of the West. Another potential danger that should be watched is the revival of Communist-sponsored Kurdish nationalism.

IX

TURKEY AND THE WORLD

Turkey's vital role in the stabilization and defense of the Middle East and in the overall global strategy has become an undeniable axiom of our day. That she stands unequivocally with the West is one of the very few known factors in the present, enigmatic world equation. These are sources of comfort and strength for the West; one must not forget, however, that recognition of Turkey's mission and position as such has not come easily. It must also be kept in mind that the residues of misconceptions which dominated Turkey's relations with the West in the past can yet cloud and mar her relations with her Western allies in the future.

The Leit-Motif of History. In retrospect, mistakes and miscalculations made in evaluating the true character, mission and orientation of the Turks seem to be present throughout history as a fantastic leit-motif. The fallacies are so well established that it would perhaps be difficult to convince the average Westerner that to become a part of the West has always been the driving force in Turkish history.

Blame for being misunderstood cannot, with any justice, be put entirely on others. Turks were never clever publicists. Overconfident about their good intentions and about their basic integrity, they seldom made an effort to make their motives and objectives clear. When they were misunderstood or disappointed they became remorseful and, often, their reactions were indeed strong. The Turk thus remained as a stranger both in Europe, which he wanted to join, and in the East, whence he came. The West used Turkey when it deemed it strategically or economically necessary or profitable and turned against her when it considered her usefulness ended. Suleyman the Magnificent was obliged to turn eastward in his disappointment; Young Turks joined the German-Austro-Hungarian alliance in theirs.

The miscalculations of the Western allies concerning Turkey, prior to and after the First World War, should be briefly mentioned here as object lessons. They could have easily kept Turkey out of the war or even won her over to their side, had they evaluated her importance correctly. But they considered Tsarist Russia as a more substantial and dependable ally which should be appeased at all costs. They failed to recognize the potential threat against their interests in the Middle East and in the Mediterranean by a Russia dominating Istanbul and the Straits. Rather than giving guarantees to Turkey against Russia, they tacitly accepted the Russian aspirations.

After the war, the Allies were intent on breaking Turkey down into small states and encircling her with hostile Kurdish, Arab and Armenian States. It now seems absurd that even after the establishment of the Turkish Republic, the British and the French continued their intrigues to provoke Arab and Kurdish nationalism against the Turks and persisted in this until the mid-1930's. One cannot refrain from asking what the current situation in the Middle East would have been had the British-French intentions concerning Turkey then been carried out? Or conversely, whether it would not have been better for the Western interests if Britain had not insisted on annexing the Mosul oil region to Iraq?

The Turks under the leadership of Kemal Ataturk were able to rise above their bitterness against the West and to continue their drive to become a part of it. The West itself played a scant part in this reconciliation. A Turkish writer wearily wrote that Turkey has had very little trouble in making herself understood to her enemies, but "what an unsurmountable task it is to be understood by our friends!"

The Expendable Out-Post Conception. The struggle (and it was a true struggle) to become a part of the North Atlantic Alliance proved indeed to be a difficult task. The West again wanted to use Turkey as an expendable out-post, but the basic objections of Francois and Charles to accepting "the Turk" into their exclusive European Club in the sixteenth century was still very much alive in the minds of some of their twentieth century successors. Even to this day there is a suspicion in some Turkish minds that the West has never accepted them completely and that there are still the vestiges of the "expendable out-post" conception. If there is today indeed a gap—even a shade of a difference—between the Turkish conception of being an integral part of the West and the conception of other Western countries that Turkey is after all an out-post, pitfalls and frictions will be ultimately unavoidable.

Especially for the Turkish intellectual, "to be with the West" is a matter of basic philosophy and it transcends strategic and economic mutual interests. One Turkish writer has expressed this in these words: "There are different ways of being with the West. Spain, Portugal, South Korea, Formosa, and even the Sheikdoms of Omman, Kuwait and Quatar are with the West—or rather out-posts of the West. But these are not truly members of the Western-North Amer-

ican world.   Their joining the West is not a result of identical world
outlook, identical social philosophy or identical ideals and principals. . .
They are with the West because of strategic or economic requirements
and of other calculations of self-interest.   Turkey cannot be included
in this category."

A Period of Ordeal. It cannot be denied that after the NATO
debacle of 1951 Turkish suspicions and apprehensions concerning the
West were once again aroused in 1954 and this time relations with the
United States were primarily involved.   Turks were somewhat stunned
when the United States assumed a stern and strict attitude in her
relations with Turkey.   American officials openly hinted that Turkey
should not be "spoiled any longer."   At that time, when the Soviet
danger in the Middle East had to some extent lost its intensity, these
officials clearly relegated strategic and political considerations to the
background and took Turkey to task for what they termed as her
"ambitious economic development program" which they refused to
underwrite.

It was perhaps unavoidable that the "honeymoon period" would
one day come to an end and that Turkish-American relations would
enter a realistic course.   But Washington's new realism brought back
the memories of their past experience with the West; they were again
being taken for granted by being used when necessary, and by being
pushed to the background when not!   There were even hints in some
segments of the Turkish public opinion that the "Spirit of the Crusades," the subconscious antagonism to the "infidel" was at the roots
of American coolness.

Was the United States justified in her criticism of the Turkish economy and in refusing further large scale aid to Turkey?   It is conceivable that strictly from the point of view of economic theory and
statistics, some objections were valid.   I am not an economist and it
is not within the scope of this book to go into a detailed examination
of the facts and figures.   But, frankly, I share the views of most of
my countrymen that it was unrealistic and damaging to consider Turkey solely from an economic and financial point of view, completely
oblivious to the human and political factors involved.   The need to
raise the living standard and economy of Turkey from that of a
medieval state to modest, contemporary well-being is a human
necessity which can never be measured by economic statistics.   It
was inevitable for Turkey, as it was for all other countries including
the United States, to go through a trial-and-error period, while seeking the right course for economic development.

The Turkish Ambassador to Washington, Suat Hayri Urgüplü, in a speech in January, 1958, eloquently brought out some of the human factors involved when he said: "They tell us to tighten our belts . . . I have tried to give you an idea of the living conditions and standards of the Turkish peasant and the Turkish soldier . . . And yet in these extremely tough conditions they continue to live, work and serve with the highest degree of honor, self-sacrifice and courage. I can find no place for a new hole in their belts to tighten them. Most of them even have no belts . . . If anyone can find such a place for a new hole, without pushing them into further misery, let him show it to us."

Furthermore, there is also some doubt that Turkey's economic plight was entirely due to Turkish mistakes. In the speech mentioned above, Urgüplü also said: "We have been criticized because we have no plan. And yet, there was no plan in the American aid which has largely been instrumental in our development. . ."

From a political point of view the new American "realism" towards Turkey seemed unrealistic to the Turks. According to their reasoning, aid could never be an exclusive instrument of economic charity or generosity; it was, more often than not, a political instrument which ultimately served America's interests and defense. At times the United States did not hesitate to wield the aid as such an instrument. Why then did it assume an exclusively economic aspect where Turkey was concerned? Presumably the United States was being a stern big brother to put some "economic sense" into Turkey. But in trying to attain this long range economic objective some very immediate political dangers were overlooked. Without outside assistance Turkey's economy would deteriorate and there was a danger that this deterioration might cause political instability within Turkey. Clearly, this could not be what the American "realism" really aimed at.

John C. Campbell in his *Defense of the Middle East* presents the problem more precisely:

"We should realize that the Turks tend to look at the whole question of aid as primarily political in character. They, therefore, take it amiss when the United States turns down their requests with admonitions to put their economic house in order; while offering more to Egypt or India. In the past four years Turkey has received an average of close to one hundred million dollars in economic grants per year, most of it under the label of 'defense support' but the political benefits have been lessened by the ill effects of stalling off and then turning down Turkey's request for additional support in loans . . . Certain reforms are necessary before the Turkish economy will be on a sound basis. Yet these reforms are not politically so easy to make and we should never become so stubborn in our economic arguments or set in the ways of bureaucratic routine that we lose sight of the real objective of mutual security, which must rest on the continued willingness of Turkey to see its security as tied to the West. We are, after all, giving the Turks what amounts to a continuing subsidy, not because their international payments are out of balance or because their agriculture is in need of tractors but because they are steadfast allies and are standing up against the Soviet threats and pressures. Continued haggling and pressure for changes in economic policies may obscure and even obstruct the real purpose of the subsidy."

Turkey went through a period of great economic difficulties during the last four years. The Turkish government, steadfast in its loyalty to the West, did not allow its financial ordeals to effect its standing in the Western alliance or Turkey's friendship with the United States. The Turkish leaders, President Bayar and Premier Menderes, made it clear in their various public statements that they would not be tempted by the Soviet offers of economic and financial aid. Turkey did not respond even to the efforts to expand Turkish-Russian trade relations.

During these difficult years only a strong administration and the inner strength of the nation prevented political instability in Turkey. The riots of September 6 and 7, 1955, though, were danger signals of a tension building up within the country.

In August 1958 an agreement for a joint United States-Western European financial aid to Turkey, in various categories amounting to $359 million was announced. This marked the beginning of a new phase in Turkish-American relations. The Middle East crisis of that summer had focused the attention on the political and strategic importance of Turkey. But even before that, new American personalities such as Robert B. Anderson, Secretary of the Treasury; Neil McElroy, Secretary of Defense and Douglas C. Dillon, Undersecretary of State, had taken a fresh and realistic attitude in reappraising that country's problems and its role. In conjunction with a radical stabilization program undertaken by the Turkish government, the new aid has considerably bolstered both the economy and the defense efforts of the nation.

Significant Trends in Public Opinion. It would be glossing over the realities to contend that the past four years have had no effects on Turkish-American relations or that the economic difficulties have not nurtured in Turkey some discordant opinions concerning the country's foreign relations. Some of these are obviously unrealistic, lunatic-fringe opinions expressed mostly in the coffee houses. But yet it is quite significant that such opinions are expressed and that certain misgivings concerning foreign relations have arisen. This would have been impossible four years ago.

It is perhaps not entirely irrelevant that the main opposition party, the People's Republican Party, has, for the first time since the beginning of the multi-party system, started criticizing openly the "methods and principles" of the foreign policy of the government. Ismet Inönü, the leader of that party, in a debate in the Grand National Assembly in the summer of 1958, opposed what he termed the "aggressive policies" of the administration during the recent Middle Eastern crisis. He took the government to task for allowing the use of the Adana air base by the American troops during their movements to Lebanon. It was evident from both his remarks in the Assembly, his other statements elsewhere, and from newspaper articles written by his trusted foreign affairs experts that the People's Party advocates a cautious foreign policy in general and a policy of non-involvement in the Middle East. This party is also opposed to Turkey's being too much identified with the United States. One such article criticized the United States policy in the Middle East and especially the troop landings in Lebanon; it attacked the government for making Turkey a "tool for an outpost of Western interests in the Middle East."

Some of this is clearly opposition for the sake of opposition, and is a part of the general plan to heckle and hinder the government at every opportunity. But there is, in these opinions, unmistakable traces of Ismet Inönü's well known cautious foreign policy which he practiced when he was in power from 1938 to 1950. It is, however, again, significant that such out-of-date ideas can find a context to be expressed and can also have a certain amount of political appeal within the country. This, too, could not have been possible four years ago.

I have noted these trends of thought to point out that the recent economic difficulties have indeed made certain inroads in the world outlook of the Turkish people. I must hasten to add, however, that neither the "lunatic fringe" opinions, nor the criticisms of the opposition parties are strong or substantial enough to alter Turkey's loyalties and the present course of her foreign relations. These are too deep rooted to be altered at the whim of politicians or by cross-currents of opinion.

Turkey's foreign policy is primarily based on Ataturk's legacy: to seek no territorial gains outside the present boundaries; to show vigilance and determination against Soviet threats and to stand with the West.

Then there are some basic facts: Turkey considers herself an integral part of the West not because of a temporary expedience, but as a matter of basic philosophy. She will stand or fall with the West. Her geographic and strategic position make neutrality impossible for Turkey. Her neutrality in the Second World Was war anachronistic and accidental—it cannot happen again. A general war will almost certainly extend to the Middle East; even if at the outset nuclear warfare might not require the Middle East bases, both sides will ultimately seek to deny to each other the resources and bases of the area. They will try to attain key objectives there in order to be in a strong bargaining position in an eventual peace conference. It is inevitable that Turkey would be involved in such a general war. Even if we imagined for a moment that Turkey was not in the path of Russian objectives, no Turkish leader or no Turkish party, however cautious, could take the course of waiting it out, knowing well that the Kremlin would not hesitate to turn on a "neutral" Turkey once it had beaten the West. Turkey's neutrality would merely be a delaying action. Knowing that Turkey stands or falls with the West, no Turkish leader can very well retreat into neutralism and deny the West the forces and bases which might well play a leading part in the destruction of Russia. As for a limited war in that area, this will in all probability be the result of increased Russian interference and encroachments in the area. Even if Turkey were not directly touched, she cannot remain indifferent because Russian success would isolate her. In addition to all these basic tenets and facts, a deep-seated conviction will always dominate Turkey's foreign policy: Turks know from their long and bitter experience with the Russians that the only way to deal with them is to show strength and determination.

New Expression for Basic Ideas. The present leaders of Turkey have interpreted these facts and have given expression to their convictions and principles in a dynamic foreign policy. Foreign Minister Fatin Rustu Zorlu's comments on neutralism at the Bandung Conference of 1955, for instance, was an expression of this new dynamism: "Freedom, independence, and peace are not blessings that are bestowed upon the shoulders of everyone of us . . . To fail to realize these truths, to take the line of least resistance and to hope that by shutting one's eyes to danger one may find security is a course perilous not only to the one who follows it but also to the entire community—such illusions have existed in very recent times; they have all come to disastrous ends."

When the Korean War broke out these leaders did not merely pay lip-service to lofty principles of collective security. They proceeded to put it into action. They were convinced, as Mr. Zorlu declared, that "caution and non-involvement do not pay. This line of action was the cause of the Second World War. The only way to preserve freedom and peace is to show courage and unity."

Turkey's Role in the Middle East. With such an outlook the Turkish government could not possibly relinquish the role imposed on her by geography in the Middle East. Turkey forms a land-bridge between the East and West and is, in a way, destined to link the two worlds psychologically and politically, as well as geographically. The current collusion between rampant Russian aspirations and rampant Arab nationalism has made this an urgent necessity. Turkey cannot just sit and watch while Russia settles in the Middle East; thereby encircling and isolating her. She owes it to her own security, to the security of her allies and above all to her eastern neighbors, to secure the defenses of her eastern flank and to stop Russian infiltration and interference in this region. The Baghdad Pact was pioneered in order to meet this challenge. Strategically and militarily the Pact would bring about cooperation between armed forces of the Northern Tier countries and set up a defense infra-structure. These would provide, in case of a local or global war, the spearhead and the basis for defensive action, to be supported by the naval and air forces of the Western allies. The Pact would also serve as a focus for United States commitments and assistance to the defense of the area. But admittedly the psychological and political aspects of it were to be even more important: it would be the nucleus of "first organized realization of the Soviet threat" and of a collective security spirit in the Middle East. It would also be the nucleus of cooperation with the West on an equal partnership basis.

There has been much criticism of the Baghdad Pact outside and inside Turkey. Mainly it has been said that it has provoked Russian interference and Arab nationalism. It has also been said that it connoted cooperation with unpopular leaders and was therefore not only doomed to failure but also served to increase nationalistic resentment.

"Provoking Russian interference in the Middle East" is a fallacy usually subscribed to by some segments of Western opinion and by neutralists. Turks know through their long and usually bitter experiences that there is no such thing as " provoking the Russians" in the Middle East or anywhere else. Soviet Russia, perhaps more than Tsarist Russia, has her pre-determined global objectives and a global strategy and no amount of provocation will force the Soviet leaders into action on a front or at a time when they believe it is not advantageous. On the other hand they will not hesitate to move, without the slightest provocation, if they consider it essential and timely for their purposes. In any case, Russian "interference" or "presence" was *de facto* in the Middle East, long before the creation of the Baghdad Pact—perhaps the misgivings in some segments of Western opinion helped the Soviet propaganda by providing an excuse *a posteriori*. The same can also be said for Arab nationalism; both extremism and rivalries were established facts in the Arab world before the Pact was signed.

Was the Baghdad Pact designed as an instrument against genuine Arab nationalism? Turkey, for one, never envisaged it as such an instrument. This would go against the grain of basic concepts of modern Turkey. Nationalism was, after all, the driving force which created the Turkish Republic and its leaders had singled out their support for Arab independence and freedom as far back as 1920. During the Lausanne Conference, the Turkish delegation had refused to accept or to condone the Mandates over Arab countries. When Turkey joined the League of Nations in 1932, she made it clear that her membership did not imply her approval of the Mandate system.

Turkey again showed her good intentions in 1954, when Prime Minister Adnan Menderes made distinct efforts to enlist the cooperation of Gamal Abdel Nasser in establishing a Middle East collective security alliance. Nasser openly spurned these efforts. Turks knew well from their own experiences that there is a distinction between extreme nationalism based on and nurtured by blind hatreds and unrealistic aspirations and sober, moderate nationalism based on genuine, patriotic motives. Nasser's brand, so far, proved to be of the former type and it was impossible to come to terms with it. There were, then, three alternatives for the West, in view of this intransigence: to let the Middle East go by default; to try to placate Nasser as much as possible; or to maintain positions of strength by cooperating with the leaders in the region who were willing to do so.

Turkish and Western interests were too vital to be disregarded. As for placating Nasser's nationalism, Turks were convinced that no matter how much the West atoned for past sins and no matter how many concessions and economic "gifts" it made, reconciliation with Nasser was impossible. Hatred against the West was the main driving force of his movement and he could not very well relinquish it. On the contrary, Western efforts in this direction seemed to increase his prestige and discouraged the pro-Western elements in the Middle East. The only alternative left therefore was to establish at once, the nucleus of a Middle Eastern alliance on available foundations—no matter how shaky these foundations appeared to be at the time. Admittedly, leaders like Nuri Said were unpopular in their own countries and their holds were at best temporary, but through them a start could be made, positions of strength could be maintained and an "infrastructure" of a defense system could be established. In the meantime emergence of new and popular pro-Western leaders could be encouraged. Nasser's nationalism is no doubt a reality, but perhaps not a stable one. It depends mainly on Nasser's personality, on hate and on aspirations of Arab unity; none is eternally durable.

It is inevitable that a moderate and realistic Arab nationalism or nationalisms will emerge once the dust of hate and emotionalism is settled. It is not an illusion, therefore, to hope that in the long run an understanding towards the West and the realization of Soviet threat will develop among the Arab peoples in the Middle East. The West must actively encourage this and Turkey, which has passed through the same stages, can give the benefit of her experiences to her eastern neighbors. It is necessary for the West and for Turkey, however, to maintain positions of strength and to support with determination the present allies and potential allies in the region. If, on the contrary, Turkey or the West acquiesced to Nasser's expansionism or to the Soviet "presence," Western interests will soon be choked and Turkey's survival will be threatened. Furthermore the pro-Western elements in the area would be discouraged and forced into neutralism. This, the gist of Turkey's attitude in the Middle East, was the conception behind the Baghdad Pact. Turkey repeatedly sounded warnings to her Western allies about the pitfalls in the region and urged them to show determination and to support the Baghdad Pact. She urged the United States to join it as a full member precisely because such an unequivocal commitment would have strengthened the Western position and the pro-Western forces in the area. The Eisenhower Doctrine and other United States declarations concerning the area in 1957 and 1958 were useful, but not quite adequate—psychological peculiarities and the intricacies of balance of power between various groups in the Middle East required a show of stronger determination. I venture to think that, had Turkey's warnings been heeded in time, the Lebanese crisis might have been averted or stopped at the beginning. In turn, determination in Lebanon could perhaps have prevented the coup in Iraq. It must be pointed out, however, that although the Turkish government sounded many urgent warnings and took precautions before and during the Syrian crisis in 1957 and the Lebanese-Iraq crisis in 1958, it never proposed to take action unilaterally.

The resolution adopted in the August 1958 session of the United Nations for the purpose of ending the crisis in Lebanon and Jordan was perhaps inevitable and even appropriate under the prevailing conditions. But this has not altered the basic realities in the Middle East, nor has it diminished Turkey's apprehensions. Nasser's nationalism has not yet evolved into a sober movement and is yet capable of disrupting the balance in the region. Soviet "presence" has not been negated. Unless the West maintains the remaining positions of strength and unless it expresses its determination and commitments unequivocally, the Middle East, with all its political, psychological and strategic ramifications, might be totally lost.

* * *

The situation in the Middle East seems to be the microcosm of the dilemma confronting the West in general throughout the world. Is the West in its life-and-death struggle with Communist imperialism going to be plagued by its guilty conscience and hampered by the moral principles and institutions in which it honestly believes? Communists' hands are not tied down by such considerations, and they are therefore able to seize, one by one, our positions of strength.

The Communists openly admit that they want eventually to destroy the Western society. For them co-existence is a temporary expedient. But neutralists, while they know these intentions, use a double standard in judging the West and the Communists; they are exacting in their demands concerning moral principles and propriety from the Western statesmen but are not so much bothered by Communist violations of the same principles.

I do not advocate disregard for moral principles and for the United Nations; these are fundamentals of our society. But I believe we should be more forceful and determined in the struggle for survival and should not disregard our vital interests just to placate the so-called liberals and neutralists. After all, we are confronted with an adversary who does not "play clean."

I venture to maintain that irrespective of personalities— whether of Nuri Said or Chiang Kai-shek—retreats from positions of strength will cost us dearly in the long run both strategically and psychologically.

Another thought is that we should not always be on the defensive. I realize that our system of government makes it difficult for the West to take the initiative in the cold war, but, nevertheless, we should not abandon our quest for the liberation of captive peoples.[1]

The realization that Communist imperialism is the ultimate danger everywhere and to everyone and the determination to show active resistance to this threat is the driving force of Turkey's foreign policy. A Turkish journalist once wrote that "realism and courage are the two attributes of independence." The Turkish people and their leaders have never been lacking in these qualities; nor have they defaulted in their contribution to the collective security efforts of the free world. There is no danger that Turkey's foreign policy will veer away from this course. Turkey will be with the West as long as her legitimate and vital interests are appreciated and supported. But no matter what happens, she will continue "to walk" as a Turkish poet once wrote, "on the path which she believes to be right, even if she is left all alone."

REFERENCE NOTES

CHAPTER II

[1] A teacher who was also called Mustafa added "Kemal" which means "Mature." Until 1935 Turks did not have surnames. Mustafa Kemal introduced the use of surnames—in Western fashion—and he was given the surname of Ataturk (Father of the Turks) by a grateful nation.

[2] Reportedly President Wilson fancied this idea; but there was strong opposition in the Congress against any such entanglement.

CHAPTER III

[1] This was precisely the reason why Mustafa Kemal decided to change the capital.

[2] Greeks considered this as designed against them.

[3] The same considerations also apply to the Island of Cyprus.

[4] The idea (but never the practice) of "Turkifying the Arabs" was to come after 1908.

[5] Only Vahabbis of Saudi Arabia represented a considerable difference in sect.

CHAPTER IV

[1] According to a disclosure made during a recent foreign policy debate in the Turkish Grand National Assembly, Inönü had decided to enter the war in compliance with her alliance with Great Britain and France. A code message from the Chargeé d'Affaire in the Turkish Embassy in Paris, Fatin R. Zorlu, (now Foreign Minister), warned that an Armistice was imminent and the decision was altered.

[2] An interesting sidelight to all this, has also come out in the Documents of the German Foreign office, recently published by the U.S. State Department: The Turkish Ambassador in Berlin, Mr. Hüsrev Gerede, was apparently, directly and indirectly hinting to the Germans that a Cabinet reorganization in favor of Germany was in the making in Turkey and that he was one of the candidates for Prime Minister or Foreign Minister. As far as one can gather from the Turkish sources close to the Government at that time, Mr. Gerede was never considered for these posts.

[3] The uprising was crushed by the British almost instantaneously.

CHAPTER VI

[1] There is a report, which I have not been able to document, that several Turks served in the Revolutionary Army and some of them were counted among the most rugged of Washington's Army during the winter of Valley Forge.

CHAPTER VII

[1] Inönü had opposed Ataturk's decision to participate in the NYON collective security patrol during the Spanish Civil War.

[2] U.S. Senate ratified the protocol by a vote of 73 to 2.

[3] Trade and Payments Agreement of September, 1947 between Turkey and

Yugoslavia. Trade Agreement—*Modus Vivendi* for application of preferential tariffs between Turkey and Yugoslavia—January 5, 1950. Agreement for Regulation of Frontier Railway Connections, January 12, 1951, between Yugoslavia and Greece. Agreement on Air Service—Yugoslavia-Greece—March 15, 1951.

⁴ Article 1 of this Convention of Defense Alliance between Great Britain and Turkey reads as follows: The Convention of Defense Alliance between Great Britain and Turkey with respect to the Asiatic Provinces of Turkey, signed at Constantinople on 4th June, 1878, commonly called the Cyprus Convention, runs as follows:

Article I. "If Batoum, Ardahan, Kars or any of them shall be retained by Russia, and if any attempt shall be made at any future time by Russia to take possession of further territories of H. I. M. the Sultan in Asia as fixed by the Definitive Treaty of Peace, England engages to join H. I. M. the Sultan in defending them by force of arms.

"In return, H. I. M. the Sultan promises to England to introduce necessary reforms, to be agreed upon later between the two Powers, into the Government and for the protection of the Christian and other subjects of the Porte in those territories. And in order to enable England to make necessary provision for executing her engagements, H. I. M. the Sultan further consents to assign the Island of Cyprus to be occupied and administered by England."

⁵ The idea of partition was first mentioned by Greek Foreign Minister Avengelos Averof in his conversation with the Turkish Ambassador in Athens on October 7, 1956. There was also a news item on October 17, 1956 in the *New York Times* that the partition of Cyprus as a possible solution was being discussed by the British and Americans and that the plan originated with the Yugoslavs. The Honorable Alan Lennox-Boyd, Secretary of State for the Colonies, in his visit to America in December, 1956 also mentioned partition as a solution.

⁶ Lord Radcliffe's terms of reference laid down that foreign affairs, defense, and internal security should be reserved to the Governor, and that the Constitution should be for a self-governing Cyprus under British sovereignty.

Representation in the single chamber would be roughly proportional to the population. There would be twenty-four seats for members elected on the General Roll which would comprise, almost completely, Greek Cypriot voters, six for members elected by voters on the Turkish Cypriot Roll, and six for nominated members, of whom one would be a Maronite and another a non-Cypriot British citizen.

CHAPTER VIII

¹ The State religion in Tsarist Russia was the Greek-Orthodox creed.

² Western Colonial exploitation had already started but this was done through the Capitulations and under the "shade" of the Ottoman administration, therefore the Turks drew the blame of the exploitation from which they did not even benefit.

³ Only Saudi Arabia and Yemen were truly independent.

⁴ This agreement and Vice-President Nixon's visit to Karachi in December 1953 paved the way for a military assistance pact between Pakistan and the United States which was signed on 19 May 1954 in spite of the violent opposition of India and the Soviet Union. Soviet Union had also protested the Turkish-Pakistan pacts vehemently.

⁵ The Turkish government refused to join the Arab block during the U.N. dispute on Palestine.

⁶ It has been said that Prince Abdul Illah aspired to become King of this Kingdom; King Faisal II, an amiable young man, was only a figurehead.

⁷ The pact was ratified by the Turkish Grand National and by the Iraqi parliament on February 26, 1955.

⁸ During President Bayar's visit to Pakistan in February of 1955 the ground was prepared for this accession.

⁹ In Baghdad in November 1955; in Teheran in April 1956; in Karachi in June 1957 and in Ankara in January 1958.

¹⁰ An incident involving the expulsion of the Turkish Ambassador in Cairo, Hulusi Fuat Tugay, had created a lot of ill-feeling between Egypt and Turkey in 1957. But in 1955 Prime Minister Menderes of Turkey had actively sought a rapprochement with Nasser. Even before the announcement of the pact with Iraq he had made efforts to bring about a Turkish-Egyptian mutual friendship pact. For a time in the fall of 1955 there were strong hopes that Nasser might reciprocate these efforts and even extend an invitation to Menderes to visit Cairo. But Nasser deliberately lingered and hopes vanished.

¹¹ This rapidly developed into an Egyptian-Syrian-Saudi Arabian-Yemeni alignment through a series of agreements between these countries: Egyptian-Saudi Arabian treaty was signed on October 27, 1955 and joint Egyptian-Saudi Arabian and Yemeni treaty on April 21, 1957. These provided an Egyptian leadership and Command over the military forces of the signatories.

¹² Dulles supported these misgivings in a press conference after the withdrawal of the American offer. He said: "The Egyptians, in a sense, forced upon us an issue to which I think there was only one possible response. The issue was, do nations which play both sides get better treatment than nations which are stalwart and work with us?" This, though, was evidently an after thought because the Arms Deal which was announced earlier should have been a clear indication of the uncompromising attitude of Nasser.

¹³ A day before the announcement, the Appropriations Committee of the U.S. Senate had approved a resolution asking the Administration not to give any money to Egypt without consulting the Congress.

¹⁴ Turkey opposed Egypt's unilateral decision of nationalizing the Suez Canal Zone. At the United Nations General Assembly she voted in favor of the cease-fire resolution.

¹⁵ King Saud offered to mediate in the crisis. Turkey, anxious to satisfy genuine Syrian fears, immediately accepted. Fatin R. Zorlu, at that time State Minister, flew to Saudi Arabia. The Syrian government, however, did not take up Saud's offer.

¹⁶ As of January 1959 Iraq had not formally withdrawn from the Baghdad Pact. Recently members of the new government have expressed in no uncertain terms that their "destiny" lies with the U. A. R., that Arab unity should not be broken by alliances with outsiders, and that Iraq has no reason to fear Soviet Russia. Turkey recognized the new Iraqi regime on July 31, 1958.

CHAPTER IX

¹ Turkish foreign policy cannot take an expansionist course. The basic tenets are prohibitive to such a trend. But neither Turkey nor her allies can long remain indifferent to the potential ties of the affinity between the Turks of Turkey and more than 50 million Turkish peoples living under Soviet or Communist Chinese domination in Asia.

BIBLIOGRAPHY

Acheson, Dean, *Strengthening the Forces of Freedom*, U.S. Department of State Publication 3852, 1950.

Atay, Falih Rifki, *Buyuk Gazinin Hatirat Sahifeleri*, Istanbul, 1937.

Abrevaya, Juliette, *La Conference de Montreux et le Régime des Detroits*, Paris, Editions Internales, 1937.

Apeiser, E. A., *The United States and the Near East*, Cambridge, 1947.

Basgil, Ali Fuad, *La Question des Detroits*, Paris, Pierre Bossuet, 1928.

Bilsel, Cemil, *Dunya Baris Buhraninda Bogazlar* (Straits in the World Crisis), an article in the University of Istanbul Historical Review, 1930.

Bruel, Erik, *International Straits*, 2 volumes, London, 1947.

Bayur, Yusuf Hikmet, *Yeni Turk Devletinin Harici Sivaseti*, Istanbul, Burhaneddin Matbaasi, 1935. *Turk Inkilabi Tarihi*, Ankara, Devlet Matbaasi, 1954.

Bisbee, Eleanor, *The New Turks*, University of Pennsylvania Press, Philadelphia, 1951.

Brookings Institute, *Major Problems of the United States Foreign Policy, 1948-1954*.

Brown, W. A., *American Foreign Assistance*, Washington, D.C., Brookings Institute, 1953.

Cemal, Ahmed, *Pasha: Memoirs of a Turkish Statesman, 1913-1919*, New York, 1922.

Campbell, John C., *Defense of the Middle East: Problems of American Policy*, Harper, New York, 1958.

Churchill, Winston S., *The World Crisis*, New York, Scribners, 1928. *Step by Step*, London, Butterworth, 1939. *The Unrelenting Struggle*, London, Cassel, 1946. *The Gathering Storm*, London, Cassel, 1942-46. *Their Finest Hour*, Houghton Mifflin, 1949, New York. *The Hinge of Faith*, New York, Houghton Mifflin, 1950.

Ciano, G., *Journal Intime*, Vols. I and II, Neuchatel, 1946. *Storia d'Europa*, Milan, Mandaderi, 1948.

Connolly, Violet, *Soviet Economic Policy in the East*, Vol. I, Oxford University Press, 1936.

Curl, P. V., *Documents on American Foreign Relations 1954*, New York, Harper Brothers, 1955.

Dallin, David J., *Soviet Russia's Foreign Policy, 1939-1942*, New Haven, Yale University Press, 1942.

Davison, Roderic H., *Turkish Diplomacy From Mudros to Lausanne*, (Reprinted from *The Diplomats, 1919-1939*), Princeton University Press, 1953.

Driault, Eduard and L'Heritier, Michel, *'Histoire Diplomatique de Grese de 1821 a nos jour*, Vol. V, Paris, 1926.

Durrell, Lawrence, *Bitter Lemons*, New York, Dutton, 1957.

Earle, E. M., *Turkey, the Great Powers and the Baghdad Railway*, New York, Macmillan, 1923.

Edip, Halide, *Memoirs*, New York, Century, 1926. *The Turkish Ordeal*, New York, Century, 1928.

Edmonds, C. J., *The Kurds of Iraq*, Middle East Journal, Winter, 1957.

Elphinson, W. G., *The Kurdish Question*, International Affairs, January, 1946.

Emin, Ahmet (Yalman), *Turkey in the World War*, New Haven, Yale University Press, 1930.

Einzig, Paul, *Bloodless Invasion*, London, Duckworth, 1939.

Esmer, Ahmed Sukru, *The Straits: Crux of World Politics*, Foreign Affairs Quarterly of January, 1947.

Folliot, Denise, *Documents on International Relations 1951*, Oxford University Press, London, 1954. *Documents on International Relations 1953*, Oxford University Press, London, 1956.

Frangulis, F., *La Question de Proche Orient*, Paris, 1922.

Gaulis, B. C., *Angora et la politique Anglaise en Orient*, Paris, Colin, 1924. *La Novelle Turquie*, Paris, Colin, 1924. *La Question Turque*, Paris, Berger-Levault, 1931.

Geshkoff, Theodore I., *Balkan Union: A Road to Peace in Southern Europe*, Columbia University Press, 1940.

Gordon, Leland, *American Relations With Turkey 1830-1930*, Philadelphia, University of Pennsylvania Press, 1932.

Graves, Philip, P., *Briton and Turk*, London, Hutchinson, 1941.

Hartmann, Hans W., *Die Auswartige Politik der Turkei*, Zurich Geber Leeman and Co.

Hedlam, Morley J. W., *The Black Sea, the Bosphorus and the Dardanelles, Studies in Diplomatic History*, London, Methuen, 1930.

Heyd, Uriel, *Foundations of Turkish Nationalism*, London, Harvell Press, 1950.

Hoskins, Halford, *The Middle East, Problem Area in World Politics*, New York, Macmillan, 1954.

Hostler, C., *Turkism and the Soviets*, London, Allen and Unwin, 1957.

House, E. M. and Seymour C., *What Really Happened at Paris*, New York, Scribners, 1921.

Howard, Harry M., *The Partition of Turkey*, Norman, University of Oklahoma Press, 1931. *The Straits After the Montreux Conference*, Foreign Affairs Quarterly, October, 1936. *Germany, the Soviet Union and Turkey During World War II*, Department of State Bulletin 472, 1948. *The Problem of the Turkish Straits*, U.S. Government Printing Office, Washington, 1947. *The United States and the Turkish Straits*, U.S. Government Printing Office, 1947.

Hurewitz, J. C., *Diplomacy in the Near and Middle East*, 2 vols., D. Van Nostrand Co., Inc., Princeton, 1956.

Inonu, Ismet, *Turkey, The Ten Eventful Years 1938-1947*, Reprint from Encyclopedia Britannica.

Jackh, Ernest, *Background of the Middle East*, New York, Cornell University Press, 1952.

Kannengeisser, General, *Gallipoli*, Paris, 1925.

Karal, Enver Ziya, *Atatürkten Düsunceler*, Türk Tarih Kurumu, Ankara, 1956.

Kemal, Ataturk, *Speech*, Leipzig, K. F. Koehler, 1929.

Kennan, George F., *American Diplomacy 1900-1950*, Mentor Books, New York, 1951.

Knatchbull-Hugessen, *A Diplomat in Peace and War*, London, John Murray, 1940.

Kocu, Resad Ekrem, *Osmanli Muahedeleri, Kapitülasyonlar ve Lausanne Muahedeleri*, Istanbul, Ahmed Halit Kütüphanesi, 1934.

Kohn, Hans, *Western Civilization in the Near East,* Columbia University Press, 1936. *A History of Nationalism in the East,* 1929, Harcourt Brace, 1929.

Larchet, Commandant M., *La Guerre Turque dans la Guerre Mondiale,* Paris, Berger-Levrault, 1926.

Mears, Eliot Grinell, *Modern Turkey,* Macmillan, New York, 1924.

Mikusch, Dagobert von, *Mustafa Kemal,* Doubleday, New York, 1931.

Moorehead, Alan, *Gallipoli,* Harper, New York, 1956.

Papen, Franz von, *Memoirs,* Dutton, New York, 1953.

Peter, Calvacoressi, *Survey of International Affairs, 1951,* London, Oxford University Press, 1954.

Phillipson, C. and Buxton, N., *The Question of the Bosphorus and the Dardanelles,* London, Stevens and Haynes, 1917.

Ramsaur, Ernest E., Jr., *The Young Turks: Prelude to the Revolution of 1908,* Princeton University Press, 1957.

Ramsay, Sir William, *Historical Geography of Asia Minor.*

Rustow, Dankwart A., *Defense of the Middle East,* Foreign Affairs Quarterly, January, 1956.

Sadak, Necmeddin, *Turkey Faces the Soviets,* Foreign Affairs, April, 1949.

Seton-Watson, H., *Eastern Europe between Wars: 1918-41,* Cambridge University Press, 1945.

Shotwell, James T. and Deak, Frances, *Turkey at the Straits,* New York, Macmillan, 1940.

Su, M. K. and Su, Kamil, *Turkiye Cumhurriyet Tarihi, Istanbul,* Kanaat Publications, 1954.

Thomas, Lewis V. and Frye, Richard, *The United States and Turkey and Iran,* Harvard University Press, 1951.

Toynbee, Arnold J., *The West and the World,* New York, Oxford University Press, 1953. *The Breakdown at Lausanne,* New Republic, March 7, 1923. *The Western Question in Turkey and Greece,* London, Constable, 1922.

Truman, Harry, *Memoirs*, Vol. I and II, New York, Doubleday and Co., 1955.

Turk, Tarihi, Devlet Matbaasi, Istanbul.

Vere-Hodge, Edward Reginald, *Turkish Foreign Policy 1918-1948*, Ambilly-Annemases, Imp. Franco-Suisse, 1950.

Viaud, Julian, *Lo mort de notre chere France en Orient*, Paris, Calmann-Levy, 1920.

Ward, Barbara, *Turkey*, New York, Oxford University Press, 1942.

Webster, Donald E., *Turkey of Ataturk*, American Association of Political and Social Science, 1939.

Wint, Guy and Peter Calvocoressi, *Middle East Crisis*, Penguin Books, London, 1957.

Yalman, Ahmet Emin, *Turkey in My Time*, University of Oklahoma Press, 1956.

INDEX